ADVANCE PRAISE

'Don't read this book with a broken rib—you'll ache from cover to cover. Should become a classic of Mongolian cycling literature.'

—Tim Krabbé, author of *The Rider*

'Tom Doig is not your average traveller and *Mörön to Mörön* is not like any other travel book. Bowel-splittingly hilarious and irresistibly absurd, this book is for everyone who's ever asked themselves the golden question of travel: *Why the f**k not?*'

—Benjamin Law, author of *The Family Law*

'Funnier than Bill Bryson ... Doig is Hemingway in a unitard.'

—Chris Flynn, author of *A Tiger in Eden*

moron2moron.com

MÖRÖN ▶ TO MÖRÖN

Two men, two bikes,
one Mongolian misadventure

TOM DOIG

ALLEN&UNWIN
SYDNEY · MELBOURNE · AUCKLAND · LONDON

First published in 2013

The author gratefully acknowledges the use of excerpts from the following books:
Mongolia: Travels in the Untamed Land, Jasper Becker (Tauris Parke Paperbacks, 1992)
Wild East: Travels in the New Mongolia, Jill Lawless (ECW Press, 2000)
Mongolia, ed Michael Kohn (*Lonely Planet*, 2008) (fifth edition)
Mongolian Phrasebook, Alan J K Sanders, J Bat-Ireedui, Tsogt Gombosuren (*Lonely Planet*, 2008)
(second edition)
Swimming to Cambodia, Spalding Gray (Picador, 1985)
Genghis Khan and the Making of the Modern World, Jack Weatherford (Three Rivers Press, 2003)
The Secret History of the Mongols: A Mongolian Epic Chronicle of the Thirteenth Century,
Anonymous (trans Igor de Rachewiltz, Leiden, 2006)
Nomads and Commissars: Mongolia Revisited, Owen Lattimore (Oxford University Press, 1962)
Steppenwolf, Hermann Hesse (Penguin, 1927)

Allen & Unwin
Sydney, Melbourne, Auckland, London

83 Alexander Street
Crows Nest NSW 2065
Australia
Phone: (61 2) 8425 0100
Email: info@allenandunwin.com
Web: www.allenandunwin.com

Cataloguing-in-Publication details are available
from the National Library of Australia
www.trove.nla.gov.au

ISBN 978 1 74331 126 4

Internal design by Squirt Creative
Insert photographs © Tama Pugsley 2010
Map by Darian Causby
Set in 12/15 pt Dante by Midland Typesetters, Australia
Printed and bound in Australia by the SOS Print + Media Group.

10 9 8 7 6 5

MIX
Paper from
responsible sources
FSC® C011217
www.fsc.org

The paper in this book is FSC® certified.
FSC® promotes environmentally responsible,
socially beneficial and economically viable
management of the world's forests.

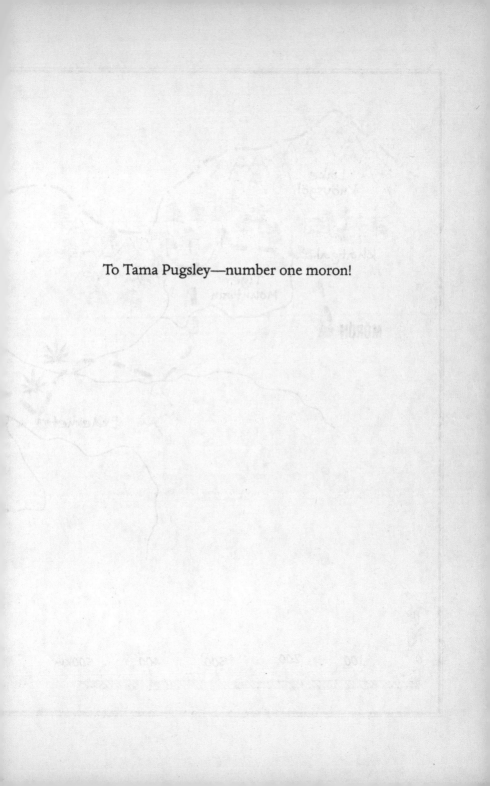

To Tama Pugsley—number one moron!

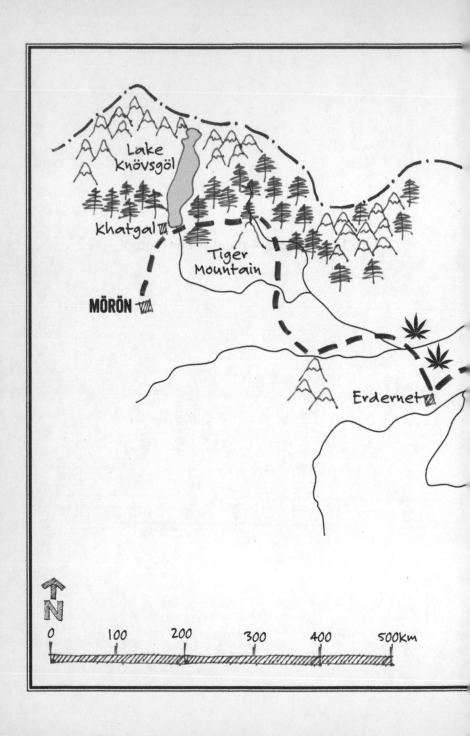

MONGOLIA

For a more detailed map go to www.moron2moron.com/map

The QR codes throughout the book and on the back cover bring videos taken during the morons' time in Mongolia directly to your phone.

Scan the QR code images and you'll be taken straight to the action.

QR code readers can be downloaded free from the web for your smartphone.

Scan the QR code on the back cover to watch the *Mörön to Mörön* trailer.

CONTENTS

PART THREE: NOT MUCH OF A HOLIDAY

Beyond the rivers
You will perhaps lose courage,
But continue to advance
In the same way;
Beyond the mountains
You will perhaps lose heart,
But think of nothing else apart from your mission.

—ANONYMOUS, *The Secret History of the Mongols*
(13th century)

Human beings must have dreams or they will go nowhere.

—DAVID HASSELHOFF, *Don't Hassel the Hoff*
(21st century)

PROLOGUE: HORDE

*F*irst, a rumbling.
  You can sense it before you can feel it: a sick sweetness in the air, a metal tingle in your mouth. Put your ear to the ground. How many? How far? You can't tell.

  On the horizon: dust clouds. A gale blowing in across the plains. Drop your hoe, leave the turnips in the fields. Hitch up your pants and run! Sound the alarm—then cross yourself. Brace yourself.

  Are there really just Four Horsemen of the Apocalypse? Looks like . . . more than four. A horde. Barbarians. Huns. Mongols. Heathens, fanatical heathens, heeding no rules or customs of civilised man, their horses snorting and frothing at the mouth, crazed, toothpaste rabid. Their entire language one unending obscenity.

  Where do they come from—the ends of the earth? The delirium of our worst fever-dreams? The depths of Lake Baikal, its bottomless black crevices leading straight to the underworld— to Hell itself?

  The steppes!

  The unharvested wastelands, home of serpent, buzzard, wolf—and death. Think of your children. Your women. Think of heads on sticks, intestines in the trees—this is the bubonic plague come uninvited, the Black Death in human form, a disease-ridden, flea-bitten foreign nightmare rampaging for no earthly reason except victory and carnage. These beasts don't bargain. They don't haggle. They storm in out of nowhere, out of the sky, reeking of unwashed stables, rancid tents, abominations on goatskin rugs. All they want is spoils. Loot. Vodka and cheese. Their unwashed hair and bloodshot blue eyes, their cracked lips, noses flaking and pink.

Tork. Tchtooork! Blye-ait-shlerg!

What are they saying? Pointing at a book. Tossing their money around. Rubbing our flag in the dirt. A peasant with gold is still a peasant. They want to guzzle devil-water and disgrace themselves in the fields of our ancestors. Steal our women. Enslave our children. Wrestle our drunkards. Shit on our country. Piss on our history—and laugh about it.

The morons are here.

PART ONE

ON THE MISSION

2000–10: GETTING MY SHIT TOGETHER

In July 2010, me and my best mate Tama Pugsley cycled 1487 kilometres across northern Mongolia from a small town called Mörön to a smaller town also called Mörön. Our motivation was brutally simple: there were two towns called Mörön, and we were two morons. It had to be done.

Even if it didn't, we were going to do it anyway.

I first noticed this moronic coincidence back in the year 2000. At the time I was an unemployed 21-year-old English Lit graduate, surprised and disappointed that Y2K had failed to cause the world's financial markets to collapse like everyone had predicted. I was living in Wellington with my parents and like most young Kiwis I spent a lot of time reading atlases and plotting my escape. One blustery winter's day I was daydreaming somewhere north of Southeast Asia when I saw the two Möröns. They were pretty close together—it was a pretty small atlas—and suddenly everything came into focus.

Some people went to Mongolia seeking the true resting place of Genghis Khan, or Chinggis Khaan, as we would come to know him. Some went to help the thousands of nomads displaced by the killer *dzuds*—literally 'white death', a winter thaw followed by a cold snap and snowfall, where the ground refreezes and prevents animals from feeding, or living. Some went to expose the awful secrets of Mongolia's commie-era purges under the dread Choibalsan. Some went to discover the truth, or lack thereof, about the fabled Mongolian death worm. But I wasn't really interested in Mongolian culture or history or geography or politics. If both Möröns had been in Kazakhstan, I would've wanted to go to Kazakhstan. If one Mörön was in Uruguay and the other in Paraguay, so be it. Like Sir Edmund Hillary's ambition to conquer Mount Everest, like Chinggis Khaan's desire to conquer the entire globe, like the guy in the song who walked 500 miles and then walked 500 more, I wanted to travel from Mörön to Mörön . . . because they were there.

It would be wrong to call it a dream, but it definitely became an obsession. The next time me and Tama went mountain-biking together I told him about the Möröns and it became an obsession of his too. Most people we mentioned it to thought it was a joke, a pretty dumb one, but we didn't care because it was *our* dumb joke. Even after I moved to Melbourne to pursue the romantic life of a struggling arts administrator and tried to forget about those Möröns, Tama kept hassling me about it.

Tama bloody Pugsley. 'Tama' means 'boy' in Maori, and he was definitely one of those, but Tama was also as *pakeha* (white, foreign) as they come. With his frosty blue eyes, blond curls and six-feet-something of tanned muscle, plus a bit of protective burger layer, he was an amiable Aryan wet dream. A mutual female friend once described Tama as a 'big, horny teddy bear' and meant it as a compliment.

In December 2005 Tama came over to Melbourne and we caught a bus to Adelaide with three of my shonky

Melbourne mates, then a train across the Nullarbor to Perth, then we cycled 800-odd kilometres around the southwest tip of Western Australia to Albany. Apart from the night I got really drunk and cycled into a fence, buckling my back tyre and nearly breaking my hand, it was a bracing, picturesque and healthful fortnight. When we finished the ride I felt better than I had in years. Then me and Tama undid all that good work on New Year's Eve by taking ecstasy and going out dancing at Albany's Insomniaxx nightclub. Insomniaxx favoured reflective metal walls, flatulent smoke machines and a variety of techno remixes of 'Smells Like Teen Spirit'. We rocked out, hard. The bouncers kept telling us to put our shirts back on. Tama met some saucy blonde jailbait and pashed on in an alley. I spent a couple of hours trying to chat up a 21-year-old trainee teacher from Perth who told me I looked 'like a skinny David Hasselhoff'. When the lights came on she let me have a bit of a kiss then laughed in my face and left.

On our way back to the campsite Tama and I went skinny-dipping in Albany Harbour while unappreciative men in utes beeped and screamed abuse; we met a drunk girl in a carpark who told us Insomniaxx had been voted 'Worst Nightclub in Australia' on Triple J the year before and wouldn't take either of us home with her; and we promised each other, just before we passed out in the tent, that *yes*, we *would* mission from Mörön to Mörön—soon.

Four and a half years later, it was finally happening. I was camped out in my bombsite of a Brunswick share house bedroom with the heater cranked, surrounded by bike gear, video equipment and thermal underwear, cramming way too many books into a couple of Ortlieb panniers while

Tama fed me duty-free whisky and tried not to stand on things. I was freshly unemployed, again, only this time I had a couple of thousand dollars saved. Tama had just flown into town and he regaled me with tales of his new life in New York, his recent documentary-making trip to the bat caves of Borneo, his hot new Kiwi-in-Vancouver girlfriend Ami, and his latest drinking-and-jumping accident—a broken collarbone sustained a couple of months ago on his thirtieth birthday and 'pretty much healed' except for a prominent alien-head lump of extra bone near his neck, which threatened to burst through his T-shirt.

'The doctor said not to do any heavy lifting for three months, and no cycling for, like, six months,' Tama said, knocking back his whisky and pouring another. 'I told him I was going to mountain-bike across Mongolia, and he said it was the worst idea he'd ever heard—but I reckon I'll be sweet.'

Four hours before our plane left, my new girlfriend Laura cycled over to my place through some particularly miserable Melbourne rain with a spandex leopard-print unitard for Tama (I'd already packed my skeleton suit). In true straight-to-DVD romantic-comedy style, Laura and I had denied our true feelings for each other for close to a decade until things came to a head on New Year's 2009/10. We were performing at the Falls Festival, on the tiniest stage there, playing a pair of incestuous hermaphroditic twins in spandex onesies. The increasingly grotesque ritual climaxed with Laura squatting over my head and spraying explosive diarrhoea—600 millilitres of chocolate milk—into my open mouth while a couple of dozen big-eyed teens gazed on, tripping balls, horrified by our overacting. After our final show Laura and I got munted and made sweet, sticky, mutant-clown love in my tent until the sun came up. Tama let us tell him the whole shonky story, laughing and cringing in the right places even though he'd heard it all before.

'So I washed the leopard suit,' Laura told Tama. 'It was pretty filthy—'

'But bro, you should've seen the *tent*!' I interrupted. Tama stopped sniggering and looked at me.

'Doig! Did you . . . you didn't, did you?'

'Did I what?'

'Did you clean the tent out *after* you filled it with chocolate milk and jizz?'

'Good question. I did . . .' I rustled through the scraps of paper on my desk, looking for my To-Do List. '. . . not. Yet. But it *is* on the list?' I grinned as innocently as possible.

'You're such a scabdog!' Tama punched me in the shoulder. I punched him back. We started play-fighting on my bed.

'Uh, boys,' Laura said, 'do you want me to leave you to it?' She dropped the unitard on the floor.

We needed the 'tards for Naadam, Mongolia's two-day national holiday of 'the three manly sports': archery, horseriding and *bökh*. *Bökh* was traditional Mongolian wrestling, a cross between between sumo and prison sex. The plan was to make it to the photogenic lakeside town of Khatgal, about 100 kilometres north of Mörön, by 11 July, where we would compete in the Khatgal Naadam *bökh* dressed up WWF style. We figured we could just rock up on the day and try our luck—it seemed like that kind of country. I was actually more excited about wrestling Mongols in spandex than riding 1500 kilometres across a blasted heath on bikes we were yet to purchase, but with a bit of luck we could have our cake and stomp on it too.

I said goodbye to Laura, then looked hopelessly around the chaos of my room until I found it: the list.

Third and final rabies vaccination—that was worth remembering. I needed to sort that out in Beijing, or Ulaanbaatar at a pinch.

Length of hose pipe filled with ball bearings—for beating off wild dogs. Laura's stepdad's suggestion from his time in the Rhodesian armed forces. Sort out in Beijing?

Other than setting fire to a forest, flying is the worst single thing an ordinary individual can do to cause climate change—no, wait, that was just a disturbing quote I copied out from *The Age of Stupid*, a doco I watched the other night. Um, cross out?

Tama threw a mini-soccer ball at my head. 'Get your shit together, bro—taxi's here in five minutes.'

We finished our whiskies. I stopped trying to jam more stuff into my panniers and stowed my rusty old single-speed racer and my conscience away in the back shed. Then a taxi arrived and took us to the airport.

Before we made it anywhere near Mongolia, Tama and I crammed in a ten-day debauch with our girlfriends in Cambodia—or *Rambodia*, as Tama was calling it, since he hadn't seen Ami for a month. Laura flew to Phnom Penh a couple of days after us, Ami came over from Vancouver the day after that, and we all went on a mini-mission. Strapped for time, we had to choose between Angkor Wat or some obscure tropical island in the south. The consensus was that Angkor Wat would still be there in a decade, but how often did we get to go swimming and eat coconuts? So we spent five days on Koh Tonsay (Rabbit Island), where we 'trained' by watching the 2010 World Cup soccer quarterfinals, choking back Mekong 'whisky' and fucking like rabbits in adjacent hutches. I sort of started smoking again. I was ready for Mörön.

On our last day in Cambodia Laura and I went to the Killing Fields while Tama and Ami stayed in their private pool, then we all got pissy on pina coladas at the Foreign Correspondents' Club. Five hours later we staggered back to the Pavilion Hotel and decided to go for a skinny-dip in the pool. This quickly degenerated into me and Laura having a surreptitious bang in the darkened deep end. After a minute or so we got self-conscious and decoupled, but when I turned around I could see our friends conjoined in the far corner of the pool, Tama's buttocks clenched and humping doggedly away.

Tama and I flew out early the next morning. Laura was too sad for morning sex.

'Goodbye babetown, I'll see you in month,' I said, trying not to sound too sad—or excited.

MONGOLIA (1) In stark geographic terms, northern Mongolia overlaps with Siberia's conifer forests, while southern Mongolia is a snaggle-toothed bite taken out of China. But in the brainpans of restless antipodeans like me and Tama, Mongolia (2) is off the charts. The precise location of Mongolia is notoriously difficult to pin down (eastern Central Asia? Northwestern East Asia? Southern North Asia?). Instead, 'Mongolia' is exotic polysyllabic gibberish

for 'middle of nowhere', to be filed next to Galápagos, Pata-
gonia, Madagascar. Mongolia: equidistant from Coventry
and Purgatory; past Timbuktu but before Moo-Moo Land.
Mongolia is the Wild West of the East, a no-man's-land of
throat-singing, stallions and ruined empires, where your
heart is as free as the open steppe and your mind is just
as empty.

Mörön (1) Mörön is a place on Earth. But Mörön is also
much more than that: it is a state of mind. Floating somewhere in the ill-defined semiotic wonderland of Mongolia,
the Möröns aren't tarnished by ideology or burdened by
backstory the way places like Tiananmen Square, Berlin or
Pearl Harbor are.

Moron (2) So, moron is a state of mind. But which state? In
1910 (save the date), psychologist and racist Henry H Goddard
coined the term 'moron' from the Ancient Greek word *moros*,
meaning 'dull', unlike *oxy*, which means 'sharp'—hence
oxymoron. According to Goddard, if an adult had a mental
age of between eight and twelve on something called the
Binet scale, this made them a moron. In intelligence quotient
terms, moron represented 'definite feeble-mindedness',
later rebranded 'mild retardation', and covered numbers 51
through 70 on the IQ charts. 'Imbecile' accounted for 26 to
50, and 'idiot' mopped up the remaining 25 points. Goddard
believed that on no account should two morons be allowed
to interbreed, so institutionalisation was best accompanied by
sterilisation to prevent the outbreak of moronic orgies and
subsequent infestations of imbecile devil-children.

In theory, if someone had called Goddard a stupid

moron for coming up with such theories, he could respond with scientific accuracy: 'Well, *you're* a retarded idiot—and that makes *me* two intelligence categories more, uh, cleverer than you!'

Years passed. People called each other morons. The scientists decided in their hipsterish way that the word wasn't cool any more, but it was too late.

And now, on the centenary of the birth of one of the English language's all-time favourite insults, two morons were poised to cycle from Mörön to Mörön.

MÖRÖN (2b) In Mongolian, *mörön*—pronounced 'muh-run'—means 'river'. Wide, flowing river.

DAY MINUS 4: BEIJING, BICYCLES, TRANS-MONGOLIAN

'Ten thousand yuan, please.'

Tama gave Heaven a thick red bundle of 100-yuan notes. It took her nearly a minute to count it. Sweat ran down my forehead into my eyes. It was just after 10 pm on 5 July 2010, six days before Naadam, a stinking hot night after an even stinkier day. Ten thousand yuan was about A$2000—one grand per bike, not much of a bargain, but it was too late to worry about that now. My credit card had glitched out when I tried to withdraw so much money so Tama spotted me 5000 yuan. We were leaning on the counter of UCC Bikes on Jiaodaokuo Dong Street, or 'Bicycle Street' as we called it. There were two bike shops to our left and seven to the right, including one that sold rickshaws and another that sold Hummer brand folding army bicycles with full camo paint jobs. We had decided to buy bikes in Beijing rather than Melbourne partly because we hoped they would be heaps cheaper, and also because the prospect of buying shonky Chinese bikes that fell apart on the third day would make for a hilarious Facebook status update: 'Failed 2 ride from moron 2 moron due 2 stinginess & idiocy LULZ.'

Heaven and Rhino, the UCC store clerks, had just finished disassembling and packing two brand-new mountain bikes into cardboard boxes for us to take on the Trans-Mongolian the next morning. Neither of us had ever heard of UCC but they were the only steel frames we could find in Beijing. Rhino couldn't speak a word of English, although he seemed to know what he was gesticulating about when he muttered 'Mongol' and pointed to the aluminium bike frames and flopped his wrist camply, then pointed to our bikes and flexed his arm with a fierce grin. More importantly, they looked flash as: mine was painted white with black writing (UCC MTB SYSTEM—ROLLING STEEL 1.0—DOUBLE BUTTED); Tama's was black with white. Our off-road tyres were chunky, gargantuan, ribbed for her pleasure; our handlebar pegs looked ready to impale a yak. On our test ride up and down Bicycle Street, my seat and its extra cushioning gel pack felt as soft as I could hope for.

Heaven rang for a taxi. Rhino helped us lug the boxes out onto the pavement. Then Heaven wished us good luck, Rhino grunted, and they both walked off into the sticky night.

It took ages for a taxi to show up. It was white and battered and not very big. The driver rolled down his window and looked suspiciously at the boxes, which were nearly as long as a person, then looked at his back seat, which was not quite as long as one. He hoicked onto the pavement and drove off. We looked around for other taxis but the street was dead. Tama got that look in his eye.

'Hey Doiggus, I reckon we should carry the boxes back to the hutongs. It'll be a great warm-up for Naadam!'

Tama had no shortage of 'great' ideas—like going on a three-day hike in Wilsons Promontory with one bottle of scotch, four rockmelons, twelve cans of baked beans and no cooker. Or scaling a thirty-storey building site at 2 am during a howling Wellington gale and dropping bricks over the edge 'to see what happens'.

'Aren't you warm enough already?' I said. 'You're sweating like a dog.'

'Yeah, but—go on, it'll be an unnecessary feat of strength! Besides, what are our options?'

I imagined cramming both boxes into a rickshaw and us running alongside the poor driver, clapping and yelling at him for encouragement—all good, except no rickshaws.

'How much do you reckon each box weighs?' I asked.

'Dunno—maybe sixteen kilos? Actually, with those ridiculous pannier racks they munted together, more like twenty?' Tama grinned. 'C'mon bro, I'm the one with the broken collarbone and I'm not fussed.'

I sighed. 'It's the shonky thing to do, huh? Okay—but I go in front.'

But Tama was already lining up the boxes either side of us, in the lead, as usual.

Following Tama's bobbing head and mutant shoulder through the muggy alleys, flanked on both sides by massive cardboard boxes, we must have looked like Fred Flintstone and Barney Rubble in a pathetic underpowered jalopy, late for some tragic cameo appearance at a theatre restaurant. The locals stared at us with a mixture of incredulity and glee as we stumbled and tripped over our jandals. Dudes eating noodles at street canteens put down their chopsticks and flexed their arms in friendly mockery. Women clapped and laughed and called out 'Jiēshi!'—Sturdy!—or maybe 'Jiétān!'—Paraplegic! We stopped to rest our arms every hundred metres or so, then every fifty metres. No one offered to help. We were perspiring through the tail end of a day that had peaked at 40.3 degrees Celsius, the hottest temperature ever recorded in Beijing. But we couldn't recognise freak Chinese weather, just that it was freakin' hot. And freakin' awesome.

At 5.45 the next morning we found ourselves bleary-eyed and sweaty on the side of Zhangwang Street, waiting for a taxi to take us to the Beijing train station. We were standing next to a small mountain of hard rubbish: two already-haggard bike boxes, plus three extra-large red, white and blue-striped plastic smuggler bags. Each bag weighed over thirty kilograms, one had a busted zip that I had wrapped up with sellotape, and all had crappy handles that broke instantly. The smuggler bags were my idea. They allowed us to aggregate all our stuff—six Ortlieb panniers, two backpacks, one tent, and half a dozen plastic bags of random bullshit, including:

- two one-metre lengths of chain, with padlocks, for securing our bikes from marauding horsemen and/or defending ourselves against rabid dogs by swinging and whacking
- two cartons of Marlboro cigarettes as payment for Mongol families who would hopefully let us stay in their gers (the round white tent of the nomads, called a yurt in Russia) and as bribes for whoever might need bribing
- two dozen plastic koalas, made in China and exported to Australia, purchased on Brunswick's Sydney Road and

flown back to China, gifts for kids we expected to meet along the way

- two psychedelic visors and two pairs of *Star Trek: The Next Generation* sunglasses I'd bought at the Beijing Alien's Street Markets to accessorise the unitards.

All this and more was crammed into the three smuggler bags, which made it much easier to keep track of and much harder to lift. Also, the ostentatiously scabby bags enabled our expensive, conspicuous and eminently stealable adventure tourism equipment to pass for worthless trash, the worldly belongings of two demented albino peasants, dissolute, down on their luck, relocating to the shantytowns of Ulaanbaatar with the rest of the unfortunates. Tama thought this second angle was a bit far-fetched, but it made me feel less paranoid about lugging 6000 bucks' worth of gear around the capital of China and the capital of Mongolia and the 1500-kilometre train ride. Six grand was a year's wages for the average Chinese worker, and nearly two years for the average Mongol, give or take.

Taxi after taxi stopped, considered our trash heap and sped off. I started to wonder if my cunning ruse was a little *too* cunning. After fifteen minutes of rejections Tama said 'Fuck this' and pushed the bike boxes behind a wall.

'You wave down a taxi, geezer, I'll do the rest.'

When the next taxi stopped I thrust a tourist map in the driver's face, bellowing '*Ni hao*! Beijing train station! *Traaain staaation!*'

Meanwhile Tama opened the back door and rammed a bike box into the back seat before the driver could stop him. The box was too long—just. Tama slammed the door into the box again and again until finally it closed with a dull crunch.

'*Ai ya!*' the driver yelled.

'Sweet dog,' Tama called to me, jumping into the front seat. 'You do the same—I'll see you at the station!'

'What about all the bags?' I yelled, but he was gone.

A couple of dishevelled minutes later I was weaving through traffic in my own taxi, smuggler bag on my lap, two more in the boot, looking out for the back of Tama's head.

I always found myself trying to keep up with the back of that head. Tama 2000: web developer, photographer, possible CIA agent. Born in the Chinese Year of the Metal Monkey, Tama was half-cyborg, half-chimp and 110 per cent sturdy ego. Tama's mum taught him to walk by dragging him by the arm through the Ontario snow, and after five years of keeping up with his parents' crazy caving, hiking, nature-loving ways, young Pugs had already developed a little sixpack. The doctors were worried, but the five-year-old girls loved it . . . There was nothing Tama couldn't do, and if there was, you'd better not tell him.

He was my yuppy Dean Moriarty, the Thelma to my Louise. When we hung out together something amoebic happened to our personalities: they started to converge, to merge. It was like we knew what each other was thinking, like we shared half a brain. If we were a Flight of the Conchords covers band—Flight of the Shonkchords—Tama would be a sexually prolific Jemaine, I'd be a tone-deaf Bret, and no one would come to our gigs, not even a fake Mel. We had a pretty much perfect symbiotic relationship, like a hippo with a bird in its mouth. Tama took care of the practical, masochistic elements—the organising and financing, the unnecessary feats of strength. I took care of the frivolous, pointless and otherwise conceptual side of things. Together, we were unstoppable.

The suburbs of Beijing flickered by, not beautiful but impressively rectangular. We were in a stuffy sleeper cabin of the Trans-Mongolian with a quiet middle-aged French couple also on their way to Naadam. They seemed a bit overwhelmed by all our luggage, not to mention the professional T-shirts that Ami had designed and printed for us and which I felt gave the trip a much-needed veneer of respectability, even when drenched with sweat. The T-shirts said MORON in big letters and had authoritative arrows that pointed—if I remembered to sit to Tama's left—at each other.

Tama had his Leatherman out and was trying to unscrew the cabin window to let in some air. The window was jammed 'forever', the conductor said. Tama had been at it for over ten minutes; most people would have stopped by now, but not Tama 2000. It was a thirty-hour train ride to Ulaanbaatar, so I was glad he was trying to sort it out. Meanwhile I gave myself a crash course in Mongolian, courtesy of our *Lonely Planet* phrasebook.

'*Sain bainuu!*' I said. '*Angilar yaridag, xun bainuu? Uh, jorlon khaana, baidiin be?* That's "Hello! Does anyone speak English? Where is the toilet?"'

'Two carriages down, bro. There's binoo all over the seat.'

'Doofus. *Zogs!*'

'Zogs?' Tama turned around and grinned. 'That sounds like "titties"!'

'True, but it means "stop". Like, "Zogs staring at my zogs, you dirty westerner!"'

'So what *is* the word for "titties"?'

'Hang on . . .' I scanned the vocabulary section. There was nothing for 'breasts', 'bosom' or 'boobs'. 'Damn, they've got "rape" but not "rack". What's wrong with the world?'

'If *I* made a phrasebook app,' Tama said, 'it'd have a whole section on shonkiness.'

'Tama Pugsley, that's not such a dumb idea. That could be your killer app!'

'Ha ha, true—zang!'

Feeling confident about my new proficiency in Mongolian, I moved on to Jasper Becker's book *Mongolia: Travels in the Untamed Land*. When the Soviet Union finally de-unioned in 1991, Becker was one of the first westerners to cross the Mongolian border and write about it. For most of the twentieth century it had been impossible enough to visit red Russia or commie China, let alone a poor little dusty paddock of a Socialist state literally sandwiched between them. *Travels in the Untamed Land* had the potential to be the Great Mongolian Travel Book. There was just one problem—Becker's writing style:

> *A land of bloody conquerors, of wandering tribes, of prophets, shamans and mystic kings. A country as immense as North America where the wolf still stalks the wild horse across a treeless plain and where the eagle hangs in a blue sky searching the bare mountains for the shy argali sheep that no shepherd has ever tamed . . .*

WTF? *Becker: Jasper and the Untamed Adjectives*! I ploughed on through the ultraviolet prose, determined to learn more about the 'untamed land' before we crossed the border. Twenty-odd years ago, Becker had been on the same train line, travelling the same direction. I discovered a second major problem with the book—Jasper's personality:

> *The train itself was dirty and uncomfortable. I had not been able to get a first class ticket, a soft seat as it is called, and sat grumpily by the aisle straining to catch a glimpse of the countryside through the window. The train was unheated and crowded . . . Soon the cigarette smoke and the body heat created a dense atmosphere thickened by the loud staccato chatter of my Chinese companions. After answering the usual questions about my origin, I lapsed into silence. The more I travelled in China, the more it irritated me . . .*

The more I read of *Mongolia*, the more it irritated me, and I was only up to page nine. To moan about a Third World train being 'dirty' and 'crowded' is like saying the tropics are 'too hot', or Finland in the winter is 'too dark'. And to complain about Chinese people talking to you in their 'loud staccato chatter', well—that's why some people pay the big yuan for the soft seats, I thought, stretching out on my soft seat.

Mr Becker reminded me of a British backpacker—let's call him Dick—I met during my first trip to China four years earlier. I was in Yangshuo, a few hours up from the Vietnamese border. Yangshuo was a mecca for domestic and foreign tourists alike, who all came to gawp at the spectacular pointy fingernail mountains that feature on the Chinese twenty-yuan note and in nature docos galore. In 2006, Yangshuo's Xi Jie (Foreigner Street) was the only place in China where you could find shops with signs in English but not Chinese, that's how touristy it was. And then there was Dick.

Dick had accidentally checked into a fake YHA ('I knew something was funny about that place, mate—they'd spelt "YHA" wrong'). He worked this out when he saw me sitting in the *real* Foreigner Street YHA, eating dumpling soup. ('What you eating that shit for, mate? *Planet* sez they got steaks here.') Dick ran back to his YAH, threatened the manager with grievous bodily harm unless he gave Dick a refund, boasted about this behaviour to me, then launched into a tirade against China. ('You have to be a total *arsehole* to every one of 'em, mate, or they'll take you for all you're fucken worth. They're worse than the Indians—you've gotta haggle till they're fucken *crying* . . .') In a few action-packed minutes, Dick moaned about his boring friends and crap family back in his miserable British hometown (I think it was Dickton). Against my better judgement, I told him where I was from.

'Wellington? What a *shit*hole, mate! Windy and rainy all the time, dark as shit too! Mate, I fucken *hated* Wellington.'

'Really? How long were you there for, Dick?'

'Overnight. What a shit night, mate. Sleeping at the airport. Shit airport. What fucken awful carpet, mate, hard as a rock . . .'

I gulped down my soup and excused myself as fast as I could, but Dick has lingered with me as a presence, a crude archetype of the Bad Tourist. Dick created his own foul weather systems everywhere he went, little self-fulfilling cyclones of antagonism and distrust. Dick could circumnavigate the world five times over and not learn a fucken thing, mate, other than to confirm what he knew all along: *people are fucked.*

Tama gave a grunt and fell back from the window. The windowpane plunged down and the whole thing almost fell out of the frame onto our French cabin-mates.

'Tama 2000!' I yelled. 'He's Bear Grylls—on crack!'

'Zang! You want a beer?'

'Always!'

I put Becker away and pulled out *Wild East* by Jill Lawless. She was heaps better than Becker, which wasn't hard. Skipping the history section, I flipped to a chapter called 'The Adventurers'. That sounded like me.

> *A certain kind of city dweller dreams of Mongolia. Land of the harshest climate. The worst roads . . . The toughest country on Earth . . . They came by the dozens. Tourists. No: travellers. The kind with serious boots . . . You'd stumble across them in summertime. Fuelling up on beer and camaraderie in the city before the arduous journey ahead: eager, confident, primed . . . They wanted to test themselves against the greatest Outward Bound course on Earth . . . Their stories always began the same way. 'I've dreamed of Mongolia,' they'd say, 'since . . . .'*
>
> *. . . 'Why on Earth are you doing it?' I asked.*
>
> *'When I get there, I will be a man.'*
>
> *Oh. It was often something like that . . .*

I was a city dweller, last time I checked. I had serious boots; I was going to bring them with me, for kicking rabid dogs, but Tama reckoned they'd be too hard to cycle in.

And 'Becoming a Man', well, sure—but the less said about that, the better.

I heard twin giggles and looked up to see Tama and my beer dawdling in the corridor, striking up a conversation with a couple of dopey young backpacker girls who oohed and aahed and stared dreamily into his cleft chin.

'You're so adventurous, like,' one of them said. 'We thought *we* was brave, just comin' on this *train!*'

I reached my hand out into the corridor. A beer landed in it. More giggles. I tried to look up 'big horny teddy bear' in the phrasebook—*tom* something teddy *baavgai?*—then gave up.

Tama's parents separated when he was in early high school. Sometimes he stayed with his mum, Pam, and sometimes he stayed with his dad, Chris, and Chris's new partner, Kris, and later their extra partner, Andy. Chris, Kris and Andy would go on to run a thriving pink-dollar homestay and a not-so-thriving gay adventure tourism business, and Koromiko Road became the preferred venue for 'Sun Boys', the Wellington Nude Sunbathers Club's monthly all-male get-together.

But while Tama was still at school, Chris Pugsley made sure to balance out all the middle-aged gayness by stocking the house with a plentiful supply of straight young female housemates. A couple of weeks after they moved in, these women would invariably be chilling out on the balcony when they would see a boy—a young man, really—walking up the path after hockey practice, sweat and mud still gleaming on his pliant flesh . . . and let's just say, young Pugs didn't have a lock on his door. So it was that, from some rather incongruous soil, Tama grew up to become the Most Heterosexual Man on Earth.

As we headed north, the concrete towers and overpasses were replaced by steep hills and dammed river valleys, then small mountains with gouged-out rockfaces, decapitated peaks. We passed trains that stretched out of sight, carriage after endless carriages stuffed with Mongolian coal and timber headed south to the sweatshops of Beijing. There were bridges and tunnels, more tunnels, blackness.

When I woke up, Tama was deep in the *Ronery Pranet*.

'Man, there are all these rules for staying in a *ger*. You should never lean on the support beam, it's bad luck.'

'What, cos the tent will fall over?'

'Probably. If you kick someone's feet, you have to shake their hand straightaway. And you have to sleep with your feet facing the door.'

'True, especially my feet.'

'This is a good one: you should *never* touch another man's hat.'

'I wish someone had told me that before I moved to Australia!'

Tama threw his hat at me. I sat up and checked out the view. Apart from the odd industrial nightmare smoking away on the horizon, Chinese Inner Mongolia was mostly flat plains, gritty terracotta villages, plantations of wind turbines. It finally clicked that this part of Mongolia was only 'inner' in relation to Beijing and the Han Chinese empire. From Ulaanbaatar's perspective, we were in deep southeast Mongolia, and 'outer' Mongolia didn't exist—it was just *Mongolia*, straight, no chaser.

But 'Inner' Mongolia has been out of Mongol hands for hundreds of years now. Since the late 1600s, a whole baffling clusterfuck of imperialism and mismanagement has gone down. These days Inner and Outer Mongolians couldn't read each other's writing, and unification was little more than a neo-fascist pipedream. Meanwhile, unregulated mining, deforestation and desertification were spawning dust storms, carcinogenic ones, that made for refugees in China, health scares in Korea and marvellous sunsets over the hazy golden steppes.

Hours passed. The dining car ran out of water, then food. We didn't know it at the time but nearly two-fifths of Inner Mongolia—about 400,000 square kilometres, half the size of New South Wales—was in a state of severe drought. Funny that a bunch of westerners on a tourist train should briefly suffer the fate awaiting *all* of northern China in a few decades—that is, unless China decides to make a grab for the melting permafrost and invade Siberia. Via Mongolia. By the time things get that dire, there probably won't be much room on the Trans-Mongolian for a couple of Kiwi adventurers and their stripy smuggler bags.

We were nearly in Mongolia.

DAY 0: THE WORST BUS RIDE OF MY LIFE

It was the middle of the night, or maybe 5 am. The scenery was still amazing, no doubt, but there wasn't a shred of moon to see it by. We'd been rattling northwest-ish out of Ulaanbaatar since the previous afternoon in a big old bus with about forty stoic locals and four tourists: Tama, me and Maya and Sharon, a couple of Israeli girls from the LG Guesthouse. We were up the very back of the bus on the right, directly above the wheel—the worst seats in the house. Our heads were about thirty centimetres below the bus's curved ceiling. As the shorter moron, I sat in the corner.

The road was bumpy, ludicrously bumpy. Theme-park bumpy. A small bump would propel us out of our seats by about ten centimetres; a medium bump, twenty to thirty centimetres. The large bumps attempted to launch us between fifty and seventy centimetres into the air. The roof prevented this.

For the first couple of hours the road was sealed and the bumps small to medium, occurring about once a minute. A few kilometres past a town called Hadasan the highway became a mess of roadworks. The driver veered sharply left, lurching us into a series of puddles, potholes and rocks that generated small, medium *and* large bumps, at a rate of All. The.Time. At first we thought this was a diversion around the roadworks, but after half an hour it became clear that this sodden minefield *was* the main road. The manager at the guesthouse in Ulaanbaatar had told us the bus would drive 'like a crazy mouse'—we were starting to understand what she meant.

We made the most of it, popping a couple of 'Relaxnol'— the not-quite-Valium I'd picked up in Phnom Penh—and washing it down with slugs of Chinggis Khaan brand vodka, which was smoother than any vodka I'd had in my life and, at five dollars a bottle, infinitely cheaper. Sharing a single pair of headphones, we rocked out to Tama's 'Big Apple Mix': Daft Punk live in New York; Notorious B.I.G.'s 'Juicy' mashed with Frank Sinatra's 'New York, New York'; Jay-Z's 'Empire State of Mind'. I told Tama he was a *teneg*—moron— for making himself a New York playlist. He nodded his head in time with the music.

For the first couple of hours we admired the jolting view, and the whole thing was amusing, even *mash sain* (very good). Having grown up in New Zealand I wasn't easily impressed by scenery, but Mongolia was like New Zealand on steroids, like someone had stretched the South Island out and shaken all the people off. Half a sleepless night later, my head was sore. My neck was sore. Hips, sore. Bum, sore. I was in a state of dazed, glazed disbelief.

This is the closest we could get to sleep: 1) use both arms as braces against the ceiling, to stop your head from pile-driving the vinyl; then 2) pass out as quickly as possible without your brace-arms slipping down. This was easier said than done. The Relaxnol and Chinggis helped with the passing out part but made the bracing much harder. I tried wrapping my thermal top around my head in a degenerate turban, but after fifty or sixty roof-kisses it would invariably fall apart. I considered getting my bike helmet out of my bag, but by the time we made it to Mörön it would be reduced to polystyrene confetti, no good for the ride. I considered getting out and walking. I considered flying there next time. When I looked over at Tama he was miraculously asleep, arms still pressed into the roof, like a somnambulist bank teller being held up at gunpoint. Then we went over a monster bump, his elbows buckled and he headbutted the ceiling. I couldn't help laughing.

'Damn,' he said, 'I was dreaming that I was back in New York at this crazy Manhattan penthouse party with Flight of the Conchords . . . Bret and Jemaine were getting mobbed by all these screaming girls with titties for Africa, they were fending them off like judo masters and I was catching all the rebounds and pashing them and ramming them into my pannier bags for later . . .'

'That was no dream,' I said.

As we high-fived, the bus plunged into a pothole. Our heads pashed the roof.

Ulaanbaatar had been all right, for a post-Soviet urban hellhole with the second-worst air pollution of any capital city in the world. After eighteen hours on the Trans-Mongolian staring at blank Gobi Desert, the outskirts of Ulaanbaatar—UB to locals and wannabe locals—were a sensory overload: a demented patchwork of shabby wooden fences, technicolour log cabins and *gers*, thousands of *gers*, round white mushroomy things that made me think of corrupt hippies selling watery chai. One third of Mongolia's three million citizens were crowded into and around the capital, and the overall impression was of arriving at a monster music festival held in a refugee camp. As we got closer to town, the nine- and twelve-storey apartment towers and potholed basketball courts with uprooted hoops reminded me of the concrete wastelands of America's less glamorous cities, as seen in *The Wire*: Ulaanbaltimore.

Then the billboards started. After decades of Soviet influence, Ulaanbaatar's signs were all in Cyrillic, which I couldn't read except by transliterating it—incorrectly—into English. Some words I could decode—хаан банк was Khan Bank; супер маркет was Super Market—but overall I had the giddy sensation that a dyslexic megalomaniac sign-writer had painted the town weird.

Getting off at the train station, I didn't feel like I was in Asia anymore. There was none of Cambodia's tropical mugginess and little of Beijing's bustle. It was probably like Russia, although I hadn't been there so I couldn't be sure, but the Soviets had definitely left the ugly stamp of their architecture everywhere. Mongolian men, I thought, generalising grossly, looked kind of like the Maori and Pacific Islander dudes I went to school with: tall, stocky, round-faced, bad haircuts.

After struggling our stuff to the nearest backpackers, me and Tama skipped the sightseeing and caught a taxi straight to the Dragon Centre bus station in the west of UB, hoping to buy tickets to морон (Mörön) for the following day from the ховсгол (Khövsgöl) counter. But that bus was full; the best they could do was the day after. This was pretty tight—

after twenty or thirty hours the bus would arrive in Mörön in the morning or maybe night of 10 July, and there was still 100 kilometres of cycling before we made it to Khatgal for Naadam, which began on the 11th and finished on the 12th. But we didn't have a choice. We bought a couple of tickets and hopped a taxi back to LG Guesthouse. On the way, we freaked out about getting all our luggage onto the bus, so we told our driver to go back to Dragon Centre. He cackled and pulled a wild U-turn into oncoming traffic. Back at the bus station we bought the last two tickets for Mörön. They were only 25,000 tugrugs—about A$25—and we figured that this way, if our voluminous cargo became an issue, we could brandish the extra tickets and demand that our bikes sit next to us on their own paid-for seats.

Which is pretty much what happened two days later. The bus driver, Bat, blocked our way, gesturing that it was impossible to take the boxes onboard. When Tama pointed to the bottom of the bus, the luggage packer, Batbold (pronounced 'Batbot'), shook his head vigorously: too long, his hands told us, much too long.

'*Ugui, ugui*,' he said, then in English, 'No.'

I flicked through the phrasebook for 'please' but I couldn't find it. The bus driver raised an eyebrow and rubbed his thumb and forefingers together.

I looked at Tama; he nodded. I took the third and fourth bus tickets out of my wallet and Bat and Batbold both smiled wide. Then Tama gave Bat a packet of Marlboros and he was our dear friend.

'*Za, za, za* (Yeah, yeah, yeah), *sain, sain*,' he said. 'We find way!'

Their way differed slightly from our way. Our bike boxes,

half-dissolved by UB acid rain and gaffer taped up with scraps of whiffy cardboard scavenged from the local markets, were crammed into an already full baggage compartment with brute force, the kicks of army boots and repeated slam-mings of baggage compartment door onto box end. Tama couldn't bear to watch, since he wasn't the one doing the kicking. I couldn't tear my eyes away. Those double-butted steel frames were already paying for themselves—alumin-ium wouldn't have stood a chance.

Just before the bus was scheduled to leave, the Israeli girls turned up. We had met Maya and Sharon at our guesthouse the day before. Both in their early twenties, Maya was cute and elfin and took an instant interest in Tama; Sharon was sullen and vaguely anaemic. The girls were hoping to make it to Khatgal for Naadam as well, and the only way there was via Mörön. They were running out of days. Tama had told Maya that our bus was sold out but suggested they come down on the day and try their luck. The driver sold them our bribe-tickets for the quite reasonable price of 30,000 tugrugs. Maya and Sharon hadn't packed, so they caught a taxi back to LG to sort their shit out while the whole bus, by now full, waited. I felt generally disgruntled. I started on the Chinggis vodka and stomped on and off the bus to piss in a ditch in full view of dozens of bemused locals, some who took photos.

'Tama, dude, those girls are pretty lame,' I said.

'I know,' he replied, 'but the cute one's pretty cute.'

An hour and a half later, Maya squeezed herself into the middle of the back seat next to Tama. Sharon ended up wedged between Maya's knees, sitting in the aisle on a sack of coal.

When the bus stopped for dinner at Hadasan, we headed into a diner with Sharon, Maya and a studious, bespectacled young man called Jamsuren who was trying to practise his English on Sharon. Jamsuren ordered us something that sounded like 'hodamic horik', a thick, muttony soup with wheat noodles that looked wrong but tasted right. I tried to memorise the name so we could order it in future, and got Jamsuren to write it in my notebook; it came out as аиттаи хоммог хуурга.

I asked Jamsuren to help me with my pronunciation in general since I was finding it harder than playing Scrabble without any vowels. Even basic phrases like 'Sorry, I don't understand'—'Uuchlaarai, bi oilgokhgui bain'—made me feel like I was a sedated dental patient coughing up half-chewed camel tongue. At least 'New Zealand' was easier: Shin Zeland. It would be hard even for us to stuff that up.

The girls picked at their soups, looking stricken. Sharon was a strict vegetarian. Being vegetarian in Mongolia was almost as much fun as being diabetic at Disneyland. We were all given complimentary cups of süütei tsai, the traditional, salty Mongol tea, but the girls refused to try it.

'What's the point in coming halfway round the world if you're not going to even try the local stuff?' I said to Tama, then struggled to gulp the lukewarm briny goop down.

'I know, lame,' he said. 'But this tea—it's scabby as.'

As we lined up to get back on the bus, Tama hissed, 'Bro, check out that boy's head.' He pointed to a little Mongol punk rocker of thirteen or fourteen dressed in double denim with a silver earring, short hair and a crude swastika shaved into his right temple.

Tama took a sneaky photo of him; in the background

you can see Maya and Sharon, laughing at something. Had they seen the swastika? What would they think? What did I think? Was the kid some kind of neo-Nazi, or did he just like the symbol? Maybe he thought it was a car brand, like the Mercedes peace sign, or something to do with the Sex Pistols.

At the next rest stop we met the kid's dad, a self-declared Tsaatan shaman from the western shores of Lake Khövsgöl. He invited us to spend Naadam with them, although unfortunately he didn't live on the way to the other Mörön. Maybe the swastika was a traditional Tsaatan symbol, and the Sanskrit crew stole it off them before Hitler stole it off everyone? How confusing.

I recalled the grumpy old Israeli retiree at LG guesthouse who had monopolised the internet and told me I acted 'like a German' after I demanded a go on the communal computer. When I told the old man where I was from he informed me that 'New Zealand is lucky—you have much less trouble with your natives than in Australia, because you killed them all'.

I sighed and asked him for a cigarette.

The bus shuddered onwards through the night. In my weakened state, it felt like this trip had been going on for many years; it was entirely reasonable to suppose it would never end. I wanted to take my shoes off, but in UB I had stashed half a million tugrugs—about A$500—under the inner sole of my left shoe, and now I was paranoid I'd lose it. To simplify expenditure when we were on the road, Tama had suggested we get out the same amount of cash and pool it, then just spend the money, like a joint bank account.

Now Tama put his backpack on his lap to make a lumpy pillow for Maya. He used his right arm to fend the roof off and his left to hold Maya's head down on his bag. She giggled, then snored. I watched this little scene for a few minutes, slightly jealous, until Tama noticed.

'You can lie down too, bro,' he said.

So I did. It was great, except that any lateral bus movement brought my and Maya's skulls together with a hollow 'tock'. Tama did his best to hold both of us down with his forearms. This worked for a little while, as our combined mass seemed to keep us all in our seats, but when we hit a really big bump Tama had no way to stop his own head from fully slamming into the roof. After a couple of those I grudgingly sat back up. Maya snuggled into Tama's bag. In the faint light I could see Sharon. She was pouting.

The whole scene reminded me of the 'good' old days, back in 2000, when I was in love with a girl called Kirsty and Tama was in love with Kirsty's best friend Lucy. Tama and Kirsty moved into the same sharehouse, and me and Lucy were around all the time. Not a vodka-and-Red-Bull-guzzling weekend or a Wednesday went by without one of the girls, usually Kirsty, losing it at someone, usually me. Tama and I spent hundreds of hours thrashing up and down the mountain-bike trails of Wellington, counselling each other and complaining about our women, and it was during those dark days that we first fixated on the distant Möröns. Was our dream of Mongolia nothing more than a sublimated fantasy of escape from our volatile, booze-soured girlfriends? I wasn't ruling it out.

The sun appeared mockingly in a pale blue sky. I popped another Relaxnol and pulled my turban over my head. Tama fastened me to the bus seat with an ockie strap across my chest. This was the only proper sleep I got. I woke twenty minutes later with a burning forehead and an extreme close-up of the moustachioed Mongolian cowboy sitting in front of me, who was staring at me and rubbing the back of his head. The ockie strap's rubbery innards were strewn across my lap. Thanks for nothing, Beijing Two-Yuan Shop.

'Easy, geezer, we need that for our bags,' Tama said between snorts of laughter. 'And you shouldn't headbutt the locals—it's not his fault the road's so shonky.'

I apologised to the cowboy in English. He nodded sorrowfully. I made a mental note to learn the word for 'sorry'. Tama gave him some dried apples.

As the bus rattled on, I looked out the window for lingering signs of the *dzud*, Mongolia's notorious 'white death'. When a mild winter brought temperatures of twenty degrees below, it was hard to imagine a *harsh* winter, but just six months earlier Mongolia had weathered its harshest *dzud* since records began, with temperatures nudging minus 50 degrees Celsius. Mongolia's overall supply of the 'five snouts'—horse, camel, yak-slash-cow, sheep and goat—plummeted from 45 million to 37 million. This would be bad news anywhere, but in a country that is still literally horse-powered, this was very bad news indeed. By April 2010, roughly 200,000 black beauties had died a white death, and thousands of nomad families were left with the grim prospect of hitching to Ulaanbaatar to become unemployed post-nomads. These *dzuds* used to occur about once every twenty years, but between 1999 and 2002 there was an unprecedented three *dzuds* in a row—and then this one, the worst ever.

A month before we left Melbourne, Tama had emailed me a *dzud* article peppered with lurid quotes: 'Two small goats had crawled into the cavity of a dead cow seeking protection. Unfortunately, even they did not survive . . . A little further on, a frozen heap of six skinned horses had been dumped in a ditch, their legs and heads twisting into a macabre sculpture . . .'

The link was followed by a perky PS saying 'Better bring some extra trail mix, bro!'

On the last ten hours of the train ride to UB, the Gobi Desert had been sprinkled with shiny white piles of bone. We had passed the time playing 'old corpse, new corpse' and wondering what we were going to eat for the next three weeks. Months later I would stumble upon an online UN report with a colour-coded map and realise that our dire bus ride to Mörön passed through most of the provinces *not* affected by the disaster, while to our west, south and east the white death had provided journalists with all the macabre sculptures they could wish for.

But that day—crossing into Khövsgöl *aimag* (province), pinballing our way across what the guidebook called 'the Switzerland of Mongolia', in the height of summer, twenty-five perfect degrees above zero—there were no bleached skeletons to be seen in the pristine green fields. In fact, even to my aching eyes the view out the window looked suspiciously like mountain-biking paradise.

DAY 1: THE FIRST MÖRÖN

Twenty-five hours after we left UB, I began to suspect we we getting close to Mörön. All the other passengers had gone quiet and were sitting very still with their bags on their laps. The road was flatter, smoother, even sealed in places. Telephone poles marched in from the left, powerlines looped from the right, both converging on the road and headed the same way as us. Tama rummaged in his backpack to get out his GoPro HERO-cam, a tiny fish-eyed thing with a suction-cup 'tripod', and convinced a nervous Jamsuren to reach out the bus window and stick it onto the outside of the bus. I filmed this interchange on the little Flip-cam Ami had lent us. Tama and I were in agreement that we were making a documentary, although what that meant in practice remained to be seen. Tama's style was Banff Mountain Film Festival, *Baraka*; mine was more *Borat*. There was nothing much to the film so far—just hills. Then a dirty off-white smudge on the horizon that didn't look like a hill.

'Mörön!' I yelled.

A baby started howling and didn't stop.

One by one, *gers* appeared in the fields. We rumbled past a pair of zangy teenage girls in matching white baseball caps marching along the road each carrying one handle of an oversized and overstuffed handbag. We passed a petrol station with a big MT logo at the front, rusted fuel cylinders on the grass out back. We passed the rotting corpse of a dog. Dirt tracks branched off to the left and right. Behind wooden fences there was a speckle of red, pink and brown roofs, steep enough to keep off the winter snow. I expected Mörön to get denser as we got closer but the houses remained spread out and as well as the dusty gers plonked next to sagging fences there were plenty of vacant lots. Apart from the odd man walking down the road or hunched over fixing a motorbike, the streets were pretty much deserted.

Mörön wasn't like a crowded Third World town, where domestic activity spilled out into the alleys, and you could wander around staring into the lives of people too poor to afford walls. There was none of the exotic mystique of the Cambodian villages we'd been traipsing through a week before, no street-corner cripples or child beggars to appal and titillate us. The place was all boarded up, tucked away. The locals were either in offices, or off in the fields, or at home, drinking quietly.

Mörön felt like it was paused in the middle of an evacuation, which was actually not far from the truth: every winter, thousands of herders would abandon the frigid plains to huddle together in Mörön and towns like it, and when the cold weather broke they would pack up their gers and disperse back into the hinterland with their yaks, leaving dusty circles stamped into the grass. Sprawled over sixteen square kilometres, home to 35,000 inhabitants in wintertime, it was hard to know exactly what the town was doing here.

Mörön was the administrative capital of Khövsgöl *aimag*, sure—but why *here*? There was no obvious difference between this dusty, treeless plain and the 200 kilometres or so of dusty, treeless plain we'd just driven through. I looked out for the wide, flowing river that would justify the town's name but I couldn't see anything.

We turned right onto a 'main' street. A woman in big sunglasses and a low-cut pink top walked along the dusty verge followed by a black, fluff-tailed wolf-dog that looked too healthy to be a stray. Tama and I tried to be fascinated by the white-painted fences and green gates, the gaudy roofs poking out at irregular angles, but it was tough. There were no towering concrete monstrosities, no kitsch Communist statues, no horribly photogenic factories belching black smoke into the sky.

Our guidebook said, 'For such a beautiful province, Khövsgöl has a rather disappointing capital . . . The town has few sights and most travellers only use the place to break up a journey to and from regions to the north.' This seemed like some outrageously optimistic *Lonely Planet* whitewash. Mörön was a not-so-Wild-West shantytown, plonked in a random chunk of Inner Asia. Mörön was a scabhole.

We pulled into an empty expanse of dirt that doubled as a bus station and staggered off the bus. Maya and Sharon were instantly whisked away by a tout in a minivan headed for Khatgal. (*Maya: 'See you at Naadam? We're staying at Garage 24 . . .' Hopeful glance at Tama.*) We pulled our battered boxes and bags out of the luggage compartment and dumped them in a heap, then took turns dragging stuff across the carpark into the shade of a log cabin. A portly man with a proprietorial manner, possibly the manager of the bus station, told us to move on—which we didn't, because we couldn't. A few minutes later he came back and told us to at least not leave our rubbish everywhere when we took off. We began assembling our bikes. The gears and disc brakes had survived the bus ride and all the necessary parts still seemed to be in the box, but after that jangled, sleepless ordeal I felt like a few essential cogs had been dislodged from my head. I needed a couple of bread rolls with salami before I passed out.

Soon enough we were accosted by what passed for Mörön's criminal underworld: half a dozen taxi drivers, hotel owners, touts and bullies who fought over the custom of the few foolhardy westerners who strayed this far from the Trans-Mongolian main trunk line. This sorry bunch of bored men who were dressed in Kmart Boxing Day sale polo shirts and track pants converged on our bike workshop to help and/or to steal some of our vital components. A round-faced bloke whose shirt read 'We can talk but MONEY TALKS so talk more' picked up one of our pannier racks and looked at it extremely doubtfully. Each luggage carrier was actually *two* luggage carriers: a long but flimsy aluminium rack that had been lashed onto a shorter but sturdier steel rack with a couple of metres of coathanger wire and some spare bike pedals. This allowed our pannier bags to sit way back, beyond the orbit of our massive *gweilo* (foreign) feet. Back in Beijing Tama had been horrified when he first saw Rhino's handiwork, and outraged at me for overseeing it, but it was that or do the whole trip on rickshaws. Money Talks helpfully gestured that we should throw this pinnacle of ad hoc Chinese ingenuity far, far away. I stopped slicing bread rolls and grabbed the mutant rack off him defensively, pretending it was *mash sain*.

'Buy Chinggis vodka now,' Money Talks demanded. He pointed to his tall friend who pulled a miniature vodka bottle out of his pocket and wiggled it in the air, trying to make me follow him across the carpark like he was the Pied Piper of Mörön and me an alcoholic rat-child.

'Just ignore them,' Tama muttered.

'*Russki, Russki*,' Money said, shaking his head sorrowfully, as if being born Russian was a tragic and dangerous misfortune.

The 'Russki', who looked pretty Mongolian to me, rolled his eyes and bared his teeth like an extra in an old *Sinbad* movie. I shook my head and cut into a tomato. Money Talks pointed insistently to my knife, then to Fake Russian, before grimacing and running his finger across his throat from ear to ear. This was mildly unnerving, but it seemed unlikely that I would be decapitated in broad daylight in the centre of Mongolia's fourth-largest town over a five-dollar bottle of vodka, so I ignored him and finished making our bread rolls.

One by one the touts lost interest and drifted over to the buses in the carpark. A few minutes later a furious screaming match broke out. Money Talks and Fake Russian were lashing out at each other, swinging wild windmill punches at stomach and head. Fake landed more punches than Money. Fake got Money into a headlock and slammed his skull into the bus's glass door. Money collapsed on the ground. After a few seconds he got up. Fake gave him a cigarette. Then they started fighting again.

It took us a couple of hours to get the bikes and gear ready. I surprised myself, and possibly Tama, with a sustained display of competence, managing to get handlebars, wheels, deformed luggage carrier and panniers onto my bike frame without too much supervision. My bike was too heavy to lift, but I didn't have to carry the fucker, just pedal it. I assumed the position: arse on seat. Sitting on my new two-wheeled home and turning wobbly circles in the dust felt good. I even had a little *Mongol tug*, a Mongolian flag, which I flew proudly from my handlebars. Tama had a *Mongol tug* too and he hung it from a short pole at the back of his pannier rack. It was bigger than mine.

Once Tama sorted out a little problem with his handle-bar stem he wanted to 'get a move on', but I insisted on stopping for lunch. I was too tired to be hungry but it was late afternoon and those rolls were all we'd eaten since the day before, and we were about to leave civilisation, such as it was, for the sub-Siberian wilderness with empty stomachs and a stove we didn't know how to use. We cycled a few blocks with our cumbersome loads until we found a canteen that was full and therefore (hopefully) good.

Tama waited outside with the bikes while I grabbed a menu and pointed to a word I couldn't pronounce, speci-fying '*khoyor bayartai*' ('two goodbye') and crossing my fingers for something edible. We waited in the gutter, watching bruised purple clouds queue up in the sky. In the silence a plastic bag tumbled down the 'main street'. I scrambled to get my Flip-cam out of my pannier to film it, but I was too slow.

'This place is pretty grim,' I said.

'Yeah, it's a shithole,' Tama said. 'But I've been in much shittier holes with you. Remember Hamilton?'

'Never again. Dude, remember Kalgoorlie?'

Tama shuddered. Near the end of our forty-hour train trip from Adelaide to Perth, itself a demoralising experience, we stopped for a dinner break in one of Western Australia's premier mining towns. We caught a taxi up to the Super Pit gold mine and admired a multi-billion-dollar hole in the ground that propped up the Melbourne art scene. The taxi driver was rough as guts, and keen to talk about it. Against my better instincts I asked him what race relations were like in town.

'What, the niggers? The *boongs*? Mate, they take our taxes and sleep outside like animals—I'll show yas!'

He pulled a U-turn, drove to the edge of town and shone his headlights onto a family making dinner next to a tree. They shielded their eyes. The taxi driver beeped at them. We begged him to take us back to town. He dropped us off outside a topless-bar-slash-brothel with a sign saying 'All The Meat You Can Eat'.

'Ya can't beat Kalgoorlie, mate—it's the best place in the world for a feed, fuck 'n' fight on a Friday night!' the driver said, and hooned off.

Compared to Kalgoorlie, Mörön was Paris-by-the-steppe.

A couple of mutton noodle soups arrived, remarkably similar to yesterday's hodamic horik. I inhaled it without chewing; it barely touched the sides. We went to a servo to get some *benzin* for our stove. The petrol station attendant pumped a solitary litre of Russian petrol—cheap as chips, full of lead—into our fuel bottle. He was a dude in his early twenties, uninterested in my spittle-flecked attempts at Mongolian, unimpressed by our bikes.

'Sucks being him,' I called to Tama as we rolled down the road. 'Wait till he turns twenty-eight and gets his Saturn return.'

'Never happen, bro. That's strictly a First World problem.'

Before leaving town, I forced Tama to bike around for a couple of blocks. I was determined to film something that captured the vibe of Mörön. *Ronery Pranet* wasn't much help; it said that Mörön had a museum with a woolly mammoth tusk in it, but we agreed this was missable. What I really wanted was a photogenic sign saying 'Welcome to Mörön' in huge letters—and in English. But instead there were just rows and rows of dilapidated timber cabins receding down dusty alleys. The overall impression was of wandering around a movie set that had been abandoned after a failed Soviet remake of *The Wizard of Oz*.

At the top of a dusty rise not far from the bus terminal we stopped by a pile of bricks with a dejected tree branch wrapped in blue plastic bags sticking up from it. It was as if a rogue fighter jet had strafed an outhouse, then the locals had used the debris as a burial mound for some poor moron caught on the crapper. But thanks to Jill Lawless I knew that this trash heap was actually an *ovoo*, a traditional Mongolian shamanic cairn. In Mongolia's north, where the steppe gives way to Sub-Arctic conifer forest, shamanism had been around for millennia. When they weren't busy guiding dead souls towards their next rebirth, shamans liked to build *ovoos*. Travellers were meant to leave a blue scarf, representing the sky, draped on an *ovoo* as an offering to Tenger, the sky god. Back in the good old days the scarves probably weren't made of plastic bin liner. Pious Mongols once left other offerings for the sky gods too—milk of horse, marmot's gizzard, skull of buzzard, et cetera. But during Mongolia's brief innings as a satellite state of the Evil Empire, when it was known to the Russians privately as 'the sixteenth republic', shamanism was brutally suppressed, almost entirely wiped out.

In 2010, Mörön's central *ovoo* seemed to double as a giant ashtray, with Mongols leaving smashed Chinggis bottles and cigarette butts in municipal quantities among the rubble. In a country with little evident interest in shamanism and no public bins that I could see, it was hard to draw the line between reverence and rubbish.

We left a couple of bread rolls among the bricks. And because *Ronery Pranet* told us to, we circled the *ovoo* three times clockwise for good luck, then three times counter-clockwise, just to be sure. Down the hill a grubby boy had tied a piece of string around an empty Chinggis bottle and was dragging it behind him like a dead pet dog. Two younger children followed the bottle around listlessly. The boy dragged the bottle over a rock; it smashed.

The first mörön
www.moron2moron.com/videos/first-moron

We had cycled a couple of hundred metres down the road when I realised I'd left my bike gloves somewhere. I went back and checked the servo, but there were no gloves at the petrol pump. I went inside to ask the attendant. He looked even more depressed at my return. I did some bad mime, trying to explain 'gloves', 'bike gloves', 'with fingers', 'I was wearing them just before'. No response. I became suspicious that the attendant had stolen them, and gave him a look that said as much. He stared back at me sullenly.

Tama suggested we check our lunch spot then get a move on. There was nothing at the counter, nothing in the dust outside. Well, a local Mörön had been overjoyed to scavenge the remnants of our bike boxes, so my gloves must've been an early Christmas for that bowser jockey. I shoved my hands into my pockets in frustration . . . and felt glove.

As we cleared the last of the ramshackle fences and unconvincingly patched roofs I felt the skank and fuzz of the bus ride lifting and was seized with an intoxicated, giddy glee. After months of (kind of) planning, borrowed GPS units, the jabbings of rabies vaccinations, queues in airports and duty-free stores and military-grade cartographical maps purchased in UB and left in a Korean restaurant and luckily still there the next day, here we finally were, on the edge of something enormous.

Mongolia.

We were really here, embarking on the ride of our lives! I could feel a Song of the Open Road coming on . . .

'Mongoooooooolia!'

'Motherfucken zaaaaaang!'

If I'd been wearing a cowboy hat, I would've whacked it against my thigh.

Khatgal was a respectable 101 kilometres to the north. In an ideal world we'd be there by the next morning, in time for the start of Naadam. But we'd lost a day waiting for that bus and now there were only a couple of hours of daylight left. Short of cycling all night with headtorches, snorting sachet after sachet of electrolytes and slapping each other in the face to keep awake, our only option was to ride ten or twenty kilometres north of Mörön, camp out, get up early and bust it hard to Khatgal, missing the first half of the festival. We could still catch tomorrow night's wild party times plus the World Cup soccer final between Spain and someone at 2 am Mongolian time, then get into the second and final day of manly sports, donning our leopard and skeleton costumes and showing the local *bökh* wrestlers what Kiwis were really made of.

A few minutes out of Mörön we saw a small path veering to the right of the main track, snaking towards a low ridge of jagged hills in the east. The high road! We could make out a U-shaped pass between the hills, soft and inviting, a cleft between two perfect breasts. We stared into it like entranced sailors.

'Bro,' Tama said, and I already knew what was coming.

'Maybe it's a shortcut to Khatgal, hey?' I said.

'It's all just random hills and valleys from here, we'll get there either way . . .'

'Bro, we're in fucking *Mongolia*! Let's do it!'

We took it. It was a good chance to test our lower gears, get our legs ready for the punishing days to come. The path was rougher, but rideable. Then we lurched off the dirt track onto the grass and headed uphill. It was much harder than I was expecting. In Melbourne the parks are pretty much as smooth as they look; the Mongolian pasture-side isn't. The velvety grass, which seemed pool-table smooth from a distance, was actually pockmarked by thousands, millions of hoof prints. We bounced up and down. I changed into low second, then low first. My gears made a strange crunching sound. The pass looked higher, further away. Above us, a nightmare sky. Without discussing it we both headed left, away from the pass, back in a vaguely northerly direction. We had successfully abandoned our first Kiwi shortcut.

Up ahead there was a grid of low rocks. It looked like a series of building foundations—the remains of a military barracks, or the beginnings of a new subdivision—but on closer inspection we realised it was the Mörön cemetery. Hundreds of coffin-sized slabs of granite rested among the grass, topped by rough lumps of rock approximating headstones. Some of the graves were enclosed by orna-mental cages; the cages looked like cots for baby ghosts. I wondered, briefly, if we should be riding our bikes here. Tama dismounted and started stuffing rocks into his pocket.

'Oi! Tomb Raider!' I yelled. 'Don't desecrate their grave-yard!'

'Rabid dogs, bro,' Tama said, and continued filling his pockets. I hesitated, then did the same.

Back on the 'main road' a couple of jeeps weaved past, loaded with people heading north to Khatgal. The drivers slowed down and leaned out the window to bellow *'Saikhan Naadaarai!'* ('Have a nice Naidam!') at the top of their lungs; passengers grinned and waved madly, some holding little Mongolian flags, others clutching vodka bottles.

We shouted *'Sain Naadam!'* back and everyone laughed raucously. It wasn't clear if this was Mongolia's fabled hospit-ality, or the excitement of seeing such nice mountain bikes, or pride that white tourists were flying *Mongol tugs*. Regard-less, it boded well for our trip, although Tama did suggest we camp a few hundred metres from the road to minimise the chance of becoming roadkill. The storm clouds were closing in so we jumped off our bikes and pushed them up a gully until we couldn't see the road. Tama boiled water for rice while I set up our tent in a rising wind.

While stoked to be surrounded by the rugged glory of nature, I also felt a bit uneasy. No one knew where we were, not even us. If two morons are run over in a field and no one hears them scream, do they make a sound?

Something made a sound. Up the gully, a man on horse-back appeared from behind a little ridge and cantered towards us.

TAMA: *Sain bainuu!* ['Are you well?']

HORSEMAN: *Sain, sain bainuu.* ['I'm well, and you?']

TOM: *Sain bainuu!* ['Are you well?']

[Awkward silence.]

TOM: Ah, *bi Shin Zelandaas irsen.* ['Ah, me from New Zealand.']

HORSEMAN: *Tiin.* ['Yes.']

TOM: Um, *unadug dugui, Mörön Khövsgöl, dugui dugui dugui, Mörön Khentii.* ['Um, bicycle, Mörön Khövsgöl, round, round, round, Mörön Khentii.']

[HORSEMAN looks at the bicycles, scratches his head.]

HORSE: *Whinny! Neigh!* ['Idiots! Peasants!']

[HORSEMAN presses his hands together, leans head on hands = 'Would you like to stay in my *ger*?']

TOM: [Makes pyramid with his hands.] Ah, no thanks, we have—*saikhan.* ['Rhubarb rhubarb rhubarb—beautiful.']

HORSEMAN: *Uuchlaarai, bi oilgokhgui bain.* [Not sure.]

TOM: Sorry, no Mongol. Um, *nyet Mongolski?* ['Rhubarb Mongol. Um, no Mongolian?']

HORSEMAN: *Vi govorite po Ruski? Vi shto, idiot?* [Not sure.]

[Awkward silence.]

TOM: [Gestures to hills.] Mongolia . . . *maikhan.* ['Mongolia . . . summer tent.']

[HORSEMAN shakes his head politely. TOM gets out phrasebook. HORSEMAN looks through phrasebook, fails to find anything useful. HORSEMAN returns phrasebook. TOM goes to pat HORSE; HORSE skitters away.]

TOM: [Fans the sweat on his forehead, gestures to horse.]
Khaluun. Amttai. ['Hot. Delicious.']
HORSE: *Neigh!*
HORSEMAN: Okay, *bayartai.* ['Okay, goodbye.']
TOM and TAMA: *Bayarllaa!* ['Thank you!']
[HORSEMAN rides away.]

This shabby exchange was to form a template for many of our future interactions. Most Mongolians we met would try to speak Mongolian with us; when this abruptly stalled, some would try a hopeful '*Russki?*', only to be repelled by our *nyets*. I had read somewhere that after Mongolian and Russian, Mandarin is the third most commonly spoken language in Mongolia, especially in the south, while Kazakh cameos in the west. English comes in a disappointing fifth, although it is more popular with the younger generation. This meant that even a basic conversation quickly became excruciating, phrasebook or no phrasebook (*neg yum dutuu bain*—'something is missing'). One misguided year of high-school Latin didn't help, nor did my precarious grasp of te reo Maori, my *ein-falafel-mit-chili-sosse-danke* Deutsch, or four weeks of a twelve-week 'Japanese for Dummies' course—all useless. Tama just spoke English at people and wasn't fussed when they didn't get it.

As we sat on the grass with our dinners the wind howled and the bottom fell out of the clouds to the north. There were solid slabs of rain, thunder, the odd spork of lightning, but the storm stayed away. We passed the Chinggis Gold vodka back and forth. It had a soft, clean burn like a single malt and you could sip it like one. I admired the patriotic Mongolian booze copywriting on the half-empty bottle:

Chinggis Gold vodka is distilled from pure wheat, grown in the land of the great Mongol emperor Chinggis Khaan, who in the 13th century ruled the largest land empire the world has ever known. CHINGGIS KHAAN: MAN OF THE MILLENNIUM.

What an awesome thing to be able to incorporate into your marketing campaign, I thought fuzzily. What would the Australian equivalent be—Captain Cook rum? Ned Kelly lager? Bindi Irwin cola? But that didn't matter now. I was half a world away from all that stuff, and grateful for the breathing space.

When the cold got too much we climbed into our tent and jumped in our sleeping bags. I'd forgotten how small it was inside, especially when high winds blew the tent wall into your face. Within seconds Tama was snoring up a storm to rival the gale outside. Tama snored like no one else I knew, a theatrical and onomatopoeic 'puff' that sounded like a kid trying to trick his parents by pretending to snore. Then he let rip a mighty fart and sniggered in his sleep. This was going to be my home for the next month.

I grinned. Cramped and noisy as it was, I knew the Great Outdoors were just Out There, all that good emptiness stretching out around me. I fell asleep as happy as a dog in a patch of sun.

PART TWO

THE ROCKY, SANDY, MUDDY, FLOODED TRACK LESS TRAVELLED

DAY 2: MANLY SPORTS

The Khatgal Naadam began without us, ninety kilometres to the north. If we missioned it we could be there in time for dinner and disco dancing. I wanted a big-arse bowl of muesli for breakfast, but we didn't have enough water to mix with the milk powder, so we just ate our last two bread rolls and gulped down the last of the liquid. I tipped everything out of the tent and packed it down, shoved my sleeping bag in its stuff-sack and into a pannier with my books and clothes and spork, jacket on top for quick access in case of storms, fastened the panniers onto my bike rack, stuffed the tent and sleeping roll into my backpack and ockie-strapped it on top of the panniers. Tama was ready before me. It was nearly 9 am.

We jolted back down to the road but kept to the far right as jeeps and SUVs were already hurtling north at top speed. One would pass us every couple of minutes, *Mongol tugs* flying from windows and aerials, '*Saikhan Naadaarai!*'s carrying above blaring Bollywood-inspired Mongol pop, reinforcing our impression that Naadam was Mongolian Christmas, New Year's and Schoolies all rolled into one. We whizzed over patchy grass and hard-packed clay.

'This is *Doig and Pugs vs Wild!*' I yelled.

'It's *Morons vs Wild!*' Tama yelled back.

'Yeah . . . hey, what about *Man vs Girls Gone Wild?*'

'Ha, yeah!'

'That'd be a show to watch,' I said, warming to the theme. 'Bear Grylls parachutes into LA with nothing to eat or drink except two litres of strawberry-flavoured lube . . .'

'He's like, "San Pornando Valley's in the middle of a ruddy heatwave, and the girls are gagging for it—I've gotta roger my way out of here by tomorrow night, without dying of dehydration—"'

'Or AIDS!'

It was smooth, flat riding for half an hour or so, but up ahead we could see the first proper hill. The morning cloud had burned off and the sun was holding court in a vast blue sky. We started to climb. And sweat. And climb.

I rode in front, hugging the right-hand ditch. Fewer jeeps passed us now; everyone was already at Naadam. In my mind's eye I could see crowds of happy, drunken Mongols gamboling on the shores of magical Lake Khövsgöl, the men stripping down to their underpants and grappling in the sun, ladies in yak-fur bikinis thrusting 'Round 1' cards high into the summer sky, sweet Chinggis vodka flowing like water . . .

Our banter had dropped off to the occasional redundant expletive. As we slogged our way upwards, cute little furry marmots would look up startled from their grass-munching and puddle-sipping and scamper almost mechanically into tiny roadside burrows. It was odd to think that every year a few Mongolians died from eating roast marmot infected with the bubonic plague. After a while, my uphill suffering and the rodents' clockwork vanishings felt deeply inter-connected, verging on religious: the Marmots of Impure Thinking were being banished by the Bicycle Wheel of Truth. I was a Holy Sweat Vessel, clearing the way for the Shining Path of Emptiness.

I was getting really dehydrated.

Also, my back gears were playing up. Cogs 4/6 kept grinding, slipping. I'd change up into 2/7 but that was too high; the pedalling was too hard. I'd change down, crunch and skip until I was in 2/3, my legs flailing around and the bike hardly moving. Tama moved past me steadily, pulled by an invisible towrope. I'd surge towards him then drop away. I couldn't find my pace. I pushed down on the pedal; it pushed back. I changed down and lunged forward, nearly toppling into the ditch. I was buggered—already.

Cycling, like masturbation, is fun and easy to do—some-times all day long. But also like masturbation, cycling is very hard to describe. When you're really doing it, really *riding*, there's almost no space left from which to observe that riding. Like on the uphills. It's only on long uphills that you know, deep in the marrow of your aching bones, what cycling is about. Every metre is earned and paid for through the thighs. The trick is to find your pace and stay in it. You can't conquer a hill with speed, or even strength. You just have to be patient and stay in your pace, no matter how slow or humbling, smiling and waving as the Range Rovers full of drunk festivalgoers thunder past you, laughing at the stupid westerners. That's the trick.

There are other things too, such as pedalling with your gluteus maximus as well as your thigh muscles—bending your back and literally putting your arse into it until you're hunched over like a constipated dog (Tama taught me that one). But mainly you just have to get slow and sweaty and sore, and smile as you suffer because you have *chosen* this for yourself, this pain that's really a luxury.

After thirty kilometres, nearly three hours and just over 500 vertical metres we made it to the top of the Hujirtin *davaa* (Hujirtin pass), which my brain kept abbreviating to Hurtin' Pass. On the summit we were greeted by a blue sign at least four metres high and half a metre wide proclaiming хатлrан vertically in white Cyrillic letters. Khatgal!

The town itself was nowhere in sight, but we were on the right track. On the other side of the sign, facing south, the sign said мороh. Looking back, we could just make out a light brown smear on the plains below: Mörön. Beyond that a tranquil rim of hills, then to the left, over the horizon and far out of sight, 700 kilometres to the southeast, Ulaanbaatar—and a few hundred kilometres east of that, our eventual destination, the other Mörön, the one in Khentii province, which we were currently riding away from for the sake of Schoolies by the Lake. Near the хатран–мороh sign was a large mound of empty bottles—no blue plastic or rocks though, so probably not a sacred *ovoo*. I rummaged through the bottles to see if there was a spare mouthful to be had. There wasn't.

'Man, I'm glad we didn't just ride over that crazy hill detour last night,' I said, licking my lips. 'We'd be fucked by now.'

'Maybe,' an unruffled Tama replied. 'Nah, we probably would've met, like, some nice cowboy and drunk his water. Or some hot Mongol girls washing each other in a lake.'

'Maybe.'

A station wagon drove up the hill and the driver stopped when he saw us. He got out and ambled over, carrying three disposable plastic cups and a bottle of vodka. He slopped over-generous 'shots' into the cups. Keen to follow protocol, Tama and I did like the internet suggested: we dipped our little fingers into the vodka, flicked a single drop upwards to the sky gods, bellowed 'Chinggis!' and sucked the vodka down. Our companion looked at us strangely, muttered 'nostrovia' and drank his shot. Tama asked the man for some us—water, pronounced 'oose'—so he fetched a plastic bottle from his wife, who was regarding us coolly from the passenger seat; we drained the bottle. The man nodded sadly and drove off.

The next few kilometres were a gentle downhill dream. The weight of our bellies and bags carried us freewheeling along. Pedalling was just a symbolic gesture. The track came in and out of focus, like someone was trying and failing to tune in an old TV—first there was one big path, then three little ones, then seven, then one again. Tama and I drifted left and right, dodging the odd puddle, looking for marmots to terrorise. I belted out a tuneless version of 'Road to Nowhere', changing the lyrics to 'We're on a road to Mörön'. Tama sped up until he was out of earshot. On the other side of Hurtin' Pass the landscape was overwhelmingly horizontal. There were no buildings, no fence posts or powerlines, not even a stunted tree to break up the sensation of boundless width. It would've been perfect if I wasn't so thirsty. I fantasised about dunking my head in a crisp mountain stream, but there were no streams— or mountains for that matter.

Thirty-five or forty kilometres from our morning campsite, I started to slow down. At first I thought something had gone wrong with my brakes, until I realised something had gone wrong with my legs. I was everyday-commuter fit, used to cycling up to thirty kilometres around Melbourne on a disaster of a bike with no gears, a perpetually slipping chain and no back brake, but now I was heading out of my comfort zone, big time. Tama looked back over his shoulder; I kicked hard to catch up.

In the distance was a bunch of dots that grew into a huddle of trucks and tents as we drew nearer. We rode over to beg for *us*. Up close we saw steamrollers, which implied road works, although our last four hours' riding suggested otherwise. A black-and-white TV sat on a little table in the middle of an otherwise empty clearing. On the screen two fuzzy dudes in embroidered speedos were bent at the waist and leaning heavily into each other like drunks at a funeral. We followed the TV's extension cord towards a *ger* and found a dungareed worker having lunch in the shade. He offered us some salty Mongol tea; we shook our heads and empty *us* bottles plaintively. The man grunted and led us over to a 1000-litre water tank mounted on a trailer where he filled our bottles. When he handed them back to us we were holding out two more empty bottles. He frowned then filled those as well and turned around to find we had drunk the first bottles dry and were holding them out again.

Possibly concerned for our health, the road worker gestured to his truck and pointed down the road to Khatgal. He mimed lifting our bikes onto the truck.

Mongolian hospitality! I turned to Tama.

'I know we're meant to be cycling the *whole* way from Mörön to Mörön,' I said, 'but we're missing Naadam . . . This way we could get there for the wrestling?'

'Dude, this is our first day! We've only gone like forty k's!'

'I know, but—'

'Definitely *not*.'

Tama was right.

Mörön to Mörön, by bicycle . . . and truck.

No.

We thanked the dude for the *us* and the offer, jumped on our bikes and rolled away. A buzzard circled slowly overhead. At first we made good time on the freshly flattened path, but the sun was relentless—it was at least thirty degrees—and my gears were getting worse. Then the roadworks ended and we blundered onto every cyclist's most hated and feared surface: sand. My wheels swerved and churned in the grit and I slowed right down. If I pedalled harder my chain slipped. I got off and pushed my bike for a bit but, with thirty kilograms of luggage on the back, this was no long-term solution. Twenty metres ahead, Tama was handling the sand just fine.

'Tama,' I shouted, 'let's stop for lunch!'

'There's no shade here, let's get a move on!'

'There's no shade anywhere!'

'True, but let's wait till we find a nice place to stop!'

'Like where?'

'Like a nice lake or something.'

He waited for me to catch up and showed me the map. Sure enough there was a blotchy soup-stain of a lake called Erhul *nuur* a few hundred metres ahead.

We were to discover that the cartographer's idea of 'lake' differed substantially from ours. To my eyes, Erhul *nuur* was less lake and more dried-up salt-puddle swarming with vicious biting flies. The salt flakes were impossible to bathe in but they were very good at blinding you with reflected sunlight.

'This lake sucks,' Tama said. 'Let's try somewhere else.'

'Let's just stop here.'

'But what about the flies?'

'Fuck. The. Flies.'

'Woah, what's the matter bro—are you getting hangry?'

'Yes, Tama Pugsley, I'm hangry—hangrier than I've ever been in my life. I've got a *really fast metabolism*. Now please, LET'S JUST EAT SOME BLOODY MUESLI.'

And so we did. I inhaled half a kilogram of muesli with powdered milk and water and promptly fell into a food coma, which came complete with visions of self-pedalling marmots. After five sweet seconds Tama poked me awake with his spork.

'Bro, you've been out for half an hour. Time to get a move on—gotta make it to Khatgal to watch the soccer final.'

'Urgh. How far do you reckon we've come?'

'About forty-five k's.'

'Sweet! So, how much further?'

'About fifty-five k's.'

The sun beat down.

'I still reckon we could hitch a lift to Khatgal. Not to avoid riding, but so we don't miss the festival . . .'

'No way.'

'It wouldn't be, like, cheating, it's just—'

'Dude, look around you. We're doing it!'

The world was split neatly in half: blue and white above, green and brown below. And us in the middle, crawling along like masochistic ants. A truck rumbled past, horn croaking. I looked longingly at its spacious back, which was only half-filled with luxurious sheep pelts.

'Don't even think about it, Doig.'

I thought about it.

We crossed a ridge and dropped into a rocky valley. The path wound down, left, hard right, then left across a little creek and up, up, up a nasty steep slope. There was the odd pine tree dotted around as well as the occasional log and plenty of tree stumps. The sun disappeared behind the ridge as we descended and the valley turned shady and cool. Whenever I pumped the brakes or changed gears I heard an ominous high-pitched jingling sound that I came to think of as 'the sleigh bells of imminent bike failure'.

Just when it felt like we had dropped off the grid, we turned a corner and were greeted by a picturesque log cabin roadhouse with a faded sign showing a bounty of bread, apples, cheese and cucumbers and a caption in English that said SHOP. Inside was a waist-high counter that wrapped around two walls and behind it some floor-to-low-ceiling shelves, sparsely stocked with packaged goods from China and Eastern Europe. No fruit or vegies. No bread. We bought four Mars Bars and a couple of 1.25-litre bottles of something yellow, sugary and carbonated from a young boy who was only slightly taller than the counter then sat down outside on a rickety wooden seat. After a few seconds it snapped neatly in the middle. As I lay sprawled and giggling in the dust, my first thought was 'I wish we'd filmed that,' followed by 'I wish we hadn't broken their only seat,' then 'Let's get out of here before the owner notices we've broken his only seat.'

As we got on our bikes the owner came out of the store, grinning and speaking loudly in Mongolian. We shrugged our shoulders and he switched to Russki, then sign language, with expressive jabs in the direction of his cabins. Tama pointed down the road and bellowed, 'Khatgal, Khatgal'.

'Khatgal—*nyet!*' He shook his head violently and counted on his fingers: one, two, three, four. '*Döch!*'

I flicked through the phrasebook to the numbers section. '*Döch*' was there all right.

'Jeez man, he reckons it's forty kilometres,' I said.

'He must be exaggerating,' Tama said. 'What's the word for twenty-five?'

'Ah. . . *khorin tav.*'

'Korna tiv!' Tama yelled at the proprietor. '*Mash sain!*' He laughed and shook his head. 'Okay, okay—*piv?*'

'*Piv?*'

'Budweiser?' The owner made a drinking motion.

'Oh—beer!'

'*Za, za, za—birra!* Pub!' The owner motioned for us to sit with him on his balcony. It was awash with afternoon sun.

'Whaddya reckon?' Tama asked in a pained voice.

'Man, I'd murder a beer right now—but we've gotta get to Naadam.'

'True.' He took a deep breath and turned to the owner. 'We must ride—Khatgal! Korna tiv, kilometre! If we have beer, we get—sleepy! We ride off road, crash into ditch!' All of this with Marcel Marceau hands. 'Goodbye—bayish tar!'

Tama turned his bike towards the road, but the owner shouted, '*Proteste! Proteste!*' and ran in front of Tama's bike to block his escape. He grabbed onto Tama's handlebars, clamped his knees around the front wheel and yelled something at his son, who had been watching proceedings from the doorway. The boy ran into the shop. I braced myself for a banjo duel.

'Maybe he noticed the broken seat,' I stage-whispered to Tama.

'Let's get the fuck out of here!' Tama yelled back, trying to shake the shopkeeper off.

'*Proteste! Proteste!*' the man cried.

'Psycho!' I replied.

Tama shook the shopkeeper off and as we were struggling out of the carpark the boy ran out of the shop towards us holding two large projectiles in his hands. I swerved but it was too late—he was on me. He deftly wedged an extra-large can of beer between my ockie straps and my backpack and did the same to Tama then nodded and ran inside. Now even more disturbed, I got out my wallet and tried to pay the man, but he refused my money.

'What the— zang!' I yelled. '*Naadam Sain!*' Then, 'Sorry about the bench!'

Half a hard hour later we stopped for a roadside piss and map check. My urine came out yellower and stinkier than the sugary drink from our pitstop. According to the map, a little town called Alag-Erdene was nestled in the handsome pines a couple of kilometres to the northeast. It was tantalisingly close, the very idea of it just oozing bed and breakfast, but we decided to push on to Khatgal even though it was at least another twenty-five kilometres. It was well past 5 pm, but last night it hadn't got properly dark until 10.30 pm, so we still had riding hours to burn. And burn we would.

I was sweating furiously, thirsty again. My bike was too heavy; I had too much luggage. Tama was struggling too. I suggested we drink the KYNEP-brand beers to lighten our loads. Tama was about to crack one open but stopped just in time.

'Dude, it's only 0.9 per cent alcohol—the scammer gave us light beers!' Tama shook his head in disgust.

We left the cans by the side of the road, figuring they'd be an exciting disappointment for a thirsty Mongol traveller. It was another hour before the penny dropped.

'Hey Tama,' I panted, 'I reckon that guy gave us light beers on purpose, so we could drink it with him and not get sleepy.' Tama looked up.

'Ah, Mongolia!'

We were riding slower now and checking the map more frequently. Tama, ever optimistic, reckoned we were nearly *here*, but when the old GPS unit finally spat out some coordinates we were only *there*, a whole valley further south. After ten hours on the road Khatgal didn't seem to be getting any closer—but the storm clouds in the north were. At first the light rain was a relief, taking the edge off the stifling heat. Then we rode into a massive wind tunnel of a valley—brisk northerly, right in the face—and the light rain got heavy. We considered sheltering under the tarp, which led to discussions about cooking dinner, but we'd need to pitch the tent to light the stove, that'd mean we'd be done for the day—and we were still miles from Khatgal, the World Cup soccer final and our precious Naadam.

Tama wasn't fussed about pushing on—but Tama was *never* fussed about pushing on. In the sixteen years I'd known him, he'd always been able to keep going, because he was the Tama-nator, impervious to cold thanks to his patented 'internal heating system', aka protective burger layer. He was able to shut out pain like it was the faint doorknocks of a half-hearted Mormon. Tama 2000 was, in the immortal words of monologist Spalding Gray, 'the kind of guy who was so in touch with his body that he was out of touch with it; the kind of guy who would climb Mount Everest for the weekend just to ski down it and videotape himself doing it'—except that Mount Everest had been done to death; Mörön to Mörön was our own.

We zipped up our jackets and pushed on. Every now and then I looked up from my front wheel and noticed I was in heaven. On each side of the chocolate-brown path the grass was almost neon. All this rich soil meant we must've been getting close to Lake Khövsgöl. A wooden shack and tollgate appeared up ahead; it was the entrance to Khövsgöl National Park, manned by a bored park ranger who was missing out on Naadam. In every direction it was lush and green.

And weird. In Australia or New Zealand when you entered a national park you could see a marked difference between the untainted wilderness before you and the taint you'd been driving through. But here, in one of the least densely populated countries in the world—1.8 people per square kilometre, compared to 2.9 for Australia and 16.6 for New Zealand—the distinction felt absurd. The ranger charged us a 10,000-tugrug entry fee and gave us an empty garbage bag each. As we biked past his office, I noticed bags and bags of rubbish stacked against the wall, next to a heap of vodka and beer bottles—a capitalist *ovoo*.

Just past the tollgate was a herd of about a dozen yaks. Before I could finish appreciating the magnificently shaggy beasts I was distracted by the view to the right: metallic loops of river curling across a vast floodplain, ablaze with the last of the afternoon sun. I shivered with joy.

Five kilometres on we reached Adzuun *dörölj*, a small rise topped with a metre-high *ovoo* and a sign saying ХАТГАЛ/ МОРОН, similar to the last one except cracked and bleached and almost impossible to read in the fading light. I was ready to curl up under the *ovoo* and pass on to the next world, but Tama put on his headtorch and kept grinding on so I did the same. I lost my pace, found it, lost it again.

'Nearly there, bro,' Tama called over his shoulder. 'Tomorrow morning we'll be wrestling!'

I was munted. After ninety kilometres of bad road my legs hurt all the time, even on the downhills, even when I wasn't pedalling. We jolted down into a stony river valley. My panniers bounced, my arse ached, the path ahead was shadows and blur. We crossed a shallow river that would've been one hell of a wide flowing *mörön* with spring's snowmelt.

'Are you sure this is the right way?' I yelled. Tama didn't answer.

We climbed out of the valley and saw something strange: a light. Then another. It was sheds—houses—a town— Khatgal!

I'd almost forgotten that this day's ride had a destination, that I wasn't Sisyphus on wheels. But we'd made it. Tama looked back and grinned. I whooped, gave him a double thumbs-up and nearly rode into a drunk Mongol.

We stopped outside the first grocery store we saw and staggered in. The lights inside were blinding. We emerged with beef jerky, some strange chips and two extra-large cans of КУПЕР. Tama had some coverage on his iPhone and sent Ami the longest text ever. I sat on the step, holding the beer with both hands and slurping at it. A cowboy in a maroon *deel*—the traditional Mongol silk robe—lurched up to talk to me, but he couldn't speak English and was so drunk he could hardly stand. He collapsed on the road, burbling; two of his friends carried him away. Then an amiable Mongolian beefcake in a leather jacket sat down beside me.

'Did you know that is light beer?' he said in perfect English. 'Locals drink Fusion.'

The dude, whose name should have been Bold Sukh ('Steel Axe'), was a tour operator based in UB with degrees in hospitality and business. Bold Sukh was laid-back and charming. He loved his job—he probably got plenty of back-packer zang. Bold Sukh had wrestled in the early *bökh* heats that day and was a contender in the quarterfinals tomorrow morning. He told me we could've entered the *bökh* heats if we'd been here in the morning—at first it was a free-for-all, old men and boys taking on the men in a series of sudden-death rounds that separated the wheat from the scrawny chaff. But we were too late: tomorrow was all business. My shoulders slumped. I couldn't believe it. Even with all that heinous riding, we'd blown it.

At that moment two blonde backpackers, both Swedish and sauna-ish, came out of the grocery store holding bottles of Fusion beer and giggling. Bold Sukh looked up.

'Very nice to meet you,' he said. 'I have to—'

'Take care of business?'

'Exactly.' When he raised his eyebrows, he looked like a Mongolian Tama.

I asked a group of tourists for directions, but they backed away, shocked. The second time this happened, Tama told me to turn my headtorch off. We accosted some Dutch tourists who were staying at Bonda Lake Hotel. Bonda Lake was booked out because it was apparently the only place in Khatgal with a big-screen television. The Dutchies didn't give a hoot about Naadam, but they were very excited about Holland taking on Spain in the soccer in three hours' time. Tama asked them if they knew how to get to Garage 24. The map in the guide-book put Garage 24 half a kilometre west of the shops with no access road, which I hoped was a mistake.

It wasn't a mistake.

In pitch dark, 'just head left towards the hill, *ja*, no problem' was easier said than done. We cycled bumpily and blindly across a muddy rutted field until Tama got a puncture.

'Cuntface!'

'You wanna just push your bike from here?' I asked.

'No way, that'll wreck the rim.'

Tama unclipped his panniers and threw his *Mongol tug* into the mud. Grunting and cursing, he flipped his bike upside down, pulled off his tyre and changed the inner tube astonishingly quickly. I stood quietly in the dark, filming him.

When we set off again I was beyond tired, beyond hungry, beyond disappointed. Garage 24 was nowhere to be seen. We headed for the only light source, which turned out to be the forecourt of a closed petrol station. I saw a half-built fence to the left with a hand-painted sign on it saying 'Tourists Ger'.

'Let's just stay here,' I said. 'They've got *gers* and stuff.'

'But Garage 24 has hot showers, and that Dutch guy said eggs, and Maya said it was—'

'LET'S JUST FUCKING STAY HERE. You can have a shower with Maya TOMORROW.'

'Dude, that's . . . don't say that.'

But I had already said it.

As we stood there blinding each other with our head-torches, a man wandered over. He introduced himself as Batbot and yes, he owned those *gers*, and yes, he had a vacancy. Batbot led us towards the light that emanated from a hobbit-sized door in a *ger* that looked soft, warm, marshmallow-welcoming. Inside, it was a low-rent pleasure dome. There were no showers, no girls and no eggs, but there was a potbelly stove with single beds to the left and right, plus enough space on the seventies linoleum flooring for all our gear. Batbot stoked up the fire. I collapsed on a bed and asked Batbot what time it was.

'Eleven-thirty. Holland versus Spain in two and a half hours! Go . . .' he looked at us, wanting to get it right, 'Holland? Spain?'

I just shrugged. Half-past eleven. We had been riding since 9 am. Tama opened me a beer.

'Holy smashface, bro,' I said, 'that was one of . . . the most . . . epic exercise days of my life.'

'True—much crazier than anything on the Albany mission.'

We drank our beers and chewed some beef jerky. I asked Tama if he was going to set his alarm for the soccer. He sighed.

'Maybe we could *not* do that, but say we did.'

'Ha, yeah, we could still tell everyone how awesome it was to watch the World Cup final . . . in a tent.' I finished my beer. 'Not just a tent, a bloody *ger*—by a beautiful Mongolian lake! . . . Tama?'

But Tama was fast asleep, shoes still on.

NAADAM

I lay motionless on my back in the *ger* in the grey morning light. Lactic acid and sunburn jostled with nerve damage. My whole body throbbed. Any sudden movement caused all the pain to pour into the hand, foot or head that was foolish enough to draw attention to itself, so I just lay there, trying not to breathe. I had a great view of the roof of the *ger*, which had a hole in the middle for the chimney. The only sounds were Tama's snore-puffing, the odd hiccup of a distant backfiring motorcycle, and a kid outside somewhere singing fragments of the Mongol World Cup soccer song in a broken loop: '*When I am older, I will be stronger, just like a waving flag, so wave your flag . . .*'

To counteract the almost total physical discomfort, my mind conjured feeble daydreams of Laura in a too-tight nurse's uniform, white cotton and elastane, bending over to tend to my wounds—checking my pulse, checking my other pulse—but the idea of even light sexual healing made my scrotum ache.

'*See the champions, on the field now, just like a waving flag . . .*'

'Tama,' I groaned.

'Whar?'

'We're missing Naadam.'

'Okay.'

I raised my head, winced, and looked over at Tama. He was sprawled face-down on his bed, unwilling or unable to move.

'Bro, we've gotta go to Naadam—Schoolies by the Lake, right?'

Tama looked up. He had the dull, squinty eyes of a grizzly bear woken mid-hibernation.

'Sheeeeit.'

We struggled out of bed and walked outside. When the singing child saw us he stopped singing and ran away. Just to the right of the petrol station there was a bunch of low, white concrete buildings: Garage 24. We had made it to within fifty metres of the place.

The southern tip of Khövsgöl *nuur* (Lake Khövsgöl) was a couple of hundred metres away so we wandered over at infirmary pace, looking out for the beach volleyball nets. The *nuur* was gorgeous, but there was no sign of Manly Sports. We trudged back to our *ger*, grabbed the unitards, dragged our mud-spattered bikes outside and looked at them suspiciously. Sitting down was not going to be pleasant.

In the daylight it was no problem finding a smooth route back to the shops. The night before we had somehow managed to stick to a muddy, bumpy, broken-bottled corridor that was no more than ten metres wide, avoiding flat paddocks on either side.

Khatgal was less than meets the eye. With fewer than 3000 residents, the place was much smaller than Mörön. Khatgal had a similar sprawl of gap-toothed fences and empty lots, but the rainier climate made for a muddy dark brown ambience rather than Mörön's light brown vibe. The town was deserted.

'Shall we try to find someone to ask for directions?'

'Nah. If this thing's half what it's cracked up to be, we'll see it a mile off.'

The Khatgal Naadam turned out to be about three miles off. From a distance, bright tents and parked cars gave the impression of a music festival without the music. Up close, it was more like a small-town agricultural show, the kind of thing I wouldn't be caught dead at in Australia. There were no beer tents, no vodka tents. Cowboys on horseback milled around aimlessly in their best *deel* robes; bored Mongols sold off their family heirlooms to drip-dry backpackers. Tama and I checked out one man's loot: wooden carvings of fighting stallions; the mighty curved horn of some deceased ramlike creature; rough-hewn soup spoons; an abacus; a giant mortar and pestle; numerous ceremonial *deel* belts, wide and silky, possibly looted from Beijing in the thirteenth century; a random pile of bones and coins and trinkets. The crowning glory of his collection was draped over the back door of his Land Cruiser: a bearskin with the head still attached, its eyes glassy and its mouth frozen in a useless roar. It was impressive, and no doubt very warm, but not the sort of thing one took on an off-road cycle tour. There was a set of shot glasses carved from reindeer antlers, delicate things that would've delighted my Melbourne friends (except the animal-rights ones), although there was no way they'd survive the battering to come.

A young Mongolian woman in a tight white T-shirt with CANADA emblazoned redly across her chest came up to us.

'Hello, where are you from?' she asked.

'*Shin Zeland*—New Zealand,' I said. 'Are you from ... Canada?'

She laughed at my bad joke. Uh-oh, I thought.

'I'm Tom, this is Tama. What's your name?'

'My name is Dolgor,' she said, 'but my nickname is Doggi.'

I blinked. Tama stifled a snort.

'Hi, uh, Dol-gi, pleased to meet you. We were about to have lunch, would you like to—'

'Yes, I will join you. I can help order your food.' She smiled cheekily.

'Cool!'

Doggi led us to the nearest food tent, which had pillows on the ground around a low table and a shadecloth made of smuggler-bag plastic. The only item on the menu was *huushuur*, a deep-fried mutton pancake slightly bigger than a potato cake. I couldn't help thinking that this was one of the only places in Mongolia where we *didn't* need help to order food.

'How many *huushuur* would you like?' Doggi asked me. 'Two?'

'Ah, how about four.'

'Each,' Tama said quickly.

Doggi raised her eyebrows, but ordered *naim huushuur*. A gasp went up around the tent. I showed Doggi my Flip-cam; she told me she had studied cinema in Toronto. She was based in Ulaanbaatar and was an aspiring filmmaker, although she had to make ads to pay the bills. Doggi knew a bit about New Zealand, mainly from watching *Flight of the Conchords*.

'I love Bret and Jemaine—they are so stupid!' she giggled. 'Bret is very cute.'

'Yeah, I know,' I said. 'I actually went to school with those guys. I know them from like way back.'

Tama coughed and muttered 'bullshit' at the same time.

'Really? What are they like?' Doggi asked.

'Well, they were a couple of years older than me, I don't really *know* them—but they were so funny, even then! One time Bret was on stage during this serious school assembly, and he made the whole school crack up laughing, just by pulling funny faces!'

Doggi nodded politely.

'Sooo . . . how long are you in Khatgal for?' I asked.

'Just yesterday and today. Tomorrow I have to go back to UB for work.'

'Do you like UB?'

'Yes, it's great. There are some very cool hip-hop clubs,' she said.

'Cool! Maybe when we're back there, you could take us out, show us around?'

'Yes, I would like to.' She smiled. 'I love, do you say, booty dancing?'

A movie trailer flashed into my head: me and Tama drinking with Doggi and her hot friends at Ismuss nightclub underneath a seven-metre-high statue of Franz Stalin . . . shots of Chinggis Gold all round . . . dancing to Beyoncé, waving at Franz . . . Tama paying for mojitos at Crystal Lounge . . . Doggi's friends asking how we met . . . smoke machines . . . blurry streetlights . . . Tama off with some girl . . . my voice: 'So, Doggi, Dog-gi: *when* are you going to show me how you earned that nickname?'.

I made a mental note to *not*, under any circumstances, look Doggi up when—if—we made it back to the capital.

When Tama and I began planning this trip, there'd been plenty of jokes about romancing and pillaging the locals, but now I had a girlfriend, a damn good one—by far the best I'd ever had. Mongolia's bangin' hip-hop scene would have to bang on without me. I said goodbye to Doggi and went to watch grown men in underpants pound each other into submission.

A couple of hundred people, about one-third of them white tourists, were sitting on the grass in a rough oval thirty metres long and fifteen metres across watching the *bökh*. The rules were simple, too simple: get your opponent onto the ground without touching the ground yourself. Feet and hands on the turf are okay, but any more than that—a knee or an elbow, an eyeball—and you're out.

It sounded good in theory; in practice, lack of rules equalled gridlock. The main tactic seemed to be to plant your feet nice and wide, bend at the waist, then bore your opponent to death. Without boxing's trusty three-minute bell, the *bökh* bouts dragged on for ten, twenty, thirty minutes. Finals could apparently take hours. The costumes were straight out of a Sydney Mardi Gras amyl-nitrate wank fantasy. Blue man-nappies with checked silver embroidery; hot-pink mini-jackets with sleeves but no shirt, leaving one's mighty hairless pecs exposed; and pointy-toed footwear best described as 'pixie gumboots'. While two burly Mongols gave each other wedgies, official-looking old men wearing berets topped with bulbous golden dildoes, possibly referees, circled around them, eyes on the grass, either checking for infractions or looking for the keys to their horse. The crowd was placid but intent, attuned to subtleties lost on me. Tama got bored and wandered off to call Ami on his mobile. I hung in there, waiting for the sport to reveal its inner magic.

The longer I watched, the more it seemed *bökh* was a slower, less exciting version of sumo wrestling, with contestants who didn't have the luxury of cultivating aristocratic warrior bellies. It was like the part of boxing where two psychopaths wrap their arms around each other and sway. I'd been hoping, unconsciously, for *bökh* to resemble the wrestling of my youth—American and televised, fake and spectacular. Men with big hair, absurd names, steroid addictions and unitards, yelling confusing insults and hitting the ref with chairs. Gymnastical moves named after metal objects—the clothesline, the piledriver, the cattle prod.

Well, WWF this was *not*.

One thing was certain, though: the wrestlers had a calm, steely brutality about them. These dudes deserved to be called Batbot. If I was out there, it'd be over in a second, skeleton print or no skeleton print.

When the best man, who might've been called Khatuu Chuluun ('Hard Rock'), finally won, the crowd surged forward, clapping and cheering. I fired up the Flip-cam but was dismayed to find that most of the 'action' was other foreigners with better video cameras than mine jostling to the front, desperate for a shot not filled with other tourists. I tripped over a boom operator who was part of a Singaporean television crew. Out of nowhere, Maya and Sharon elbowed their way past a fat German man with a camcorder. I despaired for the future of humanity. Then I broke through the paparazzi scrum and got a close-up of Khatuu Chuluun handing out pieces of *aaruul* (dried curd and/or crud) from a ceremonial bowl. Mongolian wrestling fans eagerly accepted the *aaruul* and munched it down. I tried some; it was hard and tasted of lapsed expiry dates.

As the crowd dispersed I saw Tama standing in the field with his aviators on, still talking on his phone. He looked like a wealthy spy waiting for his private helicopter. Behind him, three shepherds rode their ragged horses home. Everyone was packing up.

'How's Osama?' I asked.

'Pretty good. Busy. Work sounds full-on but Vancouver's sunny as, she's having lots of beach times. You wanna ring Laura?'

'Um . . . thanks, but nah. I shouldn't use up all your credit. D'ya wanna put on the costumes and do some filming? In the suits?'

Tama looked at me suspiciously. 'Of what?'

'Of . . . us. In costume. At Naadam.'

'There's nothing here. It'll just look shit.'

'I know, but, we came all this way . . .'

'Look bro, we can do some filming in a few days, when we're somewhere nice—the top of a mountain or something. Cool?'

'. . . I guess.'

As we biked away from Naadam my gears squeaked and crunched and my perineum burned. I was sunburnt, sore, bloated with mutton and a little distraught. I had known that Mörön was going to be a shithole, but this was different. The Naadam festival was in *Ronery Pranet*'s list of Top Ten Things to Do in Mongolia, along with eating Mars Bars and not catching the bubonic plague. Naadam was meant to be a wild, crazy party weekend that balanced out all our grim riding. I rode into a dip and pushed hard on my pedal; my chain slipped off.

When we got back to our tourist *ger* I tried to fix my bike, which in practice meant I stood around ineffectually while Tama tried to locate the mystery noise. After an hour of this we narrowed the problem down to—the bike. Probably the front or back gears. Or the derailleur. Or the brakes. Riding slowly around the outside of our *ger* to test the gears, I got a puncture.

I was in the *ger* having a sip of vodka and a sulk when I heard Tama say 'Sigh binoo!' and turned around just in time to see a round-faced man with a hefty paunch shaking Tama's crotch. Paunch Man laughed like a farmer with a prize bull.

'Get out of it,' Tama growled, slapping the man's hand away. Paunchy gave him a big thumbs-up. I stepped out of the *ger* and he reeled towards me. I could smell the Chinggis on his breath. Not knowing what else to do, I stuck out my hand for a handshake—but he went straight for my balls. I batted Paunch Man's hand away a couple of times but he was persistent, so I said, in my best Mongolian accent, 'Bhonk?'

He looked at me blankly.

I placed my left hand on his right shoulder, like I'd seen them do at Naadam.

'Ah, *bökh!*' Paunch Man said, and broke into a sloppy grin. 'Okay, okay. *Bökh!*'

At this cry, Paunch Man's friend came running out from behind our *ger*, still buttoning up his urine-splashed trousers. The second drunkard had less hair and less paunch, but the paunch was more prominent as he had rolled the bottom of his polo shirt up to let his belly breathe the way men do all across Asia, inspired by Britney Spears.

'*Bökh!*' Paunch and Britney cried. '*Bökh!*'

Paunch Man adjusted his belt and his belly. We slapped at each other for a bit then locked arms. I got a good hold with my right arm under his left shoulder and heaved. He spun right, trying to trip me, but I clung onto his armpit. We spun around a few times until without meaning to I got Paunchy in a headlock from behind, then—still spinning—I threw him onto the ground. The whole thing was over in fifteen seconds.

Paunch Man lay on the grass, chuckling in disbelief. I offered my new friend a hand up; he made a fist with his thumb and little finger extended—the Mongolian sign for 'hang loose', unless it means 'fuck you, tourist'—then grabbed my hand and pulled himself up. Britney gave Paunch a cigarette and turned to face me.

We started in the traditional *bökh* arm lock. Britney grabbed my left arm and tried to pull me down from there, but I slipped out of the hold and skipped away. He lumbered towards me like a bear sizing up an underfed goat. We locked arms and an ugly ballet began. Tama sniggered with joy; I glanced over to make sure he was filming. Britney tried to trip me, I accidentally slapped him in the face, his leg got caught between my legs and the rest of him catapulted onto the grass, cursing. Tama cheered. Those childhood after-noons spent beating up my little sister had finally paid off.

The second bout had lasted just thirty seconds, but my heart was pounding and my breath was coming fast and hard. My left shoulder felt weird. I went to shake Britney's hand, but he backed away. Paunch Man said something and stomped towards me. I shook Paunchy's hand again and we patted each other's shoulders. I was about to offer him a vodka when he went in low and hard with his right shoulder.

Rematch?!

He stayed close and low this time, pushing fiercely, not giving me a chance to prance around. I flexed my knees and pushed back, hard, then rocked onto my heels and pulled backwards with all my might. Paunch lost his balance and lurched forward. He spun around and nearly toppled over but stayed on his feet, then bent at the waist into the classic *bökh* attack posture and tried to give me a wedgie. We staggered around like this for half a minute until I foolishly lunged at his shoulders, too high. His centre of gravity held and Paunch Man pulled me in by my pants and gave me a colossal wedgie, lifting both my feet off the ground. I should've gone over; I should've come down on my head in a vintage WWF moment with no need to fake the concussion, but somehow my left foot got jammed between his legs; I kneed him in the balls, he dropped me and I landed on his foot with a crunch. We paused, panted, then rammed into each other again. We lurched around the paddock in crooked circles until we both slowed and gasped and winced, leaning heavily into each other, two drunks at a funeral. Tama was snorting with laughter; Britney circled us, yelling advice to his friend. I looked up. My mouth said 'fuck' as I thrust forwards, shoulders hunched, one hand clutching his jeans as I thrust into him. Paunchy went for my legs but couldn't get a good hold. I tottered backwards across the lawn pulling Paunch Man by his jeans pocket as fast as I could until he took too large a step and landed heavily, stumbled, his whole body listing to the left and plunging forwards. I heaved him past me. Paunch Man went down, left knee, left forearm, left paunch, all in a crumpled heap. I barked in elation and fell to my knees then rolled slowly onto my back and lay there, wheezing.

This epic round took one minute and twenty-five seconds.

'Very good, Tomas!' It was Batbot, the *ger* owner, leaning on the fence; he had watched the whole thing.

While Paunchy and I lay crumpled on the grass, Tama took on Britney. Tama won the first round easily enough, but in the second round—what can I say? Tama might be a beefy guy, he might *look* like a CIA agent, but he's an only child. Doesn't have the muscle memory—or the ruthlessness. Me, on the other hand . . . I could already see the future stretching ahead of me. I'd roam the Mongolian steppes on my trusty 24-speed steed, upsetting *bökh* champions near and far. They'd call me the Wobbly Wolf—the Freckled Terror! Tama would carry all my wrestling costumes and sign autographs for me when my arm was too sore. It'd be—

A little chunk of mutton forced its way up my throat into my mouth as I retched from the exertion. The top half of my left arm felt a bit like it was broken. Three minutes of *bökh* and I was munted.

Britney and Paunch tried to drag us off to their *ger* for post-*bökh* Chinggis, but Batbot made them leave us alone. They staggered off towards the lake, Paunch Man carrying a half-empty bottle of vodka and Britney a full one.

Bökh wrestling
www.moron2moron.com/videos/bokh-wrestling

It started to drizzle and didn't let up all afternoon. We dozed in the *ger*. Later I visited the long-drop in a vain attempt to coax out a bowel movement made solid and recalcitrant by Cambodian anti-malaria medication. Leaving the outhouse door open, I lit a contraband Marlboro and sucked in the view. Past the dun and crimson tin roofs, past the white dots of *ger* camps and the cookie-cutter pine trees, I could make out a thin strip of Khövsgöl *nuur*, gunmetal blue and dimpled with rain. Squatting there, head buzzing, not pooing, I decided it didn't matter that we were a day late for Naadam and had missed the proper wrestling. It didn't even matter that we'd taken on Paunch and Britney without changing into our costumes. If we *had* been wearing the 'tards, our opponents might've thought it was some weird sex thing and not come near us—or, worse, come near us. It had happened like this for a reason. Working up a sweat rolling around on the grass with a couple of middle-aged, overweight, vodka-stinking Mongols miles from the Naadam festival was a thoroughly appropriate way—the *only* way—for two Kiwi morons to observe Mongolia's independence day.

We went to Garage 24 for dinner. As its name suggested it was an old Soviet truck garage that some entrepreneur had converted into a delightful westerner-friendly guesthouse, and apparently it served 'the best food in northern Mongolia'. We half-expected to bump into Maya and Sharon again, but they weren't around. We sat down in the eating bit. I plonked my bag on the table. Tama reached into it for the maps and pulled out my packet of Marlboros.

'You dirty dog, these are for the Mongols!' he said.

'I know, I just, uh . . .'

Tama shook his head. 'From now on, I'm going to hold onto *all* the smokes, okay?'

'Okay, yes, sorry. They're *gifts*. Can I just . . . have one more?'

Tama sighed and shook out a lone cigarette.

'Friends?' I said.

'Dick.'

We spread out all our topographical maps on the table, ordered our meals and ignored the complimentary salty tea as we planned a route that would take us 1350 kilometres east–southeast to the other Mörön in Khentii within twenty-one days.

Itinerary

Day 4:   Khatgal to Khövsgöl *nuur* (camping by lake): 49 km

Day 5:   Khövsgöl *nuur* to Chandmani-Öndör: 66 km

Day 6:   Chandmani-Öndör to Tsagaan-Üür: 52 km

Day 7:   Tsagaan-Üür to Middle of Nowhere: 62 km

Day 8:   Middle of Nowhere to Middle of Nowhere: 59 km

Day 9:   Middle of Nowhere to Teshig: 88 km

(Rest day)

Day 11: Teshig to Middle of Nowhere . . .

And so on. It was a punishing schedule, but we had factored in three rest days, one a week, plus a two-day buffer for 'unforeseen circumstances', to make sure we'd be back in Ulaanbaatar by 4 August to make our flight out. Even so there was still a good chance that we'd run out of days before we made it to the final Mörön, unless we hired a minivan to drive us and our bikes the last couple of hundred kilometres. I couldn't decide which was worse: failing to cycle from Mörön to Mörön, or failing to cycle from Mörön to Mörön *and* paying some cut-throat tout to transport us to the finish line. Both options made me feel like Mongolia's Biggest Loser. In the meantime, the plan was to seek out maximum adventure with minimum civilisation, heading east and staying north, hugging the Russian border as much as possible as we avoided the main roads and steered well clear of the cities.

The most alarming part of the itinerary was a great green wedge that began at a point just north of Ulaanbaatar and stretched 200 kilometres north to Siberia, reaching 150 kilometres east to west at its widest. This region consisted of Gorkhi-Terelj National Park and the Khan Khentii Strictly Protected Area. Our guidebook observed that Khan Khentii was 'almost completely uninhabited by humans, but is home to moose, brown bear and weasel to name but a few'. It was an utterly isolated mountain wilderness: a blank spot on the map with no tracks heading in an east–west direction, hardly anything heading north–south, and nothing resembling a town to resupply in, apart from the town of Terelj at the southwest tip of the park, right by UB. There were nomadic roads crisscrossing the rest of Mongolia every which way, even in the remote Gobi Desert, even in other Strictly Protected Areas. So why not here, the best and practically *only* way for us to get to Mörön? It was outrageous.

Tama suggested that we could stock up in a place called Bugant, which was eighty kilometres west of the Khan Khentii Strictly Protected Area, and then bush-bash from there, but it would be four to seven days of hard riding on small red dotted lines, then no lines, through the absolute middle of nowhere until we made it 250 unlikely kilometres to Batshireet—not to be confused with the town of Batshit—just past the eastern border of the park. Failing that, it was a mere 175 kilometres from Bugant to

Möngönmorit in the southeast, but the most direct route was blocked by Khökh Chuluut *uul*, a 2308-metre peak with no access roads.

These modest proposals were made even more daunting by the knowledge that yesterday's killer ride from Mörön to Khatgal was marked on our map as a thick, solid red line, which represented as main a road as there was in Mongolia. We were yet to discover what a thin, broken yellow line actually represented—a piece of string? A trail of breadcrumbs? But meanwhile, our alternative—cutting 200 kilometres south around the edge of the park, back into UB and all its sprawl, then heading back out northeast through Terelj National Park to avoid the boring, straight, hellish main road—seemed much less appealing and was fundamentally at odds with our moronic ethos.

A third, more ambitious option was to bypass Khan Khentii to the north by nudging over the Russian border and zanging through Siberia for 150 kilometres. Since we didn't have Russian visas this would mean bribing the border guards on the way in and out, or sneaking across the border somewhere both discreet and lacking in razor wire. This kind of caper was *definitely* in keeping with our moronic ethos, but neither of us had the cannonballs for it.

As we nutted out the finer points of our trip—all of it— we were joined by a smiling Swiss lad with a plate of mashed potatoes, a sunburnt nose and obscene bicycle shorts. Dieter had just cycled up from Mörön Khövsgöl with his girlfriend, Anya. Whenever Dieter said Anya's name, he leered.

'How long did that take you?' I asked, meaning hours.

'Oh, three days,' he said. 'Me and Anya [leer] like to stop early, and . . .'

This was Dieter's second bike tour through Mongolia and he seemed to know what he was doing. Dieter and Anya had just spent a leisurely month cycling from Ulaanbaatar to Khatgal, with plenty of 'stopping early'; they were going to spend a few days at the lake before flying back to Zurich.

'Such a *beautiful* country, once you get off the main roads. If your bikes can take it,' he added.

Dieter took a great interest in our itinerary. He raised his eyebrows and whistled ominously at large portions of our route, especially the Khan Khentii traverse.

'It is much more beautiful in the north, yes. Almost as good as Switzerland.' He nodded, then frowned. 'But are you sure that is roads there?' he asked, pointing at a dotted yellow line.

'Yeah, man,' Tama said. 'Look, it says "road" here on the key, see . . . uh, "path".'

'*Feldweg?*' Dieter read from the Deutsch key incredulously. 'In Switzerland, *feldweg* is for the mountain goats!' We waited while he laughed at his own joke.

'But I thought you said the riding was better off the main roads,' I protested.

'Of course, but in this country you don't have to be seeking the wildness. In Mongolia, the wildness comes to you.'

'Wilderness,' I said.

'Yes, it *is* very wild,' he agreed. 'Especially in the forest.'

'It's all good,' Tama said. 'We've just bought some brand-new steel-frame mountain bikes, grunty as, we'll be sweet.'

'Ah yes—your bikes! Can I look on them?' Dieter was very excited. We explained they were back at our *ger*.

'What model do you ride—Avanti? Giant? *Kona*? Kona is a great mountain bike.'

'Our bikes are awesome,' I said. 'Mine's white with black writing and Tama's is—ow!' I looked at Tama, who had kicked me under the table.

'They're UCC brand, Rolling Steel 1.0,' Tama said. 'Have you heard of . . .' Dieter's face suggested he hadn't.

'She'll be right,' Tama said.

'Who?' Dieter asked.

'They've got Shimano gears and disc brakes, good ones.'

'*Disc* brakes! Disc brakes are excellent—unless the tube snaps. Then—goodbye!' Dieter grinned wickedly. 'For my bike and for Anya [leer], we only use replaceable brake pads—and we carry many spares.'

Tama stared at the map and so did I. There were no symbols for 'replacement brake tube' that I could see.

'Of course, *my* bike is from home—but I think yours is too?' Dieter raised his eyebrows. I shot a glance at Tama, who seemed determined to keep smiling.

'Yeah, but they're all made in China now anyway,' Tama replied.

'Of course. But there is much difference between *made* in China, and *sold* in China.'

Silence. Our meals arrived.

'Good to meet you,' Dieter said. 'I would like to stay and discuss bicycles all night long, but Anya is waiting for me—in the tent [extended leer]. Good luck!' He jogged out of the dining room.

Tama stared at the map, then out the window, then at the map. After a while, he said, 'Dude, do you reckon that guy *really* has a girlfriend called Anya?'

'What do you mean?'

'Look at his tent.'

'Yeah?'

'Do you notice anything about it?'

'It's blue?'

'Smartarse. How many bikes are next to it?'

'Oh . . . one?'

'And Dieter was in here eating dinner by himself, right?'

'So what are you saying?'

'Nothing. "Anya" is probably the name of his special wanking sock.'

DAYS 4–5: WHERE ARE ALL THE OTHER TOURISTS?

W e went to bed early, desperate to rest up for the big day and the big days to come. The rain stopped around midnight and the sudden silence woke us up. It didn't keep us awake, though—the Mongolian disco music that belched forth within seconds of the rain stopping and didn't let up until dawn kept us awake. From damaged speakers that seemed to be located just underneath our beds, the same song blared, over and over: a melancholy-yet-jazzy synth, running low on batteries and overwhelmed by a tragic male voice that boomed, warbled and trampled all over the melody, the word 'Chinggis' ringing out at regular intervals. The song evoked a once-handsome cowboy who was now rather chubby, standing tall and lonely on a mountain ridge, lamenting the loss of his Marlboros. Like all good pop, the song was both heartbreaking and infinitely trite. Tama and I groaned in disbelief. We had wanted Schoolies by the Lake and now we were getting it.

On my way back from another unsuccessful morning stagger to the long-drop I noticed that Tama's Mongolian flag was flying high from our *ger*, its red panels ultra-patriotic against the morning sky. The plastic flagpole was lashed to our doorframe with my punctured and discarded inner tube. The day before, Tama had taken his *Mongol tug* off his bike so he could detune his gears, and he must've left it lying on the grass. I looked over at our party animal neighbours from the adjacent *ger*. Four of them were outside, brushing their teeth at the same tap. A man burbled '*Saikhan Naadaarai!*' at me through a mouthful of brown toothpaste.

'*Mongol tug?*' I said, pointing.

'*Tiin, tiin: Mongol tug namiruulakh,*' he said, thrusting his toothbrush into the air like a hungover Statue of Liberty. I got it: don't leave symbols of national pride lying in the mud overnight.

We hit Garage 24 for breakfast and chowed down on crunchy muesli and fresh homemade yoghurt that was warm, smooth, creamy and blasted with sugar. Dieter and his tent and maybe-girlfriend had already disappeared. A none-too-bright British backpacker girl sat next to us and tried to order the yoghurt too, but she was told the kitchen had just run out.

'Bugger!' she said, gazing wistfully at our disappearing meals. 'That's, like, the fifth mornin' in a row I've missed out on the yoghurt, innit?'

'You should get up earlier, innit,' I hissed under my breath, pulling my bowl away from her.

In an effort to lighten my load, I decided to donate three spare pairs of socks and all my holiday reading to Garage 24. I got rid of Jasper Becker (gladly) and Jill Lawless (sadly), as well as some books on climate change I'd been meaning to read all year and Tama had told me it was silly to bring: *Heat: How to Stop the Planet From Burning*; *Climate Wars: The Fight for Survival as the World Overheats* and *Storms of My Grandchildren: The Truth about the Coming Climate Catastrophe and Our Last*

Chance to Save Humanity. It was a shame, but the last chance to save humanity would have to wait until after my holiday. Finally, and most tragically, I had to jettison *Harry Potter and the Deathly Hallows,* JK Rowling's seventh and arguably seventh-best book. These thick and surpisingly weighty lumps of dead tree were all just so much ballast that already threatened to scuttle me. This saving of two whole kilograms was immediately offset by eight litres of emergency water from the Khatgal store. Tama went to a gift shop and bought himself a fake leather cowboy hat: *Brokeback Moron.*

As we rode through the outskirts of Khatgal an old man standing by the side of the road saw Tama's *Mongol tug* flying high. He shouted out, 'Okay okay,' clicked his heels together and gave a half-mocking salute. We saluted back and yelled, 'Mongolia *mash sain!*' He laughed long and hard.

'How old do you reckon that guy was?' Tama said.

'Dunno bro . . . sixty, maybe sixty-five. How come?'

'Imagine Mongolian military service during the Cold War.'

'Spying on the Chinese . . . freezing your arse off on the frozen steppes . . .'

'Skinning people alive and chucking them down wells . . .'

'Plenty of time to practise your wrestling moves!'

We cycled out through the stony riverbed of the Egiin *gol* (*gol* means river, but isn't as amusing as *mörön*) and hung a left over a long bridge where a smiling Mongol tourist reeled a huge silver salmon up out of the river and waved for us to take a picture; we didn't. Then we climbed a small hill and turned left again. All traces of human occupation immediately vanished.

Most tourists headed up the western shore of Lake Khövsgöl by horse or Hummer in search of wild reindeer, mosquito bites and authentic shamanic trinkets to take home and put on the coffee table next to their Kenyan love beads and iPhone chargers. We were heading east, in search of . . . experience. I craved raw experience, bloody chunks of the stuff that I could cram onto the overcrowded mantelpiece of my mind, next to 'In love in Laos', 'Hard rubbish day in Budapest', 'Stoned with teenage gypsies watching *Fatboy Slim Live in Brighton* DVD in Transylvanian housing estate', 'Bronchitis in Goa'.

We rode single file, we rode parallel, we wobbled all over the show. We followed a narrow twisting rope of paths that had been a horse trail for centuries, possibly millennia, and a motorbike and jeep track for decades. Now it made an ideal mountain-bike trail; you couldn't have done a better job if you'd carpet-bombed the whole country then rebuilt it just for bikepackers. The dirt was firm, smooth and fast. With all our luggage and water the uphills were slow going but on a downhill, even a slight one, we just flew. Turn on that front suspension and—zang.

With no humans anywhere and nothing more civilised than a distant powerline among the Siberian larch trees, me and Tama were treated to that most cherished and narcissistic of touristic illusions: the sensation of breaking new ground, of being pioneers. We whooped and pedalled on, boldly going where no westerner had gone for at least a day. Near midday we came up a rise and stopped in surprise. The whole hillside was speckled with angular rocks, some the colour of caramel, but also brown rocks, black rocks and—rocks that moved? Rocks that *bleated*?

'Goats, bro!' Tama yelled.

There were hundreds of them, an entire . . . gruff of goats, mixed in with the stones and strewn across our path. Most of the goats were lying down, but the more pugnacious ones had perched themselves on precarious yet pathetic rocks that were all less than a metre high. As we approached them, the goats moved aside in a mottled wave, revealing grass chewed down to the roots.

From the top of a steep little gully we could see a stream about five metres across. Tama let out a bellow and hit it with speed, splashing his way to the other side, but when I followed it was deeper than I expected. I ground to a halt and had to get off and push, and my old running shoes were instantly drenched. This was bad news.

'Uh, Tama. . .'

'Yeah?'

'You know that 500,000 tugrugs I hid in my shoe?'

'Yeah, what about—oh for fuck's sake . . .'

Luckily I had wrapped our month's food money in gaffer tape before I stashed it in my shoe, so it was only a little bit soggy and not that stuck together. Tama punched me in the shoulder then grabbed the sodden lump and rustled around in his pannier until he found a small waterproof bag. He shoved the money into it and put that bag inside a larger waterproof bag before packing it back in his pannier.

We had lunch in a massive valley flanked by piney ridges. The valley was thick with grass and sprayed with wildflowers: a soft riot of primroses, marigolds and buttercups in purple, yellow, crimson, white, orange and blue. Even though the internets had told us how nice Khövsgöl would be, even though we had planned our entire route to take in these forests, my preconceptions of Mongolia were still flat, bleak, Gobi barren. I had been psyching myself up for unrelenting dusty badlands, emptiness and ugly, but this was some fairytale shit. We had no choice but to strip naked and frolic in the flowers.

'Man, this is so sweet,' Tama signed. 'Where are all the other tourists?'

The fields of Lake Khövsgöl National Park seemed like a colossal business opportunity, millions of dollars in construction and kitsch just begging to be made. Sure, there was a bit of illegal fishing and poaching around the lake edge, but that was small fry. Where were the gingerbread-house-themed B & Bs, the buxom Mongolian maidens done up like Bavarian *fräuleins* and struggling to carry mini-kegs to British bucks' night celebrations, the six-storey concrete *ovoo*s complete with helipad? I was, of course, forgetting the nine months a year of brutal cold, minus thirty degrees or worse. Snow thick on frozen ground. Goats crawling inside cows to die. Horses arranging themselves into macabre sculptures. But on such a splendid day, winter was impossible to imagine.

I cruised along humming the *Sound of Music* theme, startling marmots from the puddle edges where they drank. On a long gentle downhill I looked back at Tama. He was twenty metres behind me with an eagle coasting about four metres above his head, its wings spread and talons outstretched, keeping perfect pace with him. At first I thought the eagle was stalking Tama's cowboy hat, but then it dived to the right before rising sharply into the air, a hapless marmot wriggling and bleeding in its claws.

'You're welcome, eagle!' I cried.

The track wound up into the pines. At the top of the

ridge we stopped to make room for an SUV coming the other way. I got ready for 'sain bainuu' and mutual incomprehension, but the driver was a multilingual German geezer. Wolfgang had short grey hair and a relaxed smile. There was a lady sitting in the passenger seat, a Mongolian lady. An extremely beautiful Mongolian lady with high cheekbones and dark eyes, a veritable Mongolian Elle Macpherson who was easily twenty years younger than Wolfgang. She was holding a sleeping baby. In the back seat there was another sleeping child. Wolfgang explained that he had come to Mongolia in the nineties for a six-month stint as a development worker; he had been living near Erdenebulgan in Khövsgöl ever since.

'You really like it here, huh?' Tama said.

'Yes, I like Mongolia very much indeed,' Wolfgang said. There was a tinkling laugh from Elle Mongolpherson.

'Where are you going?' she asked us.

'We started at Mörön Khövsgöl, and we're headed east to the Mörön in Khentii,' I said.

'From Mörön to—ah, I see. Of course.' Wolfgang chuckled despite himself. 'So, you are keeping a blog?'

'Yeah, moron2moron.com. Tama's a web developer.'

'Indeed. And one day you will write a book of your crazy travels in the land of the crazy Mongols.'

'Uh, maybe, that'd be . . . sure!'

'And which way do you go now? Khentii is very far.'

'We're going to Chandmani-Öndör,' Tama said, 'then to Sagging, Sucking, uh—'

'Tsagaan-Üür?'

'Yeah that, then down to, uh, Teshig.'

'Teshig?!' Mongelle echoed, incredulous.

'From *here*?' Wolfgang said. 'But how will you cross the Üür *gol*?'

'There's a big bridge on our map,' Tama said hopefully.

'Maybe there will be a tractor to take you,' he said. 'And east of Tsagaan-Üür, you are in the Tiger Forest.'

'*Tiger* Forest?!' I said. 'They're extinct, right?'

Wolfgang looked at me strangely. 'There are no tigers in the forest. Or roads. Just trees: birch tree, larch tree, pine tree. It is really Siberia, not Mongolia. No one lives there. It is not . . .' Wolfgang reached for his road atlas. 'We came this way, over the Badarga *davaa*.' He pointed to a dotted yellow line and a mountain pass next to an unnamed peak. It led from Tsagaan-Üür in an S-bend southwest, southeast, southwest to Erdenebulgan, through a good fifty kilometres of wilderness. 'It is still Tiger Forest, very rough, but—I think it is better. You have a GPS?'

'Of course,' Tama said.

'A really old one,' I said.

'We're going to use it to check out Teshig,' Tama continued.

'Okay, crazy morons.' Wolfgang sighed. 'We must go. Good journey—*bayartai*.'

'Bayish tar!'

'*Bay-ar-tai!*' Mongelle corrected us. Wolfgang laughed. Their baby gurgled. Wolfgang drove away.

'That's classic—he came to Mongolia for six months, and now he's gone native!'

'Did you see his wife?' Tama said.

'Yeah. She was a total Mong-MILF!'

'Probably the hottest girl in Erdenebulgan—ten years ago.'

'I bet Wolfgang lived by himself back in like Hamburg, all frozen-wiener-for-one and *scheisse* porn!'

'Let's get a move on bro, we're gonna rock the Tiger Forest!' Tama whooped and rode off. I pedalled hard to keep up.

We headed north–northeast on a road which the *Ronery Pranet* described as 'appalling . . . the worst stretch of road we encountered in over 15,000km of overland travel! Expect mud, rocks, roots and the odd collapsed bridge.' It was definitely a bit rugged, but nothing to use an exclamation mark over. Perhaps it got gnarlier further up. If so, we wouldn't find out, because we were only going to follow it for a couple more kilometres. The plan was to spend the night camped out by Lake Khövsgöl and in the morning head east on the turn-off to Chandmani-Öndör, a town that sounded like it should be overrun with holidaying Ewoks.

We breezed through the pines for an hour then popped out into a startlingly wide valley. According to our GPS, the road to Chandmani-Öndör went up the valley to the right. On the left, beyond a kilometre of sloping paddock, the waters of Khövsgöl *nuur* beckoned.

'Sweet dog!' Tama grinned. 'Let's bust it down there!'

'Shouldn't we find a path?'

'Don't worry about a path—we've got Rolling Steel mountain bikes!'

He lurched onto the grass and I followed him, immediately riding into a hole and slamming my nuts.

'Fuck!'

'Don't pinch your tube, bro!' Tama yelled over his shoulder. I wasn't sure if he meant my tyre or my reproductive facilities.

After a couple of close calls I started looking around for a track. Goat track, marmot track, extinct tiger track, I wasn't fussy—anything but this lumpy impossibility. After ten minutes the lake wasn't any closer, but I couldn't see 'the worst road in Mongolia' anymore. Tama and I struggled along in parallel ditches that were as wide as a car tyre and deep enough that I couldn't pedal without the pedals catching on the sod banks I had to waddle along, still seated, my feet pushing awkwardly off the sides. This was fun—for the first twenty metres. At this rate we would make it to the lake by sunset, and if we hurried we could be back on the proper road by sunrise, as long as we didn't sleep. I was ready to turn back, but Tama pointed to the right: there was the faintest of brown paths whispering through the green. It got us to the lake.

Khövsgöl *nuur* was ringed by a five-metre fringe of round, flat skimming stones and bleached driftwood. Chuck in some chunks of pumice and we could've been in New Zealand on the edge of Lake Taupo. The bay we were in was a couple of kilometres wide and west-facing, flanked by a pair of symmetrical fir-covered headlands that extended into the water; in the distance there was a range of purple sawtooth mountains. The cool blue water of our bay rippled out into the immensity of Lake Khövsgöl proper, which stretched twenty kilometres south and over a hundred kilometres north. Khövsgöl *nuur* is the centrepiece of a 250-kilometre-wide, 175-kilometre-long knob of remote, resource-rich land that should consider itself very lucky not to have been annexed by the USSR seventy years ago. The *nuur* was massive, bigger than any lake I'd ever seen; it could've swallowed all the lakes in New Zealand then come back for seconds. We stripped off and threw ourselves into the gaspingly cold, Palaeozoic-fresh water, splashing around and rubbing the filth from our faces and feet. I wanted to stay and enjoy the water, but I was losing feeling in my legs.

Back on shore I had just put my undies on when a shepherd on horseback trotted down to us. A conversation took place that was much like the one with the cowboy just north of Mörön. The shepherd wanted us to follow him to his *ger*. Tama tried to explain that we were going to camp over on the northern headland to the right of the bay. The shepherd shook his head and said, '*mörön, mörön!*' I was briefly excited that our reputation had preceded us. We got onto our bikes and let the shepherd lead us along the beach until we reached a not-so-little river feeding into Khövsgöl *nuur* and separating us from our campsite. The *mörön*-mouth was twenty metres across and clogged with a foamy lattice of floating sticks. It was hard to tell how deep it was.

'No problem,' Tama said, running his hand along his waist, 'we cross. *Mash sain!*'

The shepherd shook his head emphatically. He held his hands far apart. '*Ta nar gatalj chadaxgui. Gün us. Gün!*'

We shrugged our shoulders and nodded. The shepherd jumped off his horse and picked up a branch that was about my height. He stood on the edge of the *mörön* and poked the branch into the foam. It went all the way in.

'Oh,' I said. '*Gün*. Deep.' I'd remember that one.

The shepherd invited us to stay in his *ger*, again.

'What do you reckon?' I asked Tama.

'Why don't we go back and camp on the other headland, down the other end of the beach?'

'Love it. And how do we explain that to the Lone Ranger?'

'We *maikhan* on ridge,' Tama said, making a pyramid with his hands then pointing to the south.

'We—like—being—outside,' I added, gesturing to all the good nature and wrapping up with a double thumbs-up.

'*Gatsüür?*' the shepherd said, pointing to the trees.

'*Za, za, za—maikhan* gatsa,' I said, hoping it meant, 'Yeah, yeah, yeah—we will pitch our summer tent over on that excellent headland.'

'*Gatsüür . . . modond chono bii,*' he said.

'*Za, za—*conno! Gatsa conno, *mash sain!*'

After a few more minutes of us deflecting his Mongolian hospitality, the shepherd gave up and galloped away. We pushed our bikes up to the excellent trees in question. I sat on my arse and stared at the glorious Lake Khövsgöl.

'That guy really wanted us to stay with him, huh?' I said.

'Yeah man, it's all good—it's just their way.'

It sure was. Mongols are some of the most welcoming, generous peoples in the world—it's an essential part of their nomadic lifestyle. There's none of that KEEP OUT and TRESPASSERS WILL BE PROSECUTED business, no menacing goat skulls mounted to fences—and no fences, for that matter. The whole country is pretty much public property, belonging to everyone yet no one. Nomads and tourists alike can camp wherever they please. If you're riding a horse up to one hundred kilometres a day, you have to travel light. And if you're travelling light in the Mongolian winter you best be relying on the kindness of strangers, otherwise you'll end up like Jack Nicholson at the end of

The Shining: grinning and dead in a snowy hedge-maze. So if you're counting on the salty tea and sympathy of people you've never met, it follows that you extend that same courtesy to visitors—like me and Tama.

But we come from *Shin Zeland*, Land of the Long White-Collar Summer Holiday Crowd. In *our* country, when you go out tramping and camping in the great outdoors you do it to get as far away from other people as possible. New Zealanders aren't nomads; we are misanthropes. We don't live in tents; we *escape* into them. If you happened to be out in the bush having a nature-loving moment and someone invited you to eat mutton balls and stay in their tent, you'd say: 'No thanks bro, I've got my own, cheers though, eh,' and keep walking until you couldn't see that creepy character anymore. Of course, New Zealanders with tents don't offer their hospitality in the first place. No one wants to ruin their *own* tranquillity by cramming random strangers into their extremely limited personal space. Unlike Mongolian *ger*s, New Zealand *ger*s are designed to repel visitors. There's no room, I've only got two weeks off work this year, it's time to relax, *try* to relax, meeting new people isn't relaxing, get enough of that at work, where are they from anyway, grumble grumble, vote National.

In this time-honoured fashion, every Kiwi aspires to 'get away from it all' as a rugged individual and connect with Mother Nature without being disturbed by other rugged individuals. Kiwis excel at loving thy neighbour . . . from a safe distance. Using only hand movements and grimaces, it was hard to explain our complex and unique cultural practices to the Mongolians we met. Maybe they thought we were rude, or crazy, or both. Maybe they thought we were misanthropes.

We set up camp on a small patch of grass at the edge of a clump of fir trees. Beyond the grass a sloping moor of airbrushed heath in orange and green rolled away not very wutheringly down the headland to the lake's edge a couple of hundred metres distant. Half a dozen fir trees stood to lazy attention near the shore. The bay was placid and still, reflecting everything through a Vaseline lens: the northern headland, the distant slump of mountains, the play of clouds in the sky. The sun was buried in a luminous nest of cumulus, in no hurry to set beyond the peaks on Khövsgöl *nuur*'s western shores.

It was a setting perfect for reading. Having ditched all my literature that morning, I was forced to make my own. I got my journal and scribbled some notes about an annoying young wizard who has sex with a mugwump: *Harry Potter and the Naked Lunch*. Tama looked up 'gatsa' and 'conno' in the guidebook but couldn't find anything. Instead he read me some astonishing factoids about Chinggis Khaan, then cooked up a massive feed of salami, potato, cabbage and rice.

'Thanks, Camp Dad,' I said, wolfing it down with appreciative grunts.

'No worries, Camp Mum—thanks for pitching the tent.'

It was after 9 pm. The sun seemed to be frozen in the sky a few centimetres above the mountain range. Mongolia was much further north than I'd realised. We were about fifty-one degrees north, roughly the same latitude as London, closer to the Arctic Circle than Montreal or Hokkaido. We went to bed early, watching forked lightning flash on distant peaks. Tama fell asleep and dreamt he was a fighter pilot. I dreamt about Chinggis Khaan, Ocean Lord.

. . . They came across the Tenggis—the great ocean, which was really a lake. The blue-grey wolf and the lady-reindeer came, simultaneously—and their star-crossed interracial love spawned a creature called Bodonchar Munkhag, 'Bodonchar the Simpleton', Mongolian history's first official moron. Bodonchar the Simpleton lived in a grass hut by a mörön. He hunted geese, rats and marmots and quaffed the rancid, fermented milk of a horse until he vomited goose, rat and marmot bits into the river. Some generations of kidnappings, rapings and begettings later, I was born—the baby Chinggis was born!—clutching in my fist a clot of blood the size of a knucklebone. I dressed in the skins of dogs and mice. At the age of ten I killed my elder half-brother by shooting him in the back with an arrow (the 1172 film We Need to Talk About Chinggis *is based on this true story). Growing up on the banks of the Onon gol in what is now Khentii province, I had a liberating scarcity of employment options: I could spend my life with an ox yoke around my neck and wrists as the pitiful slave of an enemy tribe, which was badly paid but steady work. I could subsist as a scavenger in a grass hut like my moronic grandpa, which was the twelfth-century equivalent of arts administration. Or I could become a warrior and try my hand at conquering most of Eurasia . . .*

I woke early in the morning and stuck my head out of the tent. Our lake had gone, the heath too. All was silvery-white and indistinct. The tent had come unmoored; we were drifting aimlessly through space. I stared into the void for a few confused seconds then went back to sleep.

The fog burned off a couple of hours later. We had a ball-shrinking swim in the lake then filled our water bottles from it, even though we had both pissed in the water. We were running late as we struck camp and struggled to ride our heavily laden bikes up the hill along the lack-of-path. Tama pinched his tube and got a puncture. A couple of dozen cows and hundreds of flies watched as he sat in the grass and patched his inner tube. There were twelve patches and four spare inner tubes left; at this rate we would run out of puncture repair options about halfway to Mörön Khentii.

Back on the path we headed north, but the turn-off to Chandmani-Öndör was not where it should've been. We checked the map, then checked again. After considering riding east up the valley anyway, we decided to continue up 'the worst road in Mongolia' instead. It turned out to be better than much of the road from Mörön to Khatgal, apart from a few hundred metres of bumpy tangled roots that would've been murder in a minivan. Five kilometres north and one valley over we saw a path heading east and took it. After half an hour's hard slog up through thick pine forest, we came over a rise and were greeted by a smooth, manicured track that snaked off down the hill. Back in New Zealand, Tama 2000 would've instantly zanged down it in his best Evel Knievel impersonation: fast, furious and foolish. But here he stopped, put on his helmet, turned on his front shocks, and made sure I knew how to use my disc brakes properly.

'Brake with both hands—never just the front, or you're over the handlebars,' he said. 'The front brake does most of the stopping, the back keeps you from flipping. Brake in pulses, a second or two at a time. The discs get really hot, and if you brake for too long they'll overheat and buckle, then you're—we're—screwed. So don't go too fast, even

Morons pre-departure, a tad overconfident. Leopard-skin: Tama. Skeleton suit, bathing cap, phrasebook and messy Melbourne bedroom: Tom.

About to bust out of Mörön, capital of Khovsgol province in northern Mongolia. *Lonely Planet* describes Mörön as 'rather disappointing'.

The last of the day's sun falls on the road to Khatgal, about eighty kilometres north of Mörön.

A victorious *bökh* wrestler at Naadam festival, Khatgal. Naadam is Mongolia's Christmas, New Year's and Schoolies rolled into one.

Naadam, part 2: Father and daughter, selling off the family heirlooms to backpackers.

A friendly nomad visits us on our first night camping out in the wilderness. His horse was scared of me.

A 'Kiwi shortcut': Tom lost in thick forest outside Tsagaan-Üür. Like tramping in Fiordland, except with a bike.

Tama halfway up Tiger Mountain. Biting flies not pictured.

Tom inspects shamanic teepee east of Chandmani Öndör, wonders if it would be more comfortable than the tent.

Like a glacier on fast-forward: a flash flood of hailstones in the process of destroying someone's wheat fields, south of Khantai.

After twelve hours riding through fields of wild marijuana north of the Selenge *mörön* (river), Tom and Tama impersonate a couple of distraught homosexual miners.

Tom humps a roadsign 172 kilometres west of the final МОРОН (Mörön), Khentii province.

Chinggis Khaan country. A young Chinggis would've honed his looting and pillaging skills on these very hills.

The final Mörön. Note the conspicuous absence of almost everything.

Done with riding, hopefully forever.

though it looks sah-weet. With all this weight on, you don't wanna buckle your wheel and have to ride hundreds of k's on it—'

'Like I did in Perth!'

'Yeah man, please don't do *that* again.'

We rode down the immaculate downhill trail at a modest pace and I practised pulsing my brakes. With thirty-five kilograms of gear and water on, the bike wanted to *move*, and after a couple of hundred metres my brakes were emitting a high-pitched whistling sound. At the bottom of the hill I tapped a gloved finger onto the front disc; it burnt a hole right through the tip before I could pull it away.

I was a bit surprised that Tama was playing it so safe; he lived for the mad downhills. His dads' house in Wellington backed onto a firebreak-cum-mountain-bike-path called the Rollercoaster, which was a gruelling half-hour burn up through pine forest to the Brooklyn wind turbine, 300 metres above sea level, followed by a hair-raising six-minute (for Tama) to eight-minute (for me) downhill blast. We'd rocked it most weekends in the late nineties, and I could never keep up with him.

One time when Tama was away, I went for a Rollercoaster mission with my old primary school friend Sam, who I didn't hang out with much anymore. Sam was much more cautious than Tama, more cautious than me, and this made me go faster. I eased off the brakes and shot ahead like I'd seen Tama do so many times before. I barrelled into the turns, leaning rather than braking, clutching the shuddering handlebars, as my younger brother's too-small bike groaned beneath me, Sam lagging behind somewhere and me flying, faster than I'd ever ridden in my life, tears in my eyes, scenery reduced to blurry slabs of colour when jolting towards me came a towering wave of dark brown. The hairpin corner! I jammed on the brakes and turned left but it was too late and too sharp. I flew over the handlebars, somersaulted and landed on my back, bouncing and skidding to a rough standstill on the edge of the trail, my right foot touching the trunk of a big-arse pine tree. I took off my helmet; it was split neatly in half. My brother's bike's front wheel was buckled, but rideable. After what seemed like forever Sam came down the path. He stopped when he saw me.

'Tom, are you all right? What happened?'

'Yeah man, it's fine,' I said. 'I broke my bro's helmet but nothing else. Let's keep going.'

I turned around and got onto my bike.

'Tom! Your back . . .'

Now that Sam mentioned it, my back was a bit tingly. I tried to look over my shoulder, but I couldn't see much, so I took off my T-shirt. The back of it was bloody and ripped to shreds.

'Damn, I really liked that T-shirt,' I said, with a bravado I didn't really feel. Sam stared at me.

'Let's get a move on,' I said, thowing the helmet into the trees and pedalling away. When I told Tama the story a couple of weeks later he thought it was awesome.

We spent the day cruising east through a succession of broad valleys, each more breathtaking and quiet than the last. A song by Of Montreal was stuck in my head but mangled by the surroundings: 'Mon-gol in the summer, zang / There aren't ee-ven any streets / Everyone's off herding goats and drin-king Chinggis . . .'

Some sights were particularly asthma-inducing: a cluster of huge *ovoos* perched on a cliff top half a kilometre distant, flying ragged blue flags against the deeper blue of the sky; a diorama of squat brown-and-red log cabins nestled snugly into the base of five conical rock-topped peaks which we rode right past without stopping. The *ovoos* and the village (possibly Hohon Huree) were worth half an issue of *National Geographic* each, but we were on a mission.

As we rode, Tama told me more stories of life in New York. Contrary to what Flight of the Conchords would have you believe, NYC *was* the greatest city in the world, ever. Tama lived on the Chinatown edge of Little Italy, ate out every night, had a homeboy drug dealer who delivered weed by scooter, and hung out with models, actual models, snorting actual cocaine and bellowing along with Big Apple-themed anthems: Blah, blah, blah, NEW YORK! One of Tama's favourite things was riding his single-speed over the Williamsburg Bridge at 3 am, midwinter, no one else on the bridge, snow on the rails, coming over the rise and seeing the Manhattan skyline loom ahead like the opening sequence of a big-budget TV show, like a Frank Sinatra song.

New York sounded awesome. In fact, Tama's stories made Melbourne, the cultural capital of . . . Australia, seem a bit lame. But now that Tama had fallen for a Vancouver girl, he was planning to move there after our trip. Vancouver sounded pretty damn awesome, too: in summer you could sail your arse off around Vancouver Island, and in winter drive to Whistler after work and get blunted and go snowboarding under lights until 11 pm. In a few weeks,

Vancouver—*Ram*couver—was set to become the world's even greater-est city.

We stopped for sandwiches in an iridescent spill of wild-flowers. Tama sat down and took a picture of his feet, then pulled up his socks and took a couple more.

'What're you doing?'

'Taking some shots of my socks. I might be able to sell them to Icebreaker. Product in the wild, y'know?' He grinned.

'Whoring out your own feet—that's a new low, Tama Pugsley, even for you.' I threw a piece of cheese at his head.

'Careful! That stuff doesn't grow on trees!' He rooted around in the flowers for the gouda and munched it down.

After lunch we crossed a shallow river over the remains of a log bridge that had collapsed into the boggy soil. The track traversed a vast plain and turned a corner and headed towards what looked from a distance like a dark, malformed and shrunken Arc de Triomphe. Up close, one of Paris's most iconic monuments resolved itself into two fir trees, one on each side of the road. They were over ten metres tall and nearly as wide and they formed a ragged yet magnifi-cent gateway. A forward-thinking medieval herdsman had probably planted two seedlings there 900 or so years ago; when he died the trees would've still just been little saplings. But the story somehow felt more *significant* than that; maybe two lovers had been slaughtered on this spot, but their spirits couldn't bear to be parted so they stayed together in conifer form, fondling each other's roots, watching and waiting to avenge their deaths by dropping pine cones onto the heads of the great-great-grandchildren of their murderers ... I wanted to film us riding under those mighty trees, but Tama was determined to get a move on to Chandmani-Öndör.

'Shall we set up the tripod and do a few ride-throughs?' I said. 'You know, from different angles and stuff?'

'Yeah . . . How about you ride through the trees and I'll take some photos?'

'Cool. And then do some reverse shots, maybe something from up in the branches . . .'

'The thing is, the cameras don't have much memory, they don't have much battery, and we're not very far into our mission. You've gotta ration yourself.' He saw me looking agitated. 'Don't sweat it, man—there'll be plenty more nice trees in Mongolia, I promise!'

As we cycled away, I looked back anxiously over my shoulder. What if that was it? What if everything else from here to Khentii was only *mildly* stunning? What if that magical elven arch was the single most beautiful, haunting, cinematic spot in all of Mongolia, and we'd failed to capture it?

We made it to Chandmani-Öndör in the late afternoon. From a distance it seemed idyllic, a settlement designed by a gifted ten-year-old: log cabins crowding up to the tree line, pastel pink and blue tin roofs. Up close, Chandmani-Öndör was a dirty little town. It was similar to Khatgal but much smaller, without the thrilling/horrific sense that great sticky dollops of tourist dollars were going to give the place an extreme makeover any day now.

We leaned our bikes against a rotting fence and wandered around the sleepy town square, poking our heads into grocery stores looking for bread and cheese and fresh vegetables, with mixed results (bread, yes; cheese and vegies, no). We sucked down a couple of bowls of bland mutton soup in a gloomy canteen with a view across the square to some downtrodden *gers*.

'*Ronery Pranet* reckons we can stay in those things,' I said. 'Fuck that,' Tama replied. 'Let's keep going.'

When we came out of the restaurant a couple of teenage boys were transfixed by our bikes. They were looking, and touching, but they didn't seem interested in stealing anything. The youths wouldn't have much use for bikes or bike gear, since they had horses and horses are self-pedalling and almost never get punctures. It felt much safer than China or Cambodia, or Melbourne, so we just left our stuff there and finished our shopping. On our way out of town we startled a huddle of massive vultures with the punched-black eyes of computer porn addicts. They stopped feasting on the back half of a dead horse and flapped heavily into the air, croaking.

Ten kilometres out of Chandmani-Öndör the main path turned right, to the southwest, and we took a much less worn path to the *züün* (*züün* means both 'left' and 'east'). After a pleasant few minutes the Arigiin *gol* drew close and we cycled alongside a verdant floodplain dotted with groves of poplars and pines. It looked as nice a spot as we were likely to find so we pulled off the road, put some КУПЕР beers in the river to cool and pushed our bikes around in circles for ten minutes looking for a campsite. We ended up in a grassy glade surrounded by pine trees where I pitched our tent, then we went for a swim and admired each other's bodies. The rains came. Back at the campsite we retired inside, and Tama cooked vast quantities of instant noodles.

'Man, I wish we'd packed some gourmet freeze-dried instant curries,' I said. 'When me and my bro went tramping with Dad last Christmas down in Fiordland, he brought heaps of them. We ate like Indian princes every night.'

'You mean like rajahs?'

'Uh, sure.'

'How was that mission?' Tama asked. 'I saw the photos on Facebook—that river crossing looked sketchy as.'

'Yeah, it was a bit mental. We had to walk up this riverbed for four hours, and the river was totally in flood, like a metre higher than normal. And freezing. All these Aussies were getting airlifted out cos they couldn't handle it.'

'Ha, awesome.'

'Dad was great too. He was a bit slow on the hill climbs, but after eight or nine hours in the mud, me and Jack were staggering and tripping over, my knee was killing me, and Dad just kept ploughing ahead, didn't complain once. He's a machine. I reckon he'd give *you* a run for your money, bro!'

'Maybe. We should take him to Pakistan.'

'Totally.' I breathed in. 'It's funny, you know I was kind of thinking that he might, like, open up on the tramp, tell me and Jack his whole life story or something. All the girls before Jenny, how he got the nickname "Hundred Hands Harry", that kinda thing.' I sipped my купер. 'Y'know, male bonding.'

'Huh.'

'It was weird. We just walked up and down some hills, then I pissed off back to Melbourne.'

'Noodles up, bro!' Tama tipped a vast slop into my saucepan-bowl. We added liberal amounts of tabasco sauce and kampot pepper to the mess, but a proper curry it was not. I drifted off listening to the rain thickening across the tent, wondering what a young Mongol warrior would do on a rainy night like this.

As a rebellious teenage Chinggis I experimented with slavery—who hasn't?—and wasted a couple of years tied to a log listening to Green Day. But I cleaned myself up, escaped, and met up with my best friend from childhood, Jamukha. Me and Jamukha expressed our brotherhood by spending the night together under a single blanket, where we shared our body smells and 'ate food that is not to be digested'. We were great friends, but we were both really aggressive, and unfortunately those steppes weren't big enough for the both of us. After a tragic falling out I spent the next two decades waging war against my ex-best friend. I united the rival tribes of the Merkid, Kereyid, Tatar and Naiman, bodies piling up around me like rotten logs, until finally I defeated Jamukha's army and had him executed on top of a hill. Thus the mighty Mongol nation was born. From that day forth, everyone knew me as Chinggis Khaan—Universal Lord. And that was just the beginning . . .

DAY 6: LOST IN A FOREST, LOST IN A BOG

Sometime before morning I half-woke with half-wet feet. I worked out I could bend my knees and fold my feet up out of the wetness, and fell asleep again. Sometime later I woke with wet knees. I turned over and got back to sleep easily enough. Next I woke up with a wet arse. This was getting pretty annoying, but it was hardly life-threatening—besides, I reasoned, the top half of my body was still pretty dry, and that's where all the important stuff was. I was getting a bit cold but I just pulled my merino top out of my pillowcase and put it on and almost got back to sleep. I lay there in a half-doze, listening to the rain and trying not to move; moving made me wetter.

When day finally came it was cloudless and blue. Tama was fresh as a daisy. I was as fresh as some manure. I was also pretty embarrassed—I had done enough camping to know better.

'Why didn't you just move away from the edge of the tent, or get up and tighten the guy ropes?' Tama asked, amused.

'I dunno—it wasn't that bad,' I said. 'Plus I didn't want to wake you up.'

'You should've got the tarp and wrapped it around your sleeping bag. That's what it's for.'

I hung my sleeping bag from a couple of pine trees using the tent's guy ropes and sat down to a bowl of grumpy muesli. We agreed to take turns sleeping on the left side of the tent, to be known henceforth as the rainy side. As I rinsed out my bowl, Tama burst out laughing.

'Doiggus—your sleeping bag!'

An entire herd of wild buffalo had trampled through the pines into our clearing and they were munching on big sloppy mouthfuls of grass—and sleeping bag, which was, as Tama pointed out in their defence, green.

'Shoo! *Zogs!* Get the buggery out of here!' I yelled, waving my arms and charging at them. The beasts snorted and skittered away, feathers stuck to their snouts. As I fixed the hole in my sleeping bag with cable ties and gaffer tape and fantasised about buffalo bolognese for lunch, a herdsman appeared riding a sleek black horse. We offered him some bread. He ate it happily and *bayarllaa*'d then *bayartai*'d into the forest after his snouted livelihood.

We had made it maybe twenty metres down the road when one of the bolts in my right pannier broke off and ripped through the canvas, leaving the bag only half attached to its plastic frame. I swore at my expensive German technology. Tama 'fixed' it with a couple of cable ties, half a metre of gaffer tape and some wire he found on the side of the road. It was not an auspicious beginning to our day in the Tiger Forest.

We rode up a small, steep hill, the path choked with roots. I kept expecting Tama's bodgie patch job on my pannier to bust, but it seemed to hold. We wobbled across a vast field that was tilted like a ship in heavy seas. On the left we saw a white *ger*, a middle-aged woman standing outside, and the woman's dogs lifting up their heads and barking and baring their fangs and running towards us. Not wanting any more adventures that morning, especially rabid ones, we took evasive action to the right, bumping off the trail and down the hill. I heard a faint clinking and looked back, worried about my bodgy pannier, but all I saw was last night's empty КУПЕР bottles rolling down the hill. I didn't stop, or say anything to Tama.

After a few hours of hard riding, my bad mood lifted and I felt great: sore, hungry, ecstatic. All that focusing on the uneven track ahead and forcing myself to keep pedalling no matter what made me realise that it actually takes heaps of energy to stay grumpy. We lay under some trees on the edge of a lush field and ate sandwiches made from fresh wholemeal bread and questionable Russian mackerel from a can, admiring an abandoned barn and some rusting farming equipment in the distance. It was like being in a G-rated rewrite of *The Road*, where the cannibals hiding in the bushes had been replaced with more bushes.

We discussed our options: ride through to Tsagaan-Üür then across the Üür *gol* and east through over 100 kilometres of Tiger Forest towards Teshig as planned. Or, we could take Wolfgang's advice and turn off ten kilometres before Tsagaan-Üür and head south to Erdenebulgan via a 600-metre vertical climb up the Badarga *davaa*—which we had christened Tiger Mountain, just to confuse things. Tiger Forest—or Tiger Mountain? That a nice German man and his hot wife expected us to perish in the trees between Tsagaan-Üür and Teshig made our original route slightly less appealing. On the other hand, if we busted south over Tiger Mountain it would still be a couple of days in the wild before we got to Erdenebulgan, and we didn't have the muesli or canned fish for that. No matter which way we went, we would have to resupply in Tsagaan-Üür first.

At the speed we were travelling—approximately ten kilometres an hour—hitting Tsagaan-Üür then backtracking to the Tiger Mountain turn-off would mean a two-hour detour, minimum. Besides, the very idea of backtracking was morally repugnant. There had to be another way.

Tama came up with a third option: a shortcut. We could ride east to Tsagaan-Üür, load up on cheese and salami then bush-bash our way around a tiny ridge (it looked tiny on the map) that stood between us and our road to Tiger Mountain, glory, our faces on commemorative lunchboxes, et cetera. This ridge-circumnavigating shortcut would shave nearly twenty kilometres off our trip, showcasing our excellent orienteering skills. All things going well, we'd be camped out on the top of Tiger Mountain by dinnertime. The plan was declared *mash sain*, even zang.

In the afternoon we reached some serious shamanic architecture. Next to the track there were a dozen wooden teepees decked out with blue plastic like toxic Guy Fawkes Day bonfires in waiting. The tallest *ovoos* were twice my height, built about five metres apart from each other like targets in an archery range. Next to the westernmost *ovoo* was a metre-high engraving of an extremely beefy Mongolian man sporting the sleeves-*sans*-shirt look favoured by *bökh* champions. This athletic carving and the shooting range aesthetic gave the shamanic temples an Olympic, or rather Naadam-ic, feel. Each of these teepees was a shrine for a separate animistic spirit: bird, fish, horse, tiger. My favourite was a monkey with huge mouse ears and an erect tail, light on his feet as if he'd stolen something or was just about to. Was he related to that rascal from *Monkey*? It was possible. Buddhism was pretty big in Mongolia until the Soviets strafed that too.

Inside the *ovoos* were carved wooden boxes where offerings were left for these noble spirits. Apart from a selection of pebbles, the tributes were predominantly vodka bottles (now broken) and cigarettes (now mush), as well as some lollies with plastic and foil wrappers that would long outlast the shrines they'd been left in.

'Hard times,' I said to Tama. He just nodded.

A few kilometres on from the *ovoos* we must've biked past the turnoff to Tiger Mountain, although I didn't notice anything. Meanwhile we zanged it through the forest on a path that was a bit muddy but not too bad. The ride into Tsagaan-Üür was a perfect fifteen-degree decline with two tracks, each a motorcycle tyre wide, curling back and forth through undulating paddock. Thanks to Tama's tinkering my gears were working fine, and I felt confident, in control, fused to my bike in a happy symbiosis of tendon and cable. We saw the log cabins of Tsagaan-Üür and startled a small herd of cows and yaks that stampeded away from us towards town.

Tsagaan-Üür was bigger than Chandmani-Öndör; the houses had white roofs and green roofs as well as pink and blue ones. They were dropped across the paddocks with the perfunctory haste of a military barracks and seemed to be sinking into the mud. I'd been looking forward to reaching Tsagaan-Üür, but as we rolled up the main street I felt uneasy. A knot of bored young men looked at us askance, and I wondered if it was because of Tama's Mongolian flag. Most people seemed to appreciate our vicarious patriotism, but still: what would happen if, say, a pair of ultra-rich, conspicuously foreign Japanese tourists or Saudi princelings came rumbling through rural Queensland on $20,000 racing bikes with an upside-down Aussie flag wedged in their Prada panniers? There'd be some confused looks. What if they cycled through Cronulla?

You could distinguish grocery shops from dwellings by the sign above the door—not what it said as much as the mere presence of a sign. We found a place that sold sugary drink and promptly chugged down 1.25 litres each. We tried to stock up on the big bottles of water we'd need in the hours and days to come, but they didn't have any, just more sugary drink, which was good for replacing electrolytes and vital anti-caking agents lost through exertion but not so good for boiling rice. Tama had some bars on his phone; he tried to work out what time it would be in Ramcouver, couldn't, and called Ami anyway. I unpacked a frisbee that had travelled over 10,000 kilometres from a Kmart in Brunswick without being thrown, and flicked it to/at a couple of curious boys. The distinction turned out to be a fine one: it was all good until I threw the frisbee to a boy who caught it between the eyes and howled and howled some more. His friend looked at me hatefully and ran down an alley. I decided I should find us some water and cheese before those kids called their older brothers and things got all Cronulla on us. In the second shop I visited there was no bottled water but I saw a fridge—itself a rarity—which contained something light yellow and promising.

'Bread? Cheese?' I asked the shopkeeper. She just stared at me.

'Tork. Tchtooork! Blye-ait-shlerg?' I begged, my voice rising as I pointed with increasing desperation at the fridge. 'Come on, you know—blye, ait, shlerg?' The shopkeeper backed away from me, wide-eyed. The store had gone stone quiet, and half a dozen shoppers were staring at me with concern. The shopkeeper thrust a plastic bag of yellow at me and signalled for 3000 tugrugs. I wiped the spit from my lips, thrust a wad of wrinkled and falling apart tugrugs at her, took the cheese and a can of emergency meat and ran. Outside, Tama was still on the phone to Ami.

I suggested we look around for a scabby restaurant and cram a second lunch in before heading into the wilderness but Tama was having none of that.

'Let's bust out of here. It's still forty k's to the top of that mountain.'

Tsagaan-Üür seemed to depress Tama, like Chandmani-Öndör had, Mörön too. But more than that, the towns put him on edge, made him panicky, alarmed. It was hard to feel urgent about making it to Mörön Khenti while lying against birch trees in an Arcadian fish-sandwiched idyll, but in places with clocks, even crappy ones, the ticking of Tama's journey clock grew louder. Every minute we stopped was a minute we weren't riding, bringing us sixty seconds closer to failure.

So we took our shortcut.

On the eastern edge of town, the ridge we would have to semi-circumnavigate jutted out to our right. It was about 200 metres tall, flat-topped and thickly wooded, and it dropped away into steep not-quite-cliffs that were forested all the way down to the flat. According to our maps, this ridge extended for about 1500 metres to the east and was just half a kilometre wide—therefore, if we rode two kilometres east, then another one south, then another one west, we would get around the fucker, easy-peasy. A narrow horse track headed east out of Tsagaan-Üür in pretty much the right direction and we stuck to it, even when it led us suspiciously close to the forest that grew up and over the left side of the ridge. Stuck to that path even when it led us past a sign hammered into the ground that exclaimed in bright red Cyrillic something like CAUTION or DANGER or MORONS PROHIBITED. Unable to heed warnings in a language we couldn't read, we made devil-may-care jokes about unexploded Soviet ordnance and boldly went where no moron had gone before.

And certainly no cyclist. Beautiful, slightly creepy birch trees closed in around us, their trunks pale and bloodless. The path became narrower and less pathlike, until I was following random hoof prints, then just Tama, who was following himself. Riding segued into walking with bike frames between our legs. We dismounted and pushed our bikes, their pedals and bike chains scraping on the forest floor. It was slow going, but we only had to make it a few hundred metres more before we passed the knob, so we soldiered on. The trees had a bit of space between them, at least.

Then they didn't. After a few minutes I realised that going back would be just as hard as going forward, because our tracks were indistinguishable among the mess of composting wood-pulp—we couldn't backtrack if we tried. This was a moral victory of sorts. Tama stopped and took a GPS reading which confirmed that a) we were very close to Tsagaan-Üür, and b) our 1:200,000 military-grade topo-graphical maps weren't detailed enough for this type of orienteering, no matter what the grizzled US Army sergeant in the UB outdoor store had said.

Lacking other options, we kept pushing 'forward'. The ridge was to the south, although we couldn't see it; the Üür *gol* was to the east and north; Tsagaan-Üür was to the west. The only question was, which way were we going? The birch trees hid the afternoon sun, which should have been directly behind us if we were heading east. The ground was still flat, ish, so we weren't accidentally scaling the ridge, but beyond that it was anybody's guess. Tama's compass helped a little but, even so, our weaving progress was dictated more by gaps in the trees than a desire to hold a straight line.

All of that aside, we were in great spirits. No one had stepped on a claymore mine, there was no sign of razor wire, animist spirits, abandoned uranium mines, tigers or anything else that warranted a warning.

'Caution: Trees!'

'Danger: This Path Sucks!'

Chuckling gamely we trudged and pushed our way through the muddy mulch. After half an hour, just as the whole escapade was turning from Funny Joke into Bad Idea, the trees thinned out. Sunlight beckoned. I was overjoyed to be out of that forest—until I realised we'd stumbled into a bog. But it wasn't too bad; the bog was never more than knee-deep, and it had an almost-dry path running along its far edge. Meanwhile, the sun that burned our sweaty faces also gave us a vague idea of where east was, which matched up with following the bog-path to the right. The trail weaved back into the forest, but it was pine forest and not so much undergrowth, so we could resume cycling. We made good progress and after five or ten minutes I was relieved to see a little clearing covered with pine needles. Now we had options: if we made it around the ridge we could make a start on our climb up Tiger Mountain and camp out halfway to the pass. If not, we could come back here and pitch the tent, eat, drink Chinggis, pray.

Beyond the clearing our track reached a little creek and followed it downstream, limping along its right bank. This stream had to be flowing away from the ridge and into the Üür *gol*, so we followed the shit out of it. The bush thickened around us: birch forest again, but with the addition of unidentifiable undergrowth. The shin-deep mud, creepers, vines and drop-offs into soggy creek beds weren't much worse than your average disused tramping track in, say, southern Fiordland. The main difference was that not many people went tramping in Fiordland with sixteen-kilogram bikes and thirty-five kilograms of luggage.

The path worsened until we were stuck in a skinny ditch half a metre deep that rose 1.5 metres up a bank thick with saplings. There wasn't any room to stand beside my bike and push it, and if I tried to push it from behind—which I did—the front wheel flailed around wildly and dug into the mud. Short of detaching the pannier bags and carrying it all up separately, which seemed like cheating, the only thing for it was to straddle the bank and pull the bike uphill by the handlebars. I managed it, bellowing to avert a hernia while saplings on both sides of the path bent over and broke. Tama followed, trampling more trees. I was dimly aware that by blazing a trail through this dead-end forest we might encourage others to make similar mistakes in the future. When I shared this pearl of wisdom with Tama, he just grunted.

After a few dozen more agonising metres of bush-and-bike-bashing, doing unmentionable damage to our gears, Tama suggested we leave our bicycles and scout ahead.

'What, just leave our bikes in the forest?'

'Yeah, just for a second.' Tama leaned his bike against a birch tree that was tangled in brambles.

'What about all our gear? What if . . . we can't find our way back?'

'Dude, don't be silly. Of course we'll be able to find our way back. We'll just go for a little mission, see if it opens up.'

I sighed, and agreed—not because it was sensible, but because it was easier. Tama marched off purposefully through the forest, and I followed the back of his cowboy hat. He was a unique mix, Tama 2000. One part logical, practical, sensible; the other headstrong, bloody-minded, maniac. I couldn't always tell who was in the lead, Dr Tama or Mr Pugs. I pretended we were on a track, pretended we were making a film: *The Blair Witch Moron*. After a few minutes it really hadn't opened up. Tama stopped and looked over his shoulder.

'Let's go back,' he said.

'Okay.'

'Cool.' Then, 'This is crazier than anything I've done before.' Tama was still grinning, but there was a slight tremor in his voice.

We backtracked to our bikes then backtracked along the path, hating it. We sweated. Cursed. Branches clawed at my broken Ortlieb. We headed upstream until we returned to the pine forest with its comforting little clearing. Rather than backtracking into the bog, we decided to keep to the creek until we found a place to cross. The far bank was thick with trees, but after a few minutes there was a little gap. Tama tested the water; it was knee-deep, okay for a bike crossing. On the other side was more forest, but it was also more open, and in a couple of minutes we pushed our cycles out onto a grassy field. In that sweet moment I understood why shipwrecked Hollywood sailors hugged and kissed the beach when they finally washed ashore.

We reached a goat track that led back into the trees and followed it in the opposite direction. I proposed that we give up on circling around 'that fucken horrible ridge' and instead cross the Üür *gol* when we came to it and head in an eighty-one kilometre loop east of Tiger Mountain to Erdenebulgan along what looked like a proper track (red, solid).

Tama agreed.

Three minutes later we made it to the banks of the Üür *gol*—all that floundering around in the bush had taken place less than a kilometre from the river—and gazed across the water. All the way across. The Üür *gol* was quite a *mörön*—easily thirty metres across and extremely fast flowing. At first I thought it was in flood, but the winter snow would've melted months ago; it was just *big*. We cycled upstream towards a point where it got wider and hopefully shallower. A long, thin, rocky shoal sat five metres off the bank. We plunged in without checking the depth first; the crossing was waist-deep, and my bike tyres lifted off the riverbed. With watertight panniers that served as buoys, the whole contraption tried to float away from me and it was a fight to make it to the shoal.

As we stood panting and dripping on our pathetic little island, in denial about how deep the rest of the *mörön* must be, a horseman trotted up to the riverbank twenty metres downstream. He made it across to our shoal no problem and paused for a second before driving his horse into the torrent. When the *mörön* reached the horse's neck the mare whinnied and reared. The horseman had to turn around; he galloped back across the floodplain, towards Tsagaan-Üür.

'I thought there was meant to be a bridge here?' I said. 'Let me see the map . . . yeah, *there*, on the bend!'

We looked at the actual Üür *gol*, which swung to the left a few hundred metres upstream. No bridge.

'Do you reckon it's further up?' I asked, unconvinced.

'Doig, I reckon this map was printed in two thousand and fucken three. A *new* map wouldn't have a bridge on it.'

I stared upstream. Tama stared downstream. In desperation I checked the *Ronery Pranet*, but it had nothing to say about Teshig or how to get there. However, it *did* mention that 'the bridge east [of Tsagaan-Üür] washed away in 2006 and the river crossing is now a bit dicey'. That was helpful.

'Uncrossable river to the east. Swamp to the south. Sheeeit,' I said. 'Why don't we go back to Tsackin, Tshaggap, however the hell you pronounce it, and have some mutton soup and, like, regroup?'

Tama screwed up his nose.

'I reckon we should try to get around that fucker again,' he said, waving at the ridge that had ruined our afternoon. 'The track should be better now we're on the river.'

He wasn't kidding. The ridge was less than a kilometre away and I could swear it was laughing at us.

'You wanna ride back into that swampy foresty hell?'

'Well, no, ride on that trail we found along the edge of the swamp—'

'And when the track goes to shit?'

'We just find a nice campsite, have a nice dinner, then tomorrow we bike back through that Suck-Sack town, then backtrack ten k's west to the turnoff to that other track, and go to Tiger Mountain that way.'

I looked down the Üür *gol*. As it swept towards the ridge, the floodplain we were standing on narrowed to an overgrown nothing.

'Look, I reckon it's pretty likely to just turn to shit, and then—'

'*If* the track turns to shit, you can say "I told you so", and we can camp and have dinner.'

While we were bickering, a red tractor arrived on the far riverbank half a kilometre downstream. The tractor proceeded to tow a jeep slowly but surely across the river. I had to admit defeat. Even if we paid that tractor driver to ferry us across the Üür *gol* to the proper track on the other side (our 'trusty' map said there was a proper track on the other side) we would still have to recross the same monster river thirty kilometres downstream if we wanted to get to Erdenebulgan before we starved to death. And there was no guarantee there'd be a tractor-chauffeur waiting for us out there in the middle of nowhere. Without a bridge, the Üür *gol* was a *mörön* too far.

We left the shoal and returned to the near bank; I nearly lost my right pannier in the process. Tama cycled over to the tractor to ask the driver for directions to Tiger Mountain. The driver frowned, then pointed out the window, very expressively. His hand went left, forward, right, then along and up, up, up, winding all the way, and finally, as high as he could reach, over the top. This corresponded roughly with what we had tried and failed to do, hours ago: circumnavigate that ridge and start an ascent of Tiger Mountain towards the pass, then bust it to Erdenebulgan.

Tama smiled at me and nodded. I took a deep breath and followed the back of his head south, back towards the forest. The track was well trodden, but it seemed like it was trying to tell us something. It kept lurching off towards the riverbank and terminating, leaving us pointed at the far bank of the Üür *gol*, waiting for a tractor that wasn't coming. The third time this happened we stumbled upon two men and a woman having a picnic next to their motorbikes. Tama asked them for directions to Erdenebulgan. They pointed across the river and said, '*Mörön, mörön, ingeed, ingeed, ingeed.*' We had no idea what *ingeed* meant. It sounded like hard work.

'No, no *ingots*,' Tama retorted, pointing southwest past the ridge. 'We want mountain pass, to Tiger Mountain, what's it called—*davaa*? Badarga *davaa*?'

'*Ugui. Mörön.*' They all pointed east across the river.

'*Davaa.*' Tama pointed southwest.

'*Mörön.*'

'*Davaa.*'

'*Mörön!*'

'*Davaa!*'

I scoured the phrasebook, then weighed in with, '*tom davaa* [big pass?]'

The blokes didn't get it, but the lady nodded her head, then shook it.

'*Tiin, tend tom davaa bii—gekhde ih xetsüü, shavartai, ih ayultai—tiishee bitgii yav.*'

'*Zang!*' Tama said.

He was happy with that confirmation, whatever it actually meant, and busted out for the pass, or the *tiishee bitgii*. The path we were following got fainter and fainter, then it turned a corner into a dry stony creekbed and disappeared completely. Staring blankly at some nondescript rocks, I felt like a tracker in the Wild West—the incompetent paleface tracker who all the Red Injuns laugh at.

But Tama 2000 squinted and sniffed at the creekbed until he picked up the trail. We were heading south now, and the ridge was to our right; we were about halfway round it. We headed away from the Üür *gol* into the forest and forded a small creek, then another, then a large creek where the water came up to our stomachs and we had to unhook our panniers and carry everything across separately to avoid further damage to our chains and brakes. On the far side of the creek it was much quieter, as if we had crossed some important yet dimly understood threshold. We rode faster. It was getting dark when we heard the sound of rushing water and emerged from the trees and found ourselves by the Üür *gol* again.

We came into a big clearing next to a half-built log cabin. One wall, a few foundation beams and a couple of doorways were in place, plus a full floor plan was staked out. But the logs and timber to finish the house were rotting in the grass. An axe stuck in a chopping block had rusted and the lumps of firewood beside it had turned to mulch. The workers were nowhere to be seen. We decided to camp a few hundred metres away from the creepy half-house, not too close to the trees either. Tama found a patch of red flowers with a fine view of Tiger Mountain, which we would have to wait until tomorrow to cross. He checked the clock on the GPS:

9:47 pm. Our shortcut to avoid two hours of backtracking had taken us five and a half hours. We had travelled a pathetic two kilometres as the buzzard flies. But we *had* circumnavigated that shitful ridge; we had well and truly beaten the knob. Tama sighed in satisfaction.

'Hey, Tama.'

'Wha?'

'You were right about the shortcut—but can I still say "I told you so"?'

'Sure.'

Now we could rest. And eat. I had cheese—we could have cheese sandwiches! I reached into my pannier. The cheese was soft, really soft; it had melted into a runny mess, the consistency of butter. I tasted it. It was butter.

Four buttery jam sandwiches and half a litre of Chinggis Gold vodka later, the afternoon's adventures felt like something I had done, rather than something that happened to—or at—me. Sleep came fast and hard as a slamming door.

DAY 7: TIGER MOUNTAIN

'Wake up bro, it's past nine o'clock—gotta get a move on.'

The early morning haze had burned away and there we were, in a flowery meadow in darkest Mongolia, at the front end of a roasting hot blue-sky day. We were out of muesli so for breakfast we had more bread and more jam with lots more butter. While Tama sorted out his gears I ambled down to the Üür *gol* to filter us some water. Sitting next to the building site I spent half a painstaking hour pumping a brown fluid that was thicker than dirty dishwater into half a dozen plastic and aluminium drink bottles with the help of Tama's charcoal-filter pump, a contraption that looked exactly how I imagined a penis pump would. It wasn't easy, but I managed to break it. Then I squatted behind a bush and, with a monstrous effort, managed to squeeze out half a dozen rabbit droppings.

Back at the campsite Tama was still trying to fix his bike. Yesterday's bush-bashing and river-fording had left his derailleur, in technical parlance, 'fucken fucked'. Tama pedalled through the crimson wildflowers at a crawl, cursing as the chain rattled and slipped. With his big shoulders hunched over and the pedals whirring he reminded me of a miserable Moscow circus bear on an oversized miniature tricycle.

'I don't know why it's so munted,' he said hopelessly.

I whipped the Flip-cam out to document Tama's grumpiness—a sight almost never seen in the wild—but when he noticed me filming he perked up, said, 'It'll be sweet' and 'We should get a move on.'

It was seventy-odd kilometres along and 600 vertical metres up then down from here to the other side of Tiger Mountain. We hoped to be in Erdenebulgan by nightfall, which was about a hundred kilometres west–southwest of Teshig, which was the next resupply point on our original and not currently relevant itinerary. From Erdenebulgan we could head to Tarialan, a town whose glamorous and romantic name conjured visions of an enchanted oasis on the Silk Road between Samarkand and Byzantium. From blessed Tarialan we could rejoin our itinerary ninety kilometres further on at Khutag-Öndör. We had lost half a day in that swamp, but with a couple of monster days we would be back on track.

As we were leaving the meadow, Tama remembered the doxycycline tablets we'd forgotten to take with breakfast. I was tempted to forget mine for the rest of the trip, but the prospect of coming down with dengue fever somewhere in the Khan Khentii mountains was scarier than cycling a thousand kilometres with bowels of congealed papier-mâché. I grimaced and washed the pills down with a mouthful of brown, burnt-tasting *mörön* water and we rode off. Tama started feeling queasy straight away but he kept riding—in 1/7, the only gear configuration where his chain didn't skip. We came to a wide but shallow-looking river crossing and pushed our bikes across. The water was cool around my thighs. We were watched from upriver by a placid father and son sitting on the bank, not doing much of anything; beyond them there were signs of a clear, sweet track winding off around the west side of the ridge—the 'long way' to Tsagaan-Üür that we had decided against the day before. On the other side of the river Tama sat down on a log and put his head in his hands. His face was pale and he was sweating profusely.

'That doxy shit's making me sick,' he gasped. 'I need to eat something.'

I cracked out the half-loaf and ripped a couple of chunks off for us to chew, even though it'd mean fewer sandwiches for lunch. I felt fine, but I pretended to feel a bit sick too, out of solidarity.

'Cheer up geezer, you'll be sweet in a second.'

Tama didn't look up. 'It's not just the doxy—it's my bike. I just, I get really fucked off when I can't fix things.'

We were still sitting on that log, dreading the climb ahead of us, when a couple of motorcycles appeared on the far bank. Two guys and a girl dismounted before pushing their bikes across the stream. One of the bikes got stuck right in the middle at the deepest spot. Tama's ears pricked up and he jumped off the log and strode into the water to help, nausea forgotten. When the guy saw Tama coming, he scowled and redoubled his efforts, managing to haul his bike into the shallows before Tama could show him up. The man's girlfriend smiled and *sain bainuu*'d at Tama; the man's scowl deepened. The dude looked stern, joyless, ex-military. A brittle sadness in his eyes reminded me of my old history teacher, Mr Murphy, a former navy man and perpetually disgruntled Presbyterian. We didn't offer Mongolian Murphy any bread.

While our new awkward acquaintances waited for their bike engines to dry out, Tama and I rolled off through gently sloping paddocks that were peppered with bright yellow trumpet-shaped flowers. It had clouded over and we were glad for it. Soon enough we heard the chesty rumble of Russian hogs, and Mongolian Murphy and his motorcycle Mama overtook us, tailed by their buddy, but as Murphy gunned his bike to burn us off, the engine sputtered, backfired and died and the bike rolled to a halt. We overtook them, trying not to laugh too loudly.

I don't know what provoked it, but as we cycled towards Tiger Mountain Tama told me about the latest advances in weapons technology. Predator drones might be getting increasingly popular with the Pentagon, especially in arid Muslim countries, and tactical nukes might be getting smaller and more accurate with each passing year, but *velocity* was the new frontier. Advances in electric pulse-cannon and railgun technology by the US military (strictly confidential, of course) meant they could now fire small ceramic plates at over 8000 kilometres per hour, so fast that the plates could burn right through tank armour and thick concrete walls, rendering conventional defences useless. These plates could potentially penetrate hundreds of metres underground, making them more effective than bunker-busting nukes. The only protection against this marauding crockery was something from the CGA computer games of my childhood: light-activated force shields. I imagined my granny's finest Christmas china, complete with gravy and minted peas, slicing through aircraft carriers, through pyramids. I saw a railgun powerful enough to fire a dinner plate through the moon.

The meadow gave way to light pine forest and the twin tyre tracks we were following became muddy, puddled, riddled with tree roots. Tama stopped talking about weapons. We both rode in silent concentration along the tracks, or the grass between the tracks, or we veered off the tracks to try to avoid getting bogged. Suddenly the trail was an eighties computer game: you had to go left, then left again, straight ahead then right, left, right, right, right, straight. If you looked away from the chunk of track directly in front of you, it was jolts and splashes and spills all round. I hadn't fallen off my bike yet, not properly, and since we weren't doing it Evel Knievel-style, I was determined to make it through the whole trip upright, left, straight.

Tama stopped for a piss break and a Mars Bar, grimacing as he chugged down the cowshit river water.

'What are you smiling at?' he said.

'Nothing. I was just thinking about computer games, old-school ones.'

'I was thinking about lying in hammocks on that beach on Rabbit Island, with my Ami. Eating crab.'

'"Eating crab"—is *that* what you call it?'

'That's what your mama calls it. You know bro, we should've arranged this differently.'

'Yeah?'

'Yeah, so we could go to a tropical paradise with our girls *after* all this shit, not before.'

'True.'

We checked the map. It was thirty kilometres or more to the top from here; we had covered less than ten kilometres. It would take us four, maybe six hours to reach the top of Tiger Mountain at this rate. My shoulders were already tense from the juddering handlebars; my arse could've done with a bit more padding. I felt good, though, ready for a brutalising uphill session.

We came up off the plain and started to ascend the mountain proper. The path was gravelly as well as muddy and our tyres would slip and spray gravel on the steep bits, so we had to slow right down and not pedal too hard or we'd just burn rubber going nowhere. Then the flies—the bitey flies, big bloated stinging things with filthy bloodsucking proboscises—came out in force to feast on our calves, our forearms and, given half a chance, our foreheads. On solid ground you could've mashed them with one hand as you rode but on this treacherous, uneven grind, one hand off the handlebars and you'd tip into a slophole. Then it started to rain.

At first I welcomed the wet, thinking it would drive the flies away, but it didn't. We ran a soggy gauntlet of clay, scree, tree branches that whipped at eyeballs, abrupt hills, shortness of breath, stabbing muscle pain. In places the track dissolved into mud and you could see where cars had got bogged and spun their wheels, leaving concave gashes that were now deep puddles. At one point we paused for a Mars Bar and filthy water break and a dance troupe of orange monarch butterflies descended on my hands and panniers and one on my nose, just for a moment. When I stopped the pain stopped too, but when we started again it was right there like it never left.

The rain fell and mixed with our sweat as we climbed through a nightmare landscape of dead trees no more than grey branchless trunks sticking out of the ground like sharpened spikes. At first we had to push our bikes some of the time, then most of the time. Tama was ahead, as always, and I fought to keep up. Through a fog of ache and disgruntlement, I managed to be grateful that we'd gotten so lost yesterday—if not, we would've had to make camp somewhere on this godforsaken hillside where nowhere was clear, nowhere flat, the best we could hope for a soft bed of mud and no lightning. Those flies would've loved it. Chinggis Khaan would've loved it, too; he would've galloped all over hills like this, maybe this exact hill, standing in his stirrups to fire backwards over his shoulder, riding his enemies down and leaving them broken-spined and dying slowly in a thickening quagmire. Chinggis wouldn't've complained.

'Soggy bog log, dog log bog!' Tama called down the hill.

'Doggy boggy log sog!' I replied.

The rain stopped and the sun came out. I noticed the wildflowers again. Brimming mud puddles reflected fire-blackened and dead tree trunks in perfect symmetry. We had the whole valley to ourselves. I yodelled as loud as I could: no echo.

We crossed a 'bridge' of half-submerged pine logs laid across a wide and pungent bog, then the muddy gouge of a path turned to the left and got steeper as it headed into the forest on Tiger Mountain. I changed down into 1/2, then 1/1. There was the body that pushed the bike, the mind that pushed the body, and the thing that pushed the mind. No one knows what that thing is, but there it was, I was it.

I put my arse into it, pedalling with my gluteus maximus, hunched over like a constipated dog. I sucked all the air that I could into my heaving lungs and still it wasn't enough. I tried to keep the handlebars steady but my shoulders spasmed and stung. I tried to get my feet into my pedal clips but I couldn't—the concentration made me slow down and tip to the side. I couldn't ride in a straight line with so much weight on. My front wheel jumped around on the loose rock like a horse made skittish by lightning; I pulled unwanted wheelies and nearly tipped over backwards. My thigh muscles strained like cheap ockie straps. I struggled and cursed and fell off my bike. My whole body swore. I couldn't ride anymore so I walked, hauling that overladen pain-machine up the hill, sweat pouring down my neck, shoes churning in the gravel.

Tama was further and further ahead of me, still pedalling, suffering but stoic. Tama 2000 was in his element, his seemingly endless reserves of energy being put to good use. But apart from that musclebound freak, plodding up that endless, interminable hill was no one's idea of fun, not even mine. Gasping and choking, blinking back tears of frustration, I stopped and looked back through the dense trees. This was why no other tourists were here with us in this 'mountain-biking paradise'—it was agony.

We had planned to have lunch on the top of the pass, but after four hours I had to stop. We might've been near the top; it was impossible to tell. We dumped our bikes on the side of the track and plonked ourselves down among the pine needles.

'Check it out, bro—stretchmarks!'

Tama was pulling the waistband of his shorts away from his rapidly shrinking belly. Seven days in and there were already thin, shiny lines around his hips from the weight he'd lost. And me, I was skinny to start with, but now my ribs were starting to show through. I cut the last of our bread into thick slices and smeared them with lashings of putrefying butter and tinned mackerel that tasted of tin. Butterflies jerked through mottled beams of sunlight before alighting on our fish sandwiches. I lay on my back and felt a smile welling up from deep in my chest. After four haggard-making hours, the simple joy of not riding was profound; I was overcome with a weightless, exhausted exhilaration. My thighs ached happily and my head was clearer than it had been in years.

Two dudes on an old motorcycle rolled up. They seemed amused to see two grown men having a romantic picnic in a sun-dappled mountain glade. The motorcyclists laughed, waved and stuttered off towards the saddle. After half an hour we brushed the butterflies off and got moving. Rugged as it was, there was also something liberating about having to keep going, not having a choice in the matter. The big decisions had been made weeks ago; made by us, sure, but it was out of our hands now.

The path ahead was flatter and with fewer puddles but more tree roots and thicker forest all around. Tiger country. With all my awareness sunk in my half-full stomach I trundled forward on autopilot, taking the lead for once. After an hour the path flattened out and we came to a grassy clearing dominated by a tall wooden *ovoo*, a funeral pyre waiting for Communist witches. The top of Tiger Mountain! From the river crossing to here, it had taken us five solid hours. We collapsed on the grass.

'Holy crap, that takes the suffercake,' I said. 'I've never gone up a hill that mental, let alone with all this heavy-arse gear.'

'Yeah, it was pretty full-on,' Tama said. 'But bro, that was *nothing* compared to Mingli Sar.'

'That right?'

'Yeah man, in Pakistan. Mingli Sar was—'

'You showed me those photos—I *believe* you. Remind me never to go there with you.'

Half a Mars Bar hit me in the face, waking me up.

'Eat up, bro—gotta bust out.'

'Already?'

''Fraid so, unless you wanna camp here?'

'Next to that *ovoo*? No way.' I shivered. 'This place is nightmare central.'

'You don't believe that shamanic shit, do you?'

'Nah, not really. But if this *is* where they help people pass through to the next world, I'd prefer to sleep down the road a bit.'

I was dreading untold hours of rough riding through mud, tree roots and miscellaneous boggy skank, but the trail on the south face of Tiger Mountain was dry, hard clay, not a puddle in sight. If we hadn't been weighted down like yuppy camels it would've been a ripping giant slalom. Instead, helmets went on and off as we went. I hooted with joy, pumping my brakes and stopping every couple of hundred metres to burn blades of grass against my overheated disc brakes until Tama told me it would warp the discs—then back to the off-road reverie. Ducking branches, weaving around pine cones, eyes watering from the speed, I existed to find that one good throughline. I drifted left, right and down, always down, reduced to reflexes and robotics, fused to my wheels, smitten with gravity. We sailed right through this bewitching corner of the world like we weren't there.

The forest fell away as we rocketed into a flowery meadow. There were explosions of violet and canary yellow, maroon flowers that reminded me of raspberries. We jumped off our bikes and frolicked in the flowers, taking some photos that would do well on Gaydar. As we lay among the buttercups terrific clouds piled up above Tiger Mountain, darkening before our eyes. A storm front was moving towards us, and fast. I knew it was conceited as well as superstitious but I couldn't help thinking the weather had come to chase us out of paradise, in retribution for a law or laws unknown that we had violated. We hammered it down through the meadow and the sky gods began to pelt us with fat, heavy raindrops. Forked lightning crashed first to the left, then the right. A flash all around, the gunshot of thunder a quarter of a second behind. I was acutely aware that we were the tallest things in an exposed field and we were sitting on chunks of metal.

'Let's get a move on!' Tama roared over his shoulder as he pedalled like a demon. I tried to keep up with him, smashing down the narrow track and flying over mini-potholes at full speed. Faint hiss and wobble of a puncture; I had to really scream before Tama heard me and stopped.

'Not a good time to get a puncture!'

I just looked at him. The rain thumped down harder, wetter. Monster roll of thunder and another flash, the thunderclap right on top of us. The rain turned to hail. We left the bikes out on the road—if they got hit, we didn't want to be nearby—and took cover in a ditch with Tama's tarpaulin, sitting on one end of the tarp then wrapping it over our backs and down over our heads. It was big enough, just. The hail noise was everywhere, magnified by the tarp; little balls of ice pinballed around our shins. Our blue cocoon flashed and echoed, the ground shook, everything rumbled. Apparently Chinggis and his fierce Mongol warriors were petrified of lightning; they saw it as the wrath of God—i.e. Tenger, and did everything in their power to avoid it, which usually involved riding fast in the opposite direction.

The idea of getting hit by lightning struck me as pretty ridiculous—it was the kind of thing that happened to cartoon characters, Wile E. Coyote's skeleton flashing through his skin and five seconds later he's fine again—but I wasn't about to go out there and do a rain dance, especially after insulting that *ovoo*.

Five minutes into the hailstorm the clouds gave up and shifted back to rain. We emerged from the tarp, blinking like marmots. The thunderhead had passed to the south; we could see it near the horizon, a thick grey vertical line of rain fusing cloud and earth. While I patched my tube, Tama cooked up some emergency instant noodles. We slurped up the warming MSG gruel with grunts of appreciation and jumped back on our bikes, sucking in cool, fresh air, the countryside quiet and still around us.

Coming down out of the foothills, we found ourselves on a vast plain in what could've been a different country. The grass was longer and thicker, with a yellow-green sheen. Usually an assortment of snouts would munch it down much lower than this but there were no snouts around, no *gers* that we could see, no people. A couple of kilometres on, the path diverged: to the left, a set of overgrown 4WD tracks wound towards a terracotta-walled farmhouse that looked long abandoned. The presence of architecture without humans made the landscape feel even more eerie. We turned right.

After a few minutes, huge wheat fields stretched out before us, disappearing south and east in endless rigid rows. Our track merged with a graded, ruler-straight dirt road, an actual road that was worthy of the word and wide enough for a truck. After one day in a bog and one on remote hilltops, the regularity, the *perpendicularity* of it all was a shock, a calculated and grievous affront to Mother Nature and her assymetrical ways. Tama starting taking photographs of the unnatural fields then stopped.

'People won't understand how weird this is.' He sighed. 'It just looks like—wheat.'

Our shadows lengthened against the crops. The sun was low in the sky but not showing any sign of setting. Tama checked the GPS clock; it was just past 9 pm. We pushed on, blathering about mutton noodle soup and sugary drink. Erdenebulgan, our next resupply point, was meant to be twenty-five kilometres south of the foothills, but there was still no sign of it. Eventually we gave up and pulled off the road onto a dim prairie, the first break in the wheat fields in ten kilometres. I pitched the tent on dry grass and tiny white wildflowers. To the right, a line of hills serrated the darkening sky; one by one, stars were being pinned to a huge purple noticeboard. The prairie was as quiet, as remote, as removed from the world as anything I had ever experienced; we could've taken a wrong turn on Tiger Mountain and slipped through a portal into a neglected corner of an alien moon. Tama cooked up a mess of rice, raisins, river water and jam; we had run out of almost everything else.

The stars glared at us. There was nothing to say, so we didn't say it.

DAYS 8–9: NO COUNTRY FOR FAT MEN

As the sun climbed into a blank sky, I convinced Tama to put on his leopard suit and novelty sunglasses and run around in the field with me while we filmed it. My plan, loosely, was to emulate the style of *Tetsuo: The Iron Man*, a neglected classic of eighties Japanese independent cinema in which two guys and a girl stick rusted fragments of scrap metal into their legs and arms, have disturbing sex, whimper and yell a lot and finally mutate into a sinister three-wheeled metal machine, the whole thing shot in strobe-tastic black-and-white stop-motion. Tama's GoPro had a time-lapse function and we made freeze-frame sequences of each other racing across the dewy steppe in our outfits, mouths jammed open in manga-esque grimaces of power and awesomeness.

We were just getting ready to stick some bicycle spokes in our legs when the ground started to rumble. To the north, the air was dusty, smoky. A figure appeared bobbing on the horizon: a horseman. Then another. Four. More than four—much more. They rode closer. Tama and I looked at each other in alarm and ran back to the tent to get normal. I had my pants off but my MÖRÖN T-shirt on when the frenzied horde came thundering down the valley, riders up out of their saddles, wailing like castrato banshees and whipping their steeds with homemade riding crops as they raced past us and off towards what we presumed was Erdenebulgan. The riders were brightly coloured midgets, or perhaps jockeys. Ah, child jockeys, dozens of preteen boys wearing caps and bibs, chased by a couple of SUVs.

'*Saikhan Naadaarai!*' a bloke in a jeep yelled.

'Manly sports!' I shouted back.

A couple of minutes later one poor straggler in bib number 634 came trotting past silently, slapping ineffectually at a white horse that seemed wholly uninterested in proceedings.

To encourage him, I yelled out, '*Mash sain!*' The boy began to weep.

We chowed down on yet another disconcerting slop of rice, raisins, milk powder and jam—tastebuds reluctant, stomach insistent—then rode off towards our second Naadam. Unlike public holidays in New Zealand and Australia, which are synchronised across every state and town to ensure maximum traffic jams, crowds at beaches and opportunities for burglars, Mongolia took a more *laissez-faire* approach to holiday-making: Mongolian towns celebrated Naadam, their one and only national public holiday, *sometime* in July. A few towns, like Khatgal, made a point of holding their festivals on a fixed date, probably for western tourists. Others just had their party when they felt like it. Like Erdenebulgan, today.

Before Erdenebulgan came into view, Tama and I described it to each other.

'Dusty streets, vacant lots . . .'

'Wooden fences, half falling down . . .'

'Ghetto ski chalets . . .'

'Scabby dogs, drunk Mongols . . .'

This was the truth, but not the whole truth about Erdenebulgan. The fences weren't that ragged, the dogs not too scabby. It also had a couple of tall concrete grain silos, painted yellow—and no Mongols. No people at all, which didn't bode well for mutton soup. Near the middle of town we saw a log cabin with the telltale grocery-store sign, this one saying НАРАН ХҮНС ВАРААНЫ ПЕПГҮҮР 08.00–22.00— which for us spelt 'sugary drink'. The clerk, a teenage boy wearing hi-top sneakers, basketball shorts and a Chicago Bulls singlet, was standing outside with a basket full of junk food and locking up the door, about to head over to Naadam to hawk his wares. We waved him down and he unlocked the store to let us stock up: two cans of Russian fish, one litre of Polish pineapple juice, six American Snickers bars and one kilo of rice, probably Chinese. A second teenage boy, less fashionable in jeans and a short-sleeved shirt, came into the shop and sat on a low couch by the counter.

'My friend,' the clerk said. 'We . . . like each other.' They both smiled. It was sweet, and a bit gay.

The boys were in Erdenebulgan for summer holidays— the shop attendant from Ulaanbaatar, his buddy from Erdenet. We asked for *tom us*—big water—but they didn't stock it. Instead, the Erdenet guy offered to fill our bottles from the *khudag* (tap?) out the back for free. Erdenet lowered a large metal milk jug on a rope down into a well, and the water came up fresh and clear, headache cold. We drank straight from the milk jug, gorging ourselves. Then the kid tipped the freezing water over our heads, and we shouted with happiness.

While Tama filled our many bottles, I went inside to buy some more instant noodles, strictly for emergencies. The clerk asked me where we came from. I told him *Shin Zeland*, but he didn't care about that—he wanted to know where we had cycled from. I pointed back up the valley, towards Tiger Mountain.

'Really?' he said. 'There are bear. And wolf.'

'Nah, it's fine. You should go, it's amazing!'

He laughed and shook his head. 'I am fear. I like . . . city. Basketball. Hip-hop. I like Jay-Z, "Empire State of Mind"!'

As we biked off through the empty streets past a falling-apart concrete building with tufts of grass sprouting from the roof, past a cow eating a fence, I told Tama what the clerk told me about Tiger Mountain.

'Well, lucky we didn't camp there, huh?'

Erdenebulgan's Naadam was on the southern edge of town. A thousand or so people were gathered around a racing track-sized oval, on foot or on horseback or cruising slowly around on motorcycles. Mongolians didn't bother racing horses around in little circles, they raced across the steppe, so probably the *bökh* bouts were going to place out there. Next to the oval there was a row of cute, waiflike teenage girls selling single cigarettes and pieces of chewing gum from little trays. Their target market was presumably the nomadic cowboys who galloped in from the wilds for one day a year and lashed out with a stick of doublemint. Overall the festival was similar to the Khatgal Naadam, minus my absurd expectations; also there were no video camera–wielding European tourists, just us. I suggested that we should enter the *bökh* in our suits this time, do it properly, film it stop-motion, mutate into an evil tricycle. Tama looked at me like I was mental.

'Didn't you see the clock in the grocery store?'

'Uh, no?'

'It's already quarter to one. We've still gotta ride like eighty k's today if we're gonna make it to Tarialan.'

'But what about Naadam?'

'What about it?'

For Tama, Naadam was a case of once bitten, twice bored. We looked around for smuggler-bag shadecloth, a sure sign of a *huushuur* tent. I ordered twelve *huushuur*, to the incredulity of the locals. We each gobbled down three deep-fried discs of battered greasy mutton then I sauced up the remaining six and put them in my pannier for later. Tama scouted around for bonus supplies, preferably fresh things, and came back with four unhappy apples that looked like they had been rolled into Erdenebulgan from south China. But now was not the time to look a gift-fruit in the mouth.

Heading east out of town towards a bridge that hopefully still existed, we spied two pale figures dressed in khaki and beige walking with hefty backpacks—backpackers! Probably English speakers!

We raced over. It was a couple of Frenchies with forgettable names—let's say Pierre and, uh, Franz. Pierre was in Mongolia visiting Franz, who had come to Tarialan as an aid worker six years earlier and never left. Franz lived fifty kilometres south of Erdenebulgan in an enchanted-sounding valley with his blushing Mongol bride. Tama asked Franz if there were any bears or wolves in the forests around here.

'Of course,' Franz said seriously, then smiled. 'But it is not so bad! The locals, they say the wolves do not attack humans. And the bears, they are not so big.'

'Have you ever seen one?' I asked.

'Only one time! Just south of here, years ago. It was in the forest, scratching a tree, and when he heard us coming he ran away. He was not so big. If you see a bear, just stand still. Or run away.'

'What about tigers?' I asked.

'Do you mean T-A-I-G-A, *taiga*?' Pierre asked, trying not to laugh. 'This is what you call the Siberian forest, how you say, conifer trees. But there are no *tigers* in the *taiga*—just landmines!' He laughed some more. We excused ourselves and got out of there.

We came to a good-sized river spanned by an actual bridge made of concrete and steel. If this was still the Üür *gol*, it was much less fierce, almost fordable. I checked the map: it wasn't the Üür *gol*. We crossed the bridge and pedalled up a track lined with pines. Tama whooped for joy to be back in nature again. I joined him once or twice, then got bored. Tama kept on whooping. It was a very regular whoop.

'Tama bro—it's not *that* beautiful here, is it?'

'Nah, it's for the bears,' he said. I snorted.

'Are you scared of little Mongol bears now—in the middle of the day?'

'Dude, I grew up in Canada. I'd rather be scared of bears than eaten by bears.'

A few seconds later I said, 'Did you know you look like a grumpy bear sometimes? In the morning, when you haven't had enough sleep.'

'You've told me that before.'

We cycled on, whooping regularly. Pines gave way to pasture as we entered a vast flat trough of a valley. A powerline looping to our left made it feel like we were back in civilisation, or at least on our way there. We didn't see any bears, not even small ones, and that was pretty much the best thing about the whole afternoon. My tyres felt like they were full of concrete. I stopped and checked the back one; it was fine. Even though the terrain was pretty much flat, I couldn't find my pace. I had to keep changing up, then down, then up again. I settled on riding in a too-high gear, and an hour later my right knee was throbbing ominously. Maybe my legs just weren't up to the job anymore. After two hours of this watered-down hell we had a look on the map at our pitiful progress.

'Damn, it's a motherfucking *faux plat*,' Tama said.

'A foewhat?'

'This—a hill that pretends it's not a hill. A fake plateau. We've actually climbed like 200 metres since Erdenebulgan.'

I peered back along the valley. It looked flat to me.

We continued riding 'up' this demoralising funhouse slope for another twenty kilometres, gaining another couple of hundred vertical metres I could've done without. I'd pedal and the bike would move, but not quite as far forward as it should; it felt like I was falling asleep on the seat, grinding to a halt. I went over a bump and my *Mongol tug* fell off my front bike rack into the mud. I rode over it and grimaced and kept going. To the left and right were unremarkable fields, bland green hills.

I was a whole thesaurus of hungry, so we stopped for an afternoon tea of cold mutton pancakes with congealed tomato sauce. A few kilometres later the road came to a T-junction where it forked down diverging valleys separated by a bare rocky ridge. It wasn't clear which way led to Tarialan. The compass wanted us to keep going straight ahead, and the map was maddeningly reticent. There was a rundown farmhouse at the junction of the tracks so we dumped our bikes and walked towards it, even though the owners were probably at Naadam. A mangy and mean-looking dog bounded out barking furiously—'Rabies! Rabies!'—and we backed off. Tama pointed at the power-lines, which stretched down the valley to our right.

'Those lines must be going somewhere,' he said. 'If not Tarialan, somewhere else with sugary drink.'

'Like where?'

'Like, I dunno . . . Tosontsengel.'

I looked at the map. Tosontsengel was about 150 kilo-metres west of Tarialan, less than a day's ride from the first Mörön.

'Maybe we should go left,' I said.

We went right.

My knee felt better with the brace I'd put on, and I felt stronger, faster, until I realised we were cruising along a down-sloping *faux plat*. The countryside was quiet yet somehow not peaceful; empty, but not beautiful. It was hard to put my finger on, but it all seemed slightly degraded. Probably just overgrazing.

The path headed uphill again and it was a proper uphill this time, nothing *faux* about it. My knee stopped feeling better. At the top of the hill was sitting an ancient petrol tanker in the middle of the road, black oil spots leading up to it. The driver was lying on his back under the axle, a ciga-rette dangling from his mouth. We called out 'Sigh binoo' but kept moving, ears cocked for the *kaboooom*.

After a couple more hours of not-so-easy riding, it was clear we weren't going to make it anywhere near Tarialan by nightfall. We came to a massive valley where lush lawn rolled away on all sides into dark stands of pine. It was six o'clock. We'd only been riding for seven hours, but we decided to stop anyway.

We scattered our sleeping bags, water bottles and woollens all over the grass, an essential first step in setting up camp. I was almost done pegging in the tent when a chestnut horse cantered towards us. On its back rode a vision of Mongolian maidenhood. Her face was dreamy, round and flat like a salt lake. Her eyes were narrow, beautifully narrow, perfect for keeping evil spirits out. And her legs . . . many years ago, young Chinggis Khaan's father, Yesugei, told him that a woman must have strong legs to please a man. Well, the way those legs gripped that stallion . . .

TOM and TAMA: *Sigh binoo!*

MAIDEN: *Sain, sain bainuu.* [Smiles radiantly.]

[TAMA blushes; TOM hyperventilates.]

TOM: *Minii neriig* Tom *gedeg.*

TAMA: Tama *gedeg.*

MAIDEN: *Za, Tomatom.* [Giggles.] *Minii neriig* Mönkhtsetseg *gedeg.* Name means 'Eternal Flower'.

TOM [eyes widen]: Mönkhetysexylegs? Ah, *maikhan!* [Smiles 'sexily'.]

ETERNAL FLOWER: *Maikhan?* [Looks at our summer tent incredulously, puts hands on hips.]

TOM: Oh—no, sorry, umm . . .

TAMA: *Saikhan, saikhan* ['beautiful']. Uh, do you speak, English?

ETERNAL FLOWER: No . . . a little.

TAMA: Yes—you speak English very good!

ETERNAL FLOWER [giggles]: No, not good.

TAMA: Better than me speak Mongolian!

TOM [stage whisper]: Better than you speak English, bro.

TAMA: Do you live [gestures to valley] here?

ETERNAL FLOWER: Yes—no. [Points across the valley to a *ger*.] My parents, mother, father. They live. I . . . live Darkhan. I study, economics.

TAMA: Awesome.

[TOM is heartbroken.]

ETERNAL FLOWER: I am home, for holidays.

TAMA: Do you like it [gestures to valley] here?

ETERNAL FLOWER [laughing]: Yes, this my home! So beautiful here.

TOM: *Saikhan* . . . [looks through phrasebook] . . . *tostoi* ['greasy'].

[ETERNAL FLOWER looks at TOM suspiciously. TOM looks at phrasebook again.]

TOM: *Ovs! Ovs!* ['Grassy!']

ETERNAL FLOWER: Are you two . . . [Pointing from TAMA to TOM.]

TOM: Oh—yes—no!

[TOM and TAMA laugh awkwardly.]

TAMA: No, no. We are . . . old friends.

[ETERNAL FLOWER nods, not convinced. TOM, TAMA and ETERNAL FLOWER spend five minutes looking through phrasebook: *taivan bain* ('it's peaceful'); *bi ömsch uzej bolokhuu?* ('can I try it on?'); *tanaikhan sainuu?* ('how is your family?'); *tavtai saikhan!* ('fattening nicely!')]

ETERNAL FLOWER: In winter, it's so nice here. Quiet. Very relax.

TOM: Where do you . . . sleep?

ETERNAL FLOWER: In *ger*.

TAMA: In your own *ger*?

ETERNAL FLOWER [laughs]: No! With family. Until I am marry.
TOM and TAMA: Oh.
ETERNAL FLOWER: I go now.
TOM and TAMA: No, oh, okay, if you must . . . Bayish tar!
ETERNAL FLOWER: *Bayartai!* [TOM and TAMA watch her gallop
   away in slow-motion, rose petals falling from the sky.]

My mind was abuzz. What was the inside of Mönkhtsetseg's *ger* like? What was the inside of her life like? How
many gold-digging Mong-zangers were out there, waiting
for a non-homosexual cycle tourist or two to sweep them off
their horse? How is your family? Do you have a hat? Is that
what happened to Wolfgang, to Pierre? Had we stumbled
into the legendary Khanui Valley, a place that according to
Chinggis Khann contained the most beautiful girls in all
of Mongolia—the Valley of the Mongolian Supermaidens?
Questions, so many questions . . .
   'Do you reckon there'd be room for her in the tent?'
Tama said.
   '. . . It'd be pretty crowded,' I said eventually. 'It'd get . . .
hot.'
   'She could . . . sleep in the middle,' Tama said.
   'Yeah. She could . . . take turns,' I said.
   'Yeah.'
   We stared out across the valley.
   'Man, I miss my girlfriend.' Tama sighed.
   'Me too,' I said. 'She's got really strong legs—*Laura*. Legs.'
   It was getting dark, and cold. We looked at the tent.
Neither of us moved.

After lubing our bikes with oil and lining our bellies with raisiny rice, we were on the road by a respectable 8 am. This was meant to be a rest day, but after a good night's sleep I was happy to keep moving, especially since we were running low on food again.

We followed a couple of narrow tracks through the knee-high grass, intrigued by a high-pitched chittering hum that filled the air, when the path ahead literally erupted with miniature wildlife. Grasshoppers, crickets, locusts and assorted hopping insects catapulted themselves into the air milliseconds before impact with our front wheels. We sailed down the hill like steam trains with invisible cattle shunts, knocking the little beasties away. Tama rode on the right-hand path and I took the left, a metre behind him. The critters parted before Tama like a biblical sea; riding in his wake, thousands of insects kamikazed directly into the spokes of my front wheel, coating my once-white bike frame with buggy gore. The really ambitious ones would jump at my face, bouncing off my sunnies or lodging in my nostrils.

We rode past a *ger* in a scenic daze. Moments later two young cowboys came galloping over. The thirteen-year-olds yelled at us, spurred their horses on and raced us across the field. Tama and I tried to pedal faster but we didn't stand a chance. The boys burned us off, laughing and whooping, then galloped triumphantly over a ridge.

'Pretty impressive for young fellas, huh?' I gasped.

'Sure, but they've been riding since they were, like, four years old.'

'True—but we've been riding bikes since *we* were four.'

'True.'

Up ahead the powerlines cut left, marching up a steep

rise that led away from the main path. We decided to follow the electricity up a narrow goat track. Tama was making heavy weather of the hill, but I was feeling fresh. I pounded it up the slope, not looking back, breathing hard but not slowing down. Partly I wanted to show Tama that I could be top dog, too; partly I just wanted to see if I could do it. At the top of the rise I looked back: no sign of Tama. I waited for a couple of minutes. When Tama reached the top, he was breathing hard. He didn't say anything. I felt good and also bad.

We pedalled on through the maelstrom of suicidal insects that we had started calling 'Mongolian phosphorescence', past an exposed loaf of red rock that could've been Uluru's long-lost midget cousin. The day got hotter and hotter. I was covered by numerous fine layers of grit and filth, and every time we put more sunscreen on it added a fresh surface for dust and insect blood to adhere to.

We neared Tarialan around midday. The name was sweet, aromatic—frankincense, tarialan and myrrh—and it promised to be a step up from the glottal orc garrisons of Khatgal and Tsagaan-Üür. But it was the same gloomy A-frames and dusty streets devoid of traffic, except Tarialan was more crowded together. There were no *gers* among the wooden houses, and much less space for nomads to make camp in winter. This was farming country, not herding country.

Riding into town I felt like we were villains in a cowboy movie: everyone had run inside and closed the shutters, fearing a massacre. We found a just-open store, run by a quiet, sleepy girl, and loaded up on sugary drink and reasonably fresh bread.

Remembering the well in Erdenebulgan, we asked her if there was a *khudag* in town. The girl nodded and shut up the shop before gesturing for us to follow her. She led us through a large, dusty, deserted courtyard with faded murals on the walls that reminded me of a Mexico I'd never visited, around a corner, through a pair of gates and down an alley just wide enough for our bikes until we reached a well. It was on the other side of a chain-link fence and the gate was locked.

'*Nyamd khaallttai*. Closed,' the girl shrugged her shoulders, smiled and walked away.

'What day is it?' I asked Tama.

'Dunno . . . Sunday?'

'I hope so. These fucking towns . . .'

Further into Tarialan we came across a small strip of lacklustre shops, none of which stocked bottled water. There were canteens, but they were closed. I found a shop that sold КУПЕР beer from a fridge that wasn't plugged in. Tama discovered a pagoda overgrown with stinging nettles and we bashed our way in, seeking shelter from the punishing sun. On an otherwise deserted street, a man too drunk to walk was screaming abuse while his friends struggled to carry him along.

We ate our fish and jam sandwiches and sipped our warm beers quietly in the shade, trying not to attract attention. None of these towns made you want to stay in them; I was glad we had our summer tent, however you pronounced it. Tama called Ami on his mobile, and I wandered off in search of quality Mongolian cheese. I was unsuccessful, although I did find a rusted metal poster of a laughing, cross-eyed potato chip man with a red star on his hat, clutching a shield and flag in his cartoon hands.

Leaving Tarialan we cycled south in a dry heat and started to drop towards a broad dirt road that stretched left and right, east and west, as far as we could see. We had been up on a vast continental plateau ever since that ride from Mörön to Khatgal where we had gained 500 metres on Hurtin' Pass and not given any of them back, but now we were about to leave the high country, perhaps for good. Peering into the haze of the south, I got a sense of how flat most of Mongolia was. The fields were chopped up into squares of agricultural green, alternating with strips of dirty yellow and light brown, the colours of dry hay, drought.

At the bottom of the hill we turned left onto the thirty-metre-wide dirt thoroughfare, churned and potholed and scoured by tyres, the odd scrap of grass continuing an unlikely existence wedged between lumps of rock. On this kind of surface, travelling by bicycle was infinitely superior to anything else. You could see potholes coming and avoid them; you only needed a few centimetres of flat ground and you were cruising. I had thought the bus driver from UB to Mörön was a maniac, but he was just driving on a maniac road.

We kept to the far right of the road, giving the odd motorbike and tourist van plenty of room to overtake us. It was much hotter down on the plain; the sun was lodged behind my right shoulder and it roasted that whole side of my body. I could feel the skin on my right leg burning through the sunscreen and was doubly grateful for my knee brace. We were on a slow, steady incline, just like yesterday, except now I knew about *faux plats* and I wasn't going to take it. Rather than changing down and settling into a slower rhythm, I changed up and stood out of the saddle. My legs screamed, but my mind was clear: it was much easier to slam the *faux plat*, not worry about pacing myself, not admit there was a hill there, mind over matter, triumph of the will, my patience is at an end and so on. Tama dropped behind. When I got to the top of the slope a walloping twenty minutes later I pulled over, euphoric and disoriented, and drank from my water bottle until it was empty.

'You're going pretty hard, bro,' Tama panted when he finally caught up. 'Maybe you should slow down—you don't wanna get heatstroke.'

I took off my hat; it was drenched with sweat. Tama was out of water too. When we cycled on in a futile attempt to escape the burning sun I took Tama's advice and lagged behind, trying not to take the hill personally.

Four hours from Tarialan we spied a ratty building on the horizon and prayed for a grocery store. Even better, it was a truck stop, so we pulled our bikes into the front 'garden'—a patch of dried mud—and leaned them against the fence where we could keep an eye on them from inside.

The truck stop was run by a grumpy young woman and a furious young man, and our arrival interrupted an argument that seemed to have been going on for years. They were both very good-looking, which made their foul moods more striking. A baby screamed in a back room.

The woman asked us something, presumably what we wanted to eat. There was no menu. I tried to remember the word for that good soup: hooroton, no . . . hodamic horik?

The lady raised two impatient fingers and we nodded, okay, yes, you choose, we're not fussed. We bought a 1.25-litre bottle of purple grape Fanta and chugged it down, and then another. There was a small cell of a room off the side of the restaurant with three single beds covered with rough woollen blankets; Mongol truckies could sleep there on nights when they ran out of Chinese pseudoephedrine. The room was dominated by a poster of a hot young Mongolian couple on an airbrushed Harley-Davidson, the man shirtless and buff, the woman in a lacy push-up bra, flying through space. It could've been the truck-stop owners in better days.

Our food came. Against all odds, it was fantastic—a rich, meaty broth with noodles the size and shape of Twisties mixed through it. I wolfed mine down and licked the bowl clean. I tried to express my appreciation but they weren't interested. Outside, the sun was less fierce. As we rode away we speculated about what the couple were doing there.

'Maybe the girl's dad owns the place,' Tama said, 'and the girl works there, and this dude was just passing through one night.'

'Yeah—on a Harley!' I said.

'Sure.'

'Their eyes met across a scabby room, and they had one night of backroom bang-cock on the scratchy blankets, zangity zang—except she got *pregnant*, so the guy had to stick around.'

'The dad hated him,' Tama said.

'Of course. Dad thought he was a no-hoper—the feeling was mutual, actually—then dad *died*, she had the baby—'

'And there they are, stuck making noodles, for the rest of their lives.' Tama sighed. 'Rugged.'

A couple of kilometres on, Tama stopped to photograph a small concrete house built in the Soviet Art Deco style, a mix of functionalism and kitsch: squat concrete walls with rounded corners, pink and cream paint flaking into the dust. Against the clarity of the plains, this slapdash architecture, plonked on the unbroken landscape seemingly at random, seemed impudent, pipsqueak, a scrap of redundant punctuation just waiting for a passing horde to edit it out.

As the afternoon dragged on, the heat leached out of the sun. It was about forty kilometres to Khutag-Öndör—a suburb of Mordor, surely—but we wouldn't be able to make it there tonight without doing lasting damage. According to the map there was a river fifteen kilometres before Khutag-Öndör and a little lake a couple of kilometres north of that. We could camp out, have a wash.

Tama led the way up a hill that would've been fine at 10 am, but this late in the day it made my thighs burn and my shoulders twinge. I groaned and huddled over my handlebars. At the top of the pass half a dozen figures appeared from nowhere and swarmed around Tama's bike, clapping and cheering. Tama had just won the hill stage, fans were congratulating him, clamouring for his autograph, an official was trying to shove the yellow leader's jersey over his head. As I got closer, I realised it wasn't cycling fans—it was gypsy-ish children, boys in striped shirts and girls in floral dresses, thrusting jars of crushed strawberries into Tama's face and now mine, yelling, 'Strawberry! Buy *straw*berry!' My stomach rumbled enthusiastically.

'How much should we get?' I asked Tama.

'I'm not touching any of that badness,' Tama said. 'We bought strawberries off some kids in Pakistan one time and I shat my guts out for a week.'

'Okay, but this isn't Pakistan—maybe these ones are sweet?'

'I'm sure the strawberries are fine,' he said. 'But bro, check out their hands.'

I checked out their hands. They were even dirtier than mine.

We shook our heads and shouted 'no' and tried to ride on, but the kids were determined to make a sale. They blocked our path, shouting louder, until we shoved them out of our way. We cruised down the far side of the hill and after a couple of minutes we stopped for a water break.

I heard the machine-gun cough of a sickly motorbike engine before I saw the rider weaving down the hill, coming right for us. Rider and bike swerved at the last moment, lurching into a ditch in a red-and-green blur. The motor-cyclist was about our age, dressed in a knee-length green silk *deel* tied with a wide gold sash and wearing a sideways baseball cap instead of a helmet. He staggered to his feet and yelled at us, mainly Tama, pointing at his motorbike and shaking his fist. Tama frowned and helped him roll his vehicle off the road; after that the Mongolcyclist was all smiles and hugs, ethanol kisses. He had the squinting eyes and varicose cheeks of an advanced binge and his head lolled around on his neck like a broken toy. Maybe he had ridden from the second day of the Erdenebulgan Naadam. Maybe he was the staggering legless dude from Tarialan, maybe he was just getting into Sunday.

He 'asked' for vodka.

We gave him some *us*, then a few Marlboros. He gave us some of his cigarettes that went by the brand of Ulaanshonk-hor (rough translation, 'red shonk'). He struggled to his feet and turned away from us to urinate on his bike and hands while I covertly filmed him, then he shook my hand moistly and gave Tama a big hug. Our new friend, whose name sounded like Wimmett, kept pointing down the road and resting his head on his hands: he wanted us to stay in his *ger*. We didn't want to stay in his *ger*. The prospect was appalling. I had visions of a blasphemous *ovoo* made from broken Chinggis bottles and cigarette butts and worse, all held together with vomit, unwashed saucepans caked with burnt mutton and rancid horseflesh strewn across a urine-soaked lawn . . .

We wanted to leave but without offending Wimmett. Actually, we wanted Wimmett to leave first so he didn't charge up from behind and reinvite us to his *ger* at sixty kilometres an hour. The 'conversation' went round in circles for ages, as did Wimmett's head. Luckily a blue flatbed truck pulled up and a sweet old couple asked us something, presumably what was going on. I pointed to Wimmett and said, in my best English, 'Vodka. Drunk.' They nodded sadly and proceeded to tell Wimmett off. Wimmett sulked, looking away in a huff. In the middle of the lecture, a motorcycle came slowly up the hill. Wimmett roared and grabbed a good-sized rock and staggered to his feet, preparing to pitch it at the rider; Tama tackled him to the ground. Wimmett laughed and gave Tama a hug. The old-timers told Wimmett off. After a couple more minutes, Wimmett finally got himself and his bike upright and rode off in a wobbly line. We were worried he'd wait for us at the bottom of the hill; there were no side roads, nowhere else for us to go. We decided to wait for a few minutes. I lit up an Ulaanshonkhor.

'Woah, he just fell off!' Tama said. 'Let's make a break for it!'

Wimmett had tumbled into a ditch, again, and was staggering around looking for his hat. We leapt on our bikes and raced towards him, teeth gritted, pedals humming. He saw us and bellowed and picked up a rock and chucked it as we flew past; it sailed over our heads. I looked back at Wimmett trying to kickstart his motorbike, then grimaced and pedalled harder. At the bottom of the hill the path narrowed to a little bridge over a creek. Dozens of gypsy urchins swarmed out of the ditches and covered the bridge, shrieking and juggling shit-stained strawberries. We didn't slow down. At the last moment they scattered like grasshoppers; we zanged across the bridge and didn't look back.

A few kilometres on there was a sign informing us that we had crossed from Khövsgöl *aimag* into Bulgan *aimag*. We breathed a sigh of relief; this arbitrary administrative distinction made us feel safe from crazy Wimmett and his fruit-peddling henchmen. The sun had just set when we made it to a stream whose name didn't feature on any of our maps. On the west side of the trickle there was a dinky little wooden lean-to of a restaurant that wouldn't have been out of place on the banks of the Mekong; it had grass growing on its roof and cuts of mutton hanging to dry from the ceiling. We decided to find a nice grassy spot on the far side of the creek to make camp and then hit the lean-to for dinner. I found a good place to pitch our tent, tipped my bike onto the grass and dropped my helmet. This disturbed a green thing that stuck its head out of the grass then slowly slithered away.

'Fuckfuckfuck, it's a snake!' I squealed.

'There aren't any snakes in Mongolia,' Tama said blandly.

'Then what the hell is *that*?' I said, pointing to the terror in the grass. Tama squinted.

'I can't see anything.'

'Take my word for it.'

'It can't be that big.'

'Oh, it's probably *just* a metre long when it's outstretched,' I said.

'Where, I can't . . . oh.' Tama chuckled. 'It's tiny.'

'That doesn't mean it's not deadly!'

'There aren't any poisonous snakes in Mongolia, are there?'

'I wouldn't know,' I replied haughtily. 'I didn't know about the bears and wolves and tigers.'

The snake *was* close to a metre long—for once I wasn't exaggerating—and it had the type of pointy head I associated with the words 'adder' and 'asp'. It might've crawled 10,000 kilometres from Hungary, it was flat enough.

We pushed our bikes back to the restaurant and asked if we could camp there. *Tiin, tiin,* the proprietor said, yes, of course. I tried to ask this sweet, maternal woman about the snake, but I couldn't find the word for it in my phrase-book, just *ömkhii* ('smelly') and *savang* ('soap'), both oddly relevant. I pointed to the grass and wiggled my arm around, and the proprietress just smiled patiently at the strange man.

A teenage boy wandered over to us, waving and smiling. He watched in amazement as I threaded the aluminium tent pole through the red canvas of the tent's fly. He giggled and gave me a two-handed thumbs-up. Then he saw Tama's bike.

'Ooooh! Waaaaah!'

He gestured to Tama's bike, to himself, could he . . .? Um, I guess. Tama hastily removed his pannier bags to lessen the potential damage. The excitable youth struggled to hoist himself over the crossbar then he was away, bumping across the field, too short to sit on the seat, yelling and laughing and banging his nuts and yelling some more.

'Change down!' Tama yelled.

He pushed the bike back to us, grinning his face off and rubbing his crotch.

'Mörön Khövsgöl,' Tama said, *'unadag dugui, dugui dugui,* Mörön Khentii.'

'Waaaoo!' the kid yelled, shaking his head and patting his hair down.

'Do you reckon he's drunk?' Tama said.

'I reckon he might be a bit . . . y'know.'

'What—a thespian?'

'I think he's . . . a moron.'

To test my hypothesis, I got the *Star Trek: The Next Generation* sunglasses out of my pack. The kid gasped in wonder. I put the blue pair on him and the yellow ones on me. He shook his head around, oohing and aahing. It might have been the first time he'd ever worn sunglasses—or the first time he'd hung out with kindred spirits.

'They suit you,' I told him. He grinned with all his teeth and put his thumbs up by his ears. Then he sat down in the tent's vestibule and started going through our bags.

'We should get him out of here,' Tama said as the kid fished a pair of undies out of my pannier. To get his attention, I grabbed an ockie strap and stretched it wide. He followed me out of the tent, mesmerised; Tama quickly zipped it up. We wandered over for dinner still wearing our shades.

As our host cooked dinner in the open restaurant, I tried to talk to her about what flavours she used, but her attitude towards spices was more British than Asian—she thought they were strange and stupid. I brought over our stash of ginger, tabasco sauce and Kampot pepper to show her.

'Ginger—*amttai*, yum!' I said enthusiastically. 'Kampot pepper—*mash amttai!*'

Before I could stop her, she popped a couple of peppercorns in her mouth and cracked them between her teeth, then yelped and began rubbing her tongue. To get rid of the harsh alien taste, she ran off to her shack and came back with a plastic 1.25-litre bottle of white liquid and poured herself a cupful.

'What's that?' I asked.

'*Airag.*'

'Milk?'

'*Za, za,* yes. Horse milk. Beer milk.'

I'd heard about this stuff. *Airag*, fermented horse milk. Fermented, arguably rancid, and most importantly *alcoholic* horse milk, a centuries-old Mongolian delicacy. She poured me and Tama a glass. *Airag* tasted pretty much how I expected fermented horse milk to taste: bittersweet, soft-sharp, nice-wrong. I spluttered and said '*Amttai!*' as politely as I could; she refilled my glass. *Airag* was pronounced 'arig', though we decided 'ay-rag' was more appropriate. It was an acquired taste, like gin and VB, and if you wanted to get drunk on the stuff you'd have plenty of time to acquire that taste since it was only three per cent alcohol. A red-blooded Aussie boozer would have to put away at least three litres of milked mare before she was ready to belt out 'Khe Sanh' at the karaoke.

An extended family group arrived at the restaurant. They were on holiday, on their way to or from a rural Naadam. We all had mutton soup. Tama and I drank beer and vodka and as little ay-rag as possible and we did our best to tell them about *Shin Zeland* and its many sheep, how central the experience of travel is to a people who grow up being told they live in a neglected Pacific backwater, the edge rather than the middle of nowhere. The father nodded and smiled and clapped his hands, then poured us more *airag*. The proprietress's daughter Enkhtuya—'Ray of Peace'—charmed us with her shy ways, rosy cheeks and fine knowledge of igneous rock formations (she was a geology major). After his fourth or fifth *airag* the father's voice rose as he tried to tell us, in a mixture of English, Mongolian, Russian and semaphore, everything we needed to know about Mongolia: its horses, its heroes—and its Chinggis, always back to Chinggis . . .

Call me Universal Ocean Fearless Strong Pants Lord. Chin— strong; fearless. Chino—casual pants made from twill cotton, usually khaki in colour. I am a man of tall stature, vigorous build, robust in body, the hair on my face scanty and turned white. I have cat eyes and am possessed of dedicated energy, discernment, genius and understanding. I am awe-striking, a butcher, just, resolute, an overthrower of enemies, intrepid, sanguinary and cruel, adept at magic and deception. Some of the devils are my friends.

I kill millions of people.

I father 20,000 children.

You do the maths.

By the time of my retirement/death at sixty-five years of age, my empire stretches from Manchuria to Persia. I am master of northern China, southern Siberia and chunks of Afghanistan and Pakistan, lord of Kazakhstan, Uzbekistan, and some of the Unpronounceable-stans. My career path is more like a career superhighway. I like long walks on the steppes and kinky concubines. Is it any wonder that I am referred to as the 'Mick Jagger of the Middle Ages'?

DAY 10: A FLASH FLOOD OF HAILSTONES

I woke up with an icepick headache. It felt like a horse had pissed in my mouth. I lay in my sleeping bag trying not to retch, struggling to remember exactly what Laura's breasts looked like, when there was a familiar noise. It sounded like me and Tama . . . pedalling our bikes?

I stuck my head out of the tent. A pair of cyclists wearing full battle spandex and aerodynamic sunglasses and riding matching racing bikes, expensive ones, had just crossed the little bridge and were cranking past us up the hill. A couple more followed, all headed west. I ran towards the road in my underwear, laughing and waving. The lead rider, a sleek, freshly shaven dude in his early forties, waved at me and pulled over. The cyclist on his tail—a middle-aged woman, tanned and stringy—gritted her teeth and rode on. The guy's shirt said AVANTI.

'Hello,' he said, 'we are *ciclisti*, from Italia. Where are you from?'

'Mörön Khövsg—uh, New Zealand!'

'*Nuova Zelanda*—in Australia!' he declared with authority. 'You 'ave many sheeps, but no people, yes?'

'No, well, sure.'

A peloton of eight riders came round the hill and whizzed over the bridge. I waved and grinned toothily and gave the riders a big thumbs-up.

'Nice bikes!' I said to the *ciclista*.

'I know,' he replied.

'How far are you going?'

'We start in Ulaanbaatar, five days ago. We ride to Mörön tomorrow, then easy day to Khatgal and the *lago*. We ride one 'undred twenty *chilometri* per day. I am, how you call, pace man.' He nodded in appreciation of his own talent.

'Sweet,' said Tama, pulling on a dirty T-shirt as he walked over. 'Where's all your luggage?'

'We 'ave *autobus* for that,' he said. Moments later a couple of grey Russian Furgon minivans came slowly round the corner. 'Our guide, they driving ahead and make us lunch, at night they set up the, the . . .' He pointed to our tent. 'The *tende*.'

'We carry all our gear ourselves,' Tama said. 'In panniers. On our mountain bikes.'

'Really?' He looked at us incredulously. 'And 'ow far does your trio ride?'

'About 100 kilometres a day,' I said.

'Or more,' Tama said.

'On *those*?' He looked at our bikes, unconvinced. 'That must be . . . please excuse me, I must to catch up with the peloton. You see, I set the pace—they need me! *Ciao!*'

He biked off extremely quickly, grunting in a too-high gear. The Furgons and their bored drivers rumbled past and overtook him. Back at our tent, the third moron was sitting in the vestibule, wearing his new blue sunglasses and playing with an ockie strap.

Tama went to wash in the river, which never got above shin-deep. I didn't. I told Tama I was scared of Mongolian water snakes, which was partly true, but being in the Mongolian wilderness was also the best excuse I'd ever had for not washing for days. So I sat in the sun with the kid and put on my matching sunnies. I rubbed a new layer of sunscreen over my dirt-caked skin and with the cooking knife cut the end off one of my socks so I could wear it high on my right calf to prevent further sunburn. The kid watched me with undiluted wonder, then took off his shoe and sock, grabbed my knife and started cutting the end off his own sock. I stopped him and tried unsuccessfully to explain about my shortage of melanin, how this brand of skin was useless south of London. He just looked at me with sad eyes.

We biked east across the bridge towards Khutag-Öndör and found ourselves on a dusty, featureless plain. The sun was raw and fierce; my salmon-coloured right leg was grateful for the extra sock. We approached a blue metallic road map atop a tall grey pole. It was eighty kilometres north to Teshig and 210 kilometres west to Mörön Khövsgöl. We had just completed a nine-day semicircle, a big wonky horseshoe arc in the wilderness. We could've been here a week ago if we'd ridden on the main road instead of detouring to Khatgal, but then we wouldn't've been able to get lost in that swamp.

In the distance there was a speck on the road. As we got closer we could make out a motorcycle with sidecar and flat tyre. An elderly woman sat in the sidecar in her best *deel*, looking grim. There were no *ger*s or houses around—just the road, stretching dusty and brown to both horizons. She stared listlessly at our bikes; we stared uselessly at her puncture. Tama fished out the cigarette stash and decided to give her a whole packet. She accepted with a subdued *bayarl-laa* and lit one up. Five kilometres down the road we passed a hunched old man who was trudging towards Khutag-Öndör in a now-dusty suit.

When we reached Khutag-Öndör it was Naadam—again. We headed straight for the *huushuur* quarter, ordered fourteen and ate nine on the spot. The *huushuur* vendor sat with us. He looked different to most of the Mongols we'd met; he could've played a Red Indian in a sloppily cast cowboy movie. No one else really talked to him, and he didn't seem to fit in with the rest of the Naadam celebrations.

We got a few funny looks from people walking past. I thought it was because we were so dirty and greedy, plus I stank. Then a drunk cowboy came panting and mutter-ing towards us and pointed angrily at Tama's *Mongol tug*, which was lashed to his pannier bags and lying sideways in the dust. The *huushuur* vendor helped Tama stand his bike up, and while Tama apologised in English, he apologised in Mongolian. The cowboy demanded to have a ride of Tama's bike. Tama refused, politely, I thought.

The cowboy spat in the dust and reeled off, shaking his head and repeating, *'Juulchin . . . juulchin.'*

'Yule kin?' Tama said quizzically to the vendor.

'Ah . . . *tourista*,' he replied with a sad smile.

We thanked the man for the food. Tama took his picture and shook his hand before we left.

'He seemed like an odd man out,' Tama said. 'He was nice, but people didn't seem to like him.'

I just nodded. The guy reminded me of photos of Tama from early high school, just after his parents divorced: hopeful, haunted eyes.

Tama wanted to call Ami again. I stalked off down a dusty street to get supplies, a bit annoyed. Did he have to call her *every single time* we saw a damn phone tower? Why couldn't he just . . . *be*, in the moment? Or keep a diary? It made me feel like I should call Laura, but I didn't want to call Laura. I wanted him to not call Ami all the time. We were meant to be in the middle of nowhere.

I found a store crammed with nomads, in from the country and plastered already, loading up on cheap vodka for the festivities to come. When I asked for Chinggis Gold a murmur went through the store—it was the fancy stuff, eight dollars instead of five. The shop also sold ice-creams in a cone, a delicious shock since refrigeration hadn't really caught on in rural Mongolia. I wandered back with a couple of double-scoop strawberry ice-creams. Tama was down a side street leaning against a fence, still on the phone. I stood around and tried not to watch as Tama's ice-cream melted in its cone. A plastic bag blew down the alley and tangled itself in my pannier bags. I kicked it loose. The wind carried it away.

Tama put down his phone. 'Mongolian tumbleweed,' he deadpanned.

'How is she?' I asked.

'Good.'

'What's going on in Ramcouver?'

'Oi, it's not *Ram*couver until I arrive. She's in bed. Tomorrow morning she's got meetings with clients from Seattle.'

'Oh.'

'It doesn't seem real,' Tama said, sounding slightly confused. 'All that . . . meetings and stuff. Crazy.'

'Totally, man, I don't wanna think about it. I'm just trying to . . . be, in *this*. Y'know?'

'If you say so.'

We rode out of Khutag-Öndör up a sprawling brown scar of a road. Heaps of jeeps rolled past us, on their way to Naadam. We weaved on and off the grassy verge. It was bursting with Mongolian phosphorescence. Tama had his map-eye on a thin red line heading up a valley to the north-east. This would lead us in a wonky 100-kilometre semicircle through to Selenge, past a little-known town called Khantai, hopefully via some more of that sweet Khövsgöl-esque wildflower meadow. From there it was two days *züün* (east) to Amarbayasgalant Khiid (say that three times quickly), Mongolia's largest surviving Buddhist monastery, where we could say some final prayers then *züün* at top speed into the Khaan Khentii wasteland, never to be seen again.

We spotted a narrow goat track winding off to the left across a steep hillside. It seemed like the way to Selenge and we took it. A couple of valleys over we came upon a tiny patch of beech trees, thriving incongruously on an otherwise parched and bleak hillside. After yesterday's battering by the sun we were keen to sit out the worst heat of the day. I wrote in my diary:

Monday, 17 or 18 July. Seventh day straight riding.
Exhausted, elated. Tama off for his daily poo. Jealousy.

Half an hour later we rode up an obscure valley. It was roasting hot in the sun and I was thankful when the tree cover began. The country was was stony and dry; this could have been southern Europe, sunstroke in Sicily. The gradient increased. My right knee creaked in complaint and sweat soaked through my shirt. Tama stopped and spread Vaseline on his inner thighs to lessen the chafing. My eyes stung and my hands were going numb. At the top of the valley a couple of hours later we were greeted by the first *ovoo* in days: welcome (back) to taiga country. Conifers stretched for the sun, alone or in clumps, and the tyre tracks we were following unrolled over endless wrinkles and ruffles of bright green hill. Blue ridges in the distant north faded into purple peaks and silver-grey sky. We had a second lunch out of the sun on the lee of a ridgeline among the bracken and larch, forcing down cold *huushuur* and fish sandwiches. The boundless paddocks reminded me of New Zealand back-country farms, except purged of fence, tractor and pie shop.

I woke from an accidental siesta to the sound of bleating and maracas. A couple of hundred goats were coming over the pass, herded by a nomad jiggling a plastic bottle full of pebbles that had been jammed onto the end of a stick. He rattled his makeshift shepherd's crook in our direction and we waved back, too tired to yell.

We clambered groggily onto our bikes and cruised on for a couple of hours. Slightly nearer the northern ranges the path cut a high line across the hillside to the left. There was also a cheeky smaller path dipping downhill and right into seemingly endless wheat fields. We strapped on our helmets and went right. It was the best riding we had all day. We sailed through someone's farm next to a grassy halfpipe of a ditch. The storm clouds gathered behind us, really gathered, piling into the sky like I'd never seen before, not even in Mongolia. Once again we were in the middle of an open field, and I rode hard towards nothing in particular, towards the idea of shelter; Tama was ahead of me, riding harder. Every time I looked back the clouds were taller and darker. Thunder rumbled in the distance. A yellow-white flash, close by. Tama pointed to the ditch and mumbled something.

'What?' I yelled.

'If the lightning gets really bad, we can hide in there!'

I nodded and changed into top gear to try to outride the storm but the rain came and kept coming. We rode past some high wooden fences hiding farm equipment and a couple of half-built log cabins and a yellow construction hut on wheels that was roughly the size and shape of a packing container. A couple of workers poked their heads out of the hut and watched us ride past. In a few frenzied minutes it got colder and the rain turned to hail. Tama jammed on his brakes.

'We should go back,' he said, shielding his face.

'Go back where?'

'To that hut.'

The hail thickened. A big one got me on the right knee.

'Okay!'

By the time we made it back to the hut hailstones the size of strawberries were vomiting out of a grey-white sky and shattering on our helmets. We banged on the door and gestured could we please come inside *please*? The workers nodded, looking at us like we were very foolish. Inside, the racket of hail on the steel roof was like being in a saucepan full of cooking popcorn. The room had metal walls on three sides and little windows on the fourth, and outside the hail made the fences and piles of timber look like they were on a badly tuned TV screen. Lumps of ice the size of walnuts lay in the mud. There were no chairs inside but Bayarmaa, a solid, kindly woman in a purple jumper and pink sandals, made room for us to sit on their beds even though we were drenched. Moments later she presented us with steaming bowls of mutton soup and a plate of *boov*—deep-fried dough nuggets, for dipping. Ah, Mongolia.

There were three men in the trailer: Chuluun, a quiet, wolf-faced dude who wore his cap low; Gantulga, affable and slightly dim; and the aptly named Batsaikhan ('Strong Nice'), Bataa for short, who had intelligent, cheeky eyes and seemed to be the team leader. They were building log cabins for the farm. I pointed out the window and shouted '*shuuraga*' ('storm') above the racket. Bataa nodded and rolled his eyes like it happened every other day, then lit a cigarette. We said we were from *Shin Zeland* and that yes, it was very *jijig*—small—and very far away. Tama got out the map of the Khantai region to explain our route. Bataa looked up from the map and shook his head sadly, then laughed with twinkling eyes.

I was just getting used to the din when, out of the far left corner of the window, I saw a geyser of white concrete spray upwards into the air. No, it was hail, but it was going in the wrong direction. I shouted and pointed; Bataa threw the door open and we all piled outside to see a river of hail and ice-melt surging through the ditch next to the road. Where the ditch turned a sharp corner the flash flood had burrowed into a nearby rubbish pit and it was spraying broken glass and plastic filth mixed with soiled ice high into the air in a toxic fountain. The ditch that we were going to shelter in to hide from the lightning now resembled a rampaging glacier on fast-forward. The workers ran inside and grabbed their jackets; Tama and I ran inside and grabbed our cameras.

On the other side of the ditch the wheat fields we had just been pedalling through were smashed flat and half-submerged in ice and water and mud. Bayarmaa stood with her hands on her head, distraught. Bataa, Gantulga and Chuluun pointed mutely at the devastation, rooted to the ground in disbelief. Tama and I couldn't believe our luck and dashed back and forth to make sure we got all the angles. This was it: *Doig and Pugs vs Wild*, meteorological carnage in the Mongolian wilderness, Steve Irwin sticking his finger up a stingray's arse. I burned through all the memory on the Flip-cam and had to delete random files on the fly, wincing as I trashed clips of our lovely dinner with the moron and the cute geologist to make room for this mess.

'Strewth, look at that flash flood. That's a real ripper right there!' I yelled in a bad Steve Irwin impersonation. 'I wouldn't wanna be caught in all those hailstones!'

'If you fell in there you'd be *dead meat*, mate!' Tama Irwin replied.

'Zang . . . this is one of the craziest . . .'

'De-va-sta-ting,' Tama said, his accent lurching towards Austria. Then in his normal voice, 'Have you seen that shit?'

'Wha?'

'It's on YouTube—California's burning to the ground, these crazy-arse forest fires roasting everything, and a heli-copter lands on a hill. Arnie jumps wearing his sunnies and the reporters are like, "Mr Governator, sir, what do you think of the fires?" and Arnie just goes [vaguely German accent] "De-va-sta-ting"—totally deadpan, jumps back in the chopper and flies off. It's awesome.'

We ran around like kids in a burning candy store, stomp-ing on banks of hailstones so they collapsed into the torrent.

The temperature had plummeted but we didn't care. Meanwhile, Chuluun was hunched over a decrepit motorcycle, tapping at the engine with a stone and a broken chisel that looked Bronze Age. The bike wouldn't start. Bataa ran up to me and motioned that he was going to take my bicycle and alert the neighbours downstream, or something—then he was gone. Five minutes later he was back; the road downstream was flooded out. He dumped my bike in the mud and took off in the tractor, which had a dishevelled little Mongolian flag fluttering sadly from its roof and a top speed of ten kilometres an hour. I had a feeling that any farmers downstream would probably know about the flash flood by now.

Flash flood
www.moron2moron.com/videos/flash-flood

We weren't going to make it to Khantai that afternoon. If we wanted to sleep in our tent that night we'd need an inflatable raft, so when Bayarmaa invited us to stay in the hut we accepted gratefully. Tama and I had changed into our wool layers, all of them, and Bayarmaa had our shirts drying over the pot-belly stove.

I dug a jar of jam out of my pannier; it went well with the deep-fried *boov*. I put some jam and dough on a plate and offered it to Gantulga and Chuluun. They looked at me strangely, said something that made Bayarmaa giggle, then smiled and tucked in. Towards sunset me and Tama went for a little cycle to see if we'd missed any destruction. The ditch was now overflowing with a steaming broth of dirty water, while inexplicable clouds of freezing fog from the melting hailstones rolled across the fields. I rode into a corridor of mist and yelped: it was five degrees colder in the fog than out. I couldn't work out why some of the hailstones were long melted while others remained piled in frosty drifts until the following morning.

When Bataa returned he was pleased to see us still there. I took him aside and gave him a couple of packets of Marlboros, gesturing that they were for the team. He looked at me in deep appreciation and quickly pocketed both packs before the others could see. We stood outside the hut and watched the doomed icebergs of hail melt into the brown soup. I wanted to ask him if this kind of thing happened often, but 'extreme weather event' and 'anthropogenic climate change' weren't in the phrasebook. Bataa pointed at the wheat fields then waved his hands, as if erasing it all. Then he pointed at the half-finished log cabins. The same motion. No more wheat fields, no more construction. No more construction, no more job.

'Where will you go?'

He pointed up the valley. Back to his village, back to his family. He stared at the ditch, motionless.

'*Muu*,' I tried to say. '*Mash muu*.' ('Very bad.')

Bataa nodded sorrowfully. Then he shrugged his shoulders and laughed, his eyes smiling.

I pointed at him. 'Buddhist?' I asked.

'*Tiin, bi Buddyn shashintan!*' he cried.

'Zang!'

That night we finished their dough and our jam and drank our bottle of Chinggis Gold vodka with some older men who had materialised on ancient but apparently sturdy motorbikes just after dark. We sat out under the stars and took turns ceremoniously throwing down shots of vodka. I snapped and bludged a Marlboro off Bataa, lit it up and sucked deeply. A little atom bomb detonated in my head and I returned shuddering to my body. I was so tired my whole face hurt.

'Damn, you smoke your cigarettes like joints,' Tama said.

'Yeah . . . you want some of this?' I coughed and giggled.

'No way. But bro, I'd kill for a joint right about now.'

'Yeah . . . not kill.'

'Not kill—maim.'

I took another gut drag. 'Just snap a spine—Chinggis style!'

I went for a high five but Tama was talking to Chuluun, trying to tell him about Pakistan.

As the night wore on, we all got a little bit drunk and taught each other the words for night (*shünü*), star (*od*), moon (*sar*), unidentified flying object (*sansriin ül medegdex biet*), alien anal probe (doesn't exist in Mongolian). It was a beautiful clear *shünü* and the *od*s were bright, as bright as they got on an obscure New Zealand beach, brighter. It was hard to comprehend that Bataa, Bayarmaa and co. had just lost their jobs. We finished the Chinggis sometime after midnight but no one showed any sign of going to bed. Finally I found the phrase for 'we are tired'—*bidnar yadarchiin*—and showed it to Bataa. Instantly he sent the old-timers packing and bundled the rest of us into the trailer. Bed was a raised platform about two metres long and four metres wide where the workers slept side by side like Kiwis in a NZ tramping hut, or Tama's three dads in their custom-made bed. Tonight it was six in the bed, tatty spare blankets, Tama's feet sticking out the end. We lay down and I promptly passed out. Later Tama told me they had waited till they thought we were both asleep then got back up and sat by the door, smoking and talking quietly about the future.

DAY 11: GOATS ON A BOAT

We woke early, keen to make up for lost time, and got ready to leave straight away. Bataa wanted us to stay for breakfast but we were worried that was a slippery slope—first we eat, then help a little with the clean-up, next we knew, we'd be married to Bayarmaa—so we shook our heads. Bataa gestured that I should stay with them to work on the cabins and/or become unemployed and move to an Ulaanbaatar slum. Then he mimed that he would take my bicycle and ride off with Tama, fly to Melbourne and get a well-paying part-time job in the non-profit sector then go back to uni and milk a postgrad scholarship for a few years. Everyone pissed themselves at that one.

The goodbyes went on for ages. I felt like I'd really connected with Bataa; in other circumstances I really would've loved to stay for a few days. I said, 'Have a nice life,' and I meant it. Then they said 'Sain yavaaria!'—'Safe journey!'—and we were out of there.

We pedalled away down a track now slick with mud. With all our weight on the back tyre it was hard to keep a clean line and not slop around in the rich brown filth. I had read somewhere that Mongolia imported two-thirds of its wheat these days because since 1990 nearly 75 per cent of its own wheat land had had to be abandoned. It didn't say why—at the time I just thought more desertification. I wobbled left, overcorrected right, my wheels gave way beneath me. I just managed to leap clear as bike, bags and water bottles slopped into a quagmire of stripped topsoil.

While Tama waited for me to collect myself a jeep roared up. It was Chuluun, chauffeuring a large man in a white polo shirt with a bloated, pockmarked face. The fat man was the farm owner, and he may have been freshly bankrupt. He was exceptionally keen to get Tama's photos off him and gestured for Tama to somehow extract them from his camera. But Tama wasn't rocking a Polaroid; the images were on a memory card, and no one had their laptop handy. Tama could find the word for computer—*kompyuter*—but not the word for email. The boss wrote down something that resembled an email address except without an '@'. Tama nodded and promised to *kompyuter* the *gerel zurags* (photos) to the boss as soon as we made it to a *kompyuter tsainy gazar* (internet cafe). The boss shook his head—this wasn't good enough. We wanted to help with his insurance claims, but there was nothing else to be done, and we were behind schedule. We said goodbye another twenty times and finally got away.

It was muddy most of the way to Khantai. The town itself was little more than a pile of ramshackle cabins and rusted farm equipment dumped in the deforested foothills of the Hantayn Nuruu mountain ranges. In this sleepy, depressing and almost entirely abandoned hamlet we managed to find a single open shop. We slammed down some detergent-green Bulgarian Fanta, failed to find any bread and loaded up on the only chocolate they had: two slabs of Alpen Gold, a 'Swiss' chocolate imported from Romania. We rode east out of Khantai to our bridge crossing over the Egiin *gol*. There was a shining stripe of river, wide and swift, flanked by a pair of crumbling concrete pilings. No bridge.

I put on my David Attenborough voice. 'And so, once again, the two morons are thwarted—by a *mörön*.'

Tama didn't laugh.

'Do you think that flash flood washed the bridge away?' I asked.

'Nah bro, there are weeds and shit growing in the pilings. It's our bloody maps. That's probably what Bataa and Gantulga were trying to tell us yesterday.'

Silence.

'So, what do we do now?'

Tama looked up. 'Why are you asking me?'

I checked out the map. The Üür *gol*, which had proved uncrossable five days earlier, flowed into the Egiin *gol* 200 kilometres upstream—and here it was again, our watery nemesis. Before we admitted defeat and biked through the mud back to Khutag-Öndör, two days lost and zero kilometres gained, we decided to at least have a swim and a wash. The rocky riverbank was garnished with shards of broken glass and ripped Chinggis labels, but the river water was marvellous—clear, cool and refreshing. I stood thigh-deep in the rushing torrent, only slightly worried about slicing off a toe, and washed my ripe armpits for the first time in a week.

After a stodgy breakfast of instant noodles I turned to Tama and said, 'I'm going for a poo. I may be some time.'

I squatted in futility behind a grove of stumpy trees and had a staring competition with a couple of dozen wild goats.

I had just hitched my shorts up when four SUVs appeared on the riverbank upstream and roared towards us.

'*Sigh binoo!*' I yelled.

'Khello!' a man shouted in a thick Eastern Bloc accent.

It was a contingent of off-road enthusiasts from Ukraine, Belarus and Kazakhstan, eight smiling men and a gloomy teenage boy. The Ukrainian group leader had a smiley round face and was wearing a T-shirt with a picture of a smiley round sun shining down on a smiley round flower, all drawn in felt-tip pen. I complimented him on the shirt.

'Zank you,' he said. 'My daughter draw it for me and I wear every day—to bring luck!'

The teenager cringed; it was his little sister's crummy drawing on his dad's fat belly.

'We drive from Kiev,' Smiley Man said, 'through Kazakhstan, meet our friends—'

'Khello!' bellowed the other drivers.

'And now we drive to Lake Baikal for off-road festival. We do zis every year, always by different route!'

Tama asked the Ukrainian about the Khantai bridge. His jeep had a Sat Nav device with up-to-date GPS maps on it. The maps didn't show any bridge at Khantai.

'Maybe ten years ago,' he said, and the whole convoy laughed.

'How are you guys gonna cross the river?' Tama asked.

'We go downstream for eighteen kilomet, and zis river it split into three, ah, rivers.' He showed us on the Sat Nav. 'It is wide there, maybe shallow. We hope. You should follow us—over that saddle,' he said, pointing to a mountain range ten kilometres distant. 'We would take your bikes—but no room!' The convoy laughed again.

'How high is the saddle crossing?'

'I not sure—1600, 1700 metres maybe. Good luck, try to keep up!'

More laughter, slightly cruel, then they jumped in their jeeps and sped off. Since it was follow the SUVs or backtrack like losers, we followed the SUVs. The scabby muddy path gave way to river sand, which was much worse. If I pedalled hard my back wheel slipped; if I turned the handlebars too suddenly, or at all, my front wheel ploughed into the sand and tipped me over. Tama managed to keep upright and was grinding slowly along in lowest gear, but I had to get off and push. The base of the mountain range we had to cross wasn't getting any closer. My knee throbbed. The sun beat down.

Our track turned left and cut through low dusty scrub then came out onto a stony floodplain. We could make out an elaborate chunk of rusted machinery at least three metres tall with steel cables that stretched across to the far bank—the sort of thing you'd find on eBay if you searched for 'ruined chairlift'. Attached to the cables was the most beautiful thing I'd seen in days: a pontoon. It was a battered orange metal thing shaped like a catamaran without any sails or masts, just two long hollow hulls and a raised wood platform between them. It was old and rusty and parked on our side of the river.

'Thank fucking Christ for that!' Tama said, and high-fived me so hard my hand stung.

Three nomads were in the process of loading the pontoon with goats, a gang of scrawny black, white and brown things with blue dots spray-painted on their backs. A couple of rogues made a break from the pack and tried to escape downstream. A farmer grabbed the first goat but the second one kept thrashing around, then it went under. When it came up five metres downstream it was floating on its side. As the farmers splashed after the goat-corpse, the first goat got away again. Tama took off his bike gloves and plunged into the river. He grabbed the living goat by its curled horns and dragged it up onto the barge. Once aboard, the goat shook Tama off, made to charge at us, then joined its friends at the far end of the pontoon with a belated bleat.

'Goaty,' Tama declared. It was true: the goats did smell extremely . . . goaty, especially now they were wet. Especially the dead one.

The pontoon's locomotion was an ingenious affair. It didn't have an engine but it did have a giant double rudder, and when the rudder was turned to portside, the whole craft was shunted across the river by the power of the current, its little pulleys creaking on the steel cables above. We were prepared to pay Americans-in-Vietnam prices to get across that cursed river. But a little sign said 1500 tugrugs for cars and 700 tugrugs for motorcycles, and they charged us the motorcycle rate: about seventy Australian cents. I felt like telling the pontoon owner that he should make a special tourist price with an extra zero on it, but I didn't.

East of the Egiin *gol* the landscape changed dramatically. Grass sprouted improbably from golden sandy soil and the plains were dotted with little groves of puffy trees no taller than me. It was how I imagined the savannah would be, and I half-expected to see a pride of lions having a cheeky nap in the shade. All it needed was a cardboard cutout of Mount Kilimanjaro to complete the African illusion.

The next couple of hours passed in a hot, happy daze.

We rode up hill and down dale and sometimes got snarled in sand. We left the Egiin *gol* for ten kilometres then rejoined it, saw towering sandy cliffs dropping away into the river. We rode up a hill past a sleepy *ger* with its obligatory growling dog. A naked child ran out of the *ger* and stood staring at us in utter astonishment. I felt like Ewan McGregor, or possibly Charley Boorman.

We came over the long soft crest of a ridge and drifted downhill through a fragrant breeze, the track wavering and blurring in the distance, no sound except the whirring of our tyres. To the left were three iconic trees, bulbous explosions of green against a cloudless sky. It was a Stunning Mongolia calendar scene with no one around to appreciate it—just me and Tama, and we were passing through like ghosts on greased cables, the trees already sepia-stained, half-forgotten.

At the bottom of the hill we entered a narrow sandy valley with a wall of scrubby bushes on the right and rocky outcrops like piles of melted caramel on the left. It was hard riding and my good mood cracked on the sand and rocks. I was hungry, sore, smashed by the sun. We were nowhere near done for the day; but we were near the river again— you could hear it through the bushes—so we pulled off the track for a late lunch and found a spot with a great view of the river. Tama got that look in his eye.

'Man, imagine sailing down this river on a *raft*! We could totally do it—cut down a couple of sapling trees and lash them together, ockie-strap our bikes on top . . . Or make our own pontoon—yeah, we could use our *panniers* to make a pontoon, empty 'em out and zang! We could even catch some *fish*!'

'Never work,' I said gruffly.

'Why not?'

'Not enough cable ties.'

'Yeah, but how good would it be—lazing in the sun, letting the river carry us downstream, not having to pedal . . .'

'All our stuff'd get wet. Waterfalls. Capsize and drown.'

'Fine, you can keep cycling.' Tama lay back in the grass. 'I'll make my *own* imaginary raft.'

'Go for it, Huck Finn.' I didn't even have enough *imaginary* cable ties.

The whole conversation was a distraction from the matter at hand: what were we going to eat for lunch? We were low on everything. There was a quarter-loaf of two-day-old Tarialan bread, no butter, and we were down to our last can of Russian fish. I don't know who suggested it—I'm going to say Tama—but *someone* said we should crack out the tin of emergency meat I'd being carting around since Tsagaan-Üür. The can was red and silver with a retro silhouette of a cow on it and a curly font that said PYSSKAR. I thought of it, hopefully, as corned beef. Tama got out his Leatherman and cracked the PYSSKAR open.

It wasn't corned beef.

The PYSSKAR was a greyish pink and extremely gelatinous. It looked and smelled like jellymeat. Surely it wasn't meant for human consumption? But then again, we hadn't seen a single cat in Mongolia . . . The neighbourhood flies were very excited by it. We weren't.

In Warsaw years ago I had forced down some *nóżki w galarecie*, a local delicacy that was basically good beef ruined by immersion in gelatine. Maybe PYSSKAR was the Chernobyl version of *nóżki*.

Tama speared a chunk of meat on the tip of his knife, extracted it from the glue and raised it hesitantly towards his mouth. He chewed it for a couple of seconds, then his face clouded over and he retched and spat into the bushes, spluttering and spitting again and again to get rid of the taste.

'Good?' I asked hopefully.

Tama placed a much smaller piece of PYSSKAR in his mouth. This time he chewed it with his front teeth, trying to keep it away from his tongue, but he gagged again and spat it all out.

'It's just . . . the texture's really bad,' he said. 'It's not what meat should be.'

'Oh.'

'I think you should try some.'

Tama handed me the can and the knife. I looked at the mystery meat with mild terror. When I was little and had to feed the family cat, the jellymeat smell would make me retch.

'I don't know if I can eat that,' I said.

'I thought you and Laura *loved* getting freaky with jelly-meat.' Tama smirked.

'We might've rubbed it on each other once or twice,' I said defensively, 'but that was for a show—and we didn't *eat* it!'

I stared into the can. The stench of jellied entrails, the congealed sludginess of it all . . . but now was no time to be fussy. I stabbed a chunk of PYSSKAR and put it in my mouth. The combination of coldness, slime, cow anus and childhood trauma was potent, to say the least. I chewed at the PYSSKAR with my central incisors, trying not to vomit. I managed to gulp a piece down but I instantly regretted it. Tama was right; it was not what meat should be.

Meat in a can
www.moron2moron.com/videos/meat-in-a-can

After a troubled nap we continued on our arbitrary odyssey, hoping but not expecting to make it another 40 kilometres to the Selenge *mörön*. A kilometre down the road a small van drove up next to us and stopped. The driver nodded and made a pillow with his hands. I shook my head, tapped myself on the chest, made a pyramid with my arms and said '*maikhan*'. He nodded and drove off.

The path forded a boggy creek with logs strewn across the mud then turned left and headed uphill. With storm clouds massing to the west, we began to climb the first of three passes we had to cross that afternoon. I changed down and pedalled and changed down again and kept pedalling. The sweat ran down my face and back and drenched my shirt. I pushed from the knees, from the thighs, from the gluteus maximus for five minutes, ten minutes.

I looked at the ground beneath me. I looked as far ahead as I could. My breath came ragged and uneven; I gasped, coughed and spat out last night's cigarettes. I burped and tasted cat food. I forced myself to keep going. Fifteen, seventeen, eighteen trembling minutes. At the top I waited for Tama, feeling scattered and dizzy. We turned a corner and stopped to put on our helmets before a downhill that was over too soon. The path bottomed out in an epic valley and there were no more trees, just waist-high grass all around. No nomads, no munching snouts.

Tama slowed down, jumped off his bike and ran into the field, I presumed for an emergency poo break.

'This grass . . . is grass,' he said.

'Profound, bro.'

'No—it's *grass*. Weed. Ganja.'

'Really?'

'Hell yeah man, it's totally marijuana. Have a smell of it.'

I had a smell of it: it was totally marijuana. Fields, hectares, acres of weed—a moron's paradise. But it was still early in the summer and the plants weren't budding yet, or possibly they were all males. To get properly high we'd need to dry and smoke half a salad bowl of the stuff. Cooking up hash butter on the petrol stove was a much better option, except we were out of butter. I wandered deep into the fields, pleased at the lack of shotguns mounted on tripwires at knee-height. Tama found some plants that were a bit taller, almost budding, and we filled a small plastic bag with promising tips.

I made a mental note to write *Ronery Pranet* an email so they could update their guide. Pedalling on I was shocked not to see any Mongol hip-hop stoners camped out in the fields smoking cones through an ibex horn. The weed grew so close to the track that I could reach out and pluck the densest tips and shove them in my pocket without slowing down.

The next pass was easier at first, but got harder. My legs hurt, they burned, and gradually that pain took over my whole body until every downstroke of my pedal made my elbows ache, my toes throb, my neck pinch. Random flashes of pain in my left hip, right shoulder, both thumbs. My thighs were ravenous, with a life of their own—insatiable baby birds shrieking shrilly at mother stomach, sucking all the life out of me and croaking for more.

I didn't have any more. My body groaned, a sob ripped from my chest. My lungs were goat lungs and I was running underwater. I'd joked about this at Melbourne house parties, made light of it from a drunken hammock in Cambodia. I had wanted some unadulterated suffering—and here it was.

But it was too much. I couldn't go on. I had to go on. I can't.

Just one more pedal. No. Yes. One more. And another. But. It. Hurts.

You don't have to push. Just take it easy. See, the bike pedals itself. Let go. Okay. There's no pain here. You don't have to make it up the whole hill, just one more metre. Yeah. Don't worry about dinner, there's just this. Your legs are light, your legs are empty. You can go on like this forever.

The thigh muscles stopped screaming through the skin. I floated gently up the hill in an adrenaline-soaked satori. This was why chief financial officers who wouldn't be caught dead at meditation classes ran ultra-marathons every weekend. Once the pain takes over and knocks all the thoughts out of you, there's a shortcut to a patch of clarity. You find yourself helped along by a little voice in a far corner of your head—someone enlightened, or at least bossy.

Then my legs stopped having visions and demanded more chocolate. I reached the top of the hill with Tama just behind me. He had his top off and the sweat was pouring off him. We ate one Mars Bar and saved the last for later. It was dinnertime but this was no place to stop; we were on an exposed rocky ridge and the wind had picked up. There was a long downhill and the whole time I knew we'd have to claw every one of those metres back.

The third climb was on rocky ground. My stomach howled, my legs howled, I felt feeble and shaky. After ten minutes I asked Tama if we could eat the last Mars Bar. We did and for ten minutes I could ride hard as the sugar ripped through my lungs and poured out my knees. Then I ran out of steam. My body was used up, ransacked. It was past 9 pm but the clouds still had a silvery shine to them; the sun wasn't going anywhere. Neither were we.

'This is a really fucking big day,' I panted.

'Yep.'

Tama dug in his pannier bags for our last resort—the Alpen Gold chocolate. They had liquified in their packets. I opened one end and put the packet inside my mouth then clamped down with my teeth and pulled the bag out, forcing the sugary molten goop into my gullet like a third-rate astronaut eating third-rate astronaut food. Tama did likewise, mumbling and growling. Then he looked up to the ridgeline and smiled.

'We're gonna make it,' he said, a calm lightness in his voice and chocolate all over his face. 'Another half an hour and we'll be up there.'

Then the sugar hit me and I felt like Gandhi on Ritalin. We pedalled on. I tried to stay inside the burn because within the sharpest pain there was always a not-pain. I reached for that not-pain and wrapped it around me. I went somewhere else. I panted and cursed and begged to no one in particular. I gritted my unbrushed teeth and made it to the top of that pass.

We were too tired to celebrate. There was no celebration chocolate left anyway, plus there was still eight or nine kilometres to go until we reached the river. A four-metre strip of undulating clay stretched ahead of us in a stupendous grey waterslide.

'I wish I didn't have these Ortliebs!' Tama yelled over his shoulder as he accelerated away from me.

We were finally moving but the sun was moving too. The hills were turning to flat shades of grey and dark grey and black. I whizzed right and left over the smoothed-off ruts and ridges and widening cracks, the road ahead chunking into blocks of fuzz. Don't ride into the shadows. Stay on the path. I rode into a little shadow and my back tyre blew out. I yelled at Tama who had to turn around and ride back. He changed my tyre in a hurry while I stood there, useless and spent.

'It's nearly dark,' he said when he was finished. 'We should be riding with headtorches.'

In a few minutes it was pitch-black. We came down onto the flat but there was no way of knowing how far it was to the river. We rode along in the dark, bumping in and out of little ditches we couldn't see.

'Tama,' I called out.

'What?'

'We don't have to make it to the river tonight.'

'Why not?'

'It doesn't make any difference.'

'So?'

'So let's stop. Now.'

'Where?'

'Here.'

He pulled over to the side of the road. 'I was just going to keep riding,' he said. 'I get to this point where I don't get tired, or sore, or hungry. I can just keep going.'

'I know.'

'You need to tell me if I have to stop, because otherwise—'

'I know, bro. I will.'

I set up the tent in an invisible field surrounded by god-knows-what. Tama boiled up a slop of raisin rice. Hooves sounded in the darkness.

'Hide the weed,' Tama hissed. I scrambled around in the chaos of our panniers, struggling to find the plastic bag—in retrospect probably a sign that we didn't need to worry about hiding it—and threw it into the vestibule just as the horseman arrived. What followed was one of the more frustrating conversations of our trip. The man tried extremely hard to tell us something. He kept gesturing and pointing down the hill and wouldn't give up. Were we in a landslip area? Near an abandoned mine? Did he want to cook us a proper dinner and let us sleep in his *ger*?

'WE-ARE-NEW-ZEA-LAN-DERS,' I said. 'LEAVE-US-A-LONE.'

Finally he left, but not before the rice went mushy. I wolfed down a mountainous bowlful and wanted more. There wasn't more. I wanted vodka, but there wasn't vodka. Right before we passed out Tama set up his tripod and took a photo of us. We are wearing our headtorches, chests bare and gleaming, an arm around each other's shoulder, staring into the lens like distraught homosexual miners.

DAY 12: THE LAKE ON TOP OF THE HILL

'Tama, are you dead?'

Tama grumbled and pulled his jacket over his head. I filmed him sleeping for a bit then got up to take a piss. I could see a whisker of the Selenge *mörön* at the end of the valley, less than a kilometre away. The tent was pitched in the middle of a grassless clearing about six metres across: not an alien crop circle, but rather the mark a *ger* leaves after a few months. The grass beyond looked soft, but it was full of rocks; on balance I had done good.

I felt anything but good. After eight consecutive days of hard riding, twenty-three crummy meals and not enough of them overcompensated for with way too much chocolate and cheap sugary drink, I was wrecked. The frenzied opening-night thrill of Really Being in Mongolia had curdled into a vague but constant sense of panic that buzzed away at the base of my neck.

Meanwhile, the end was nowhere in sight. I put on the same rancid underpants, the same stinking shorts and the same browning T-shirt I'd been wearing for an unwashed week and tried to do some yoga, but I went straight from child pose to corpse pose and stayed there.

When Tama got up we had a meeting about breakfast. It was moved that we should not have raisiny rice with milk powder *again* but should instead hold out until we reached the township of Selenge, where we could have a good meaty soup with hunks of fresh bread. Tama had read somewhere that Selenge was 'the bread-basket of Mongolia' and this boded well—the motion was seconded and zanged.

Another, more far-reaching motion was tabled: that instead of heading northeast from Selenge through to Kyalganat and the Amarbayasgalant Khiid monastery, taking care to avoid the city of Erdenet due to its presumed toxic and dystopian nature, we should actually cycle south towards this Erdenet place as fast as humanly possible. Once there we could check ourselves into a hotel, have a hot shower or two, do some laundry, go to a restaurant with cold beers and menus in English, get drunk, sleep in and HAVE A REST DAY.

I was half-curious to check out the monastery, but I'd already stared at my share of temples in Thailand and India, not to mention all those boring churches in Europe. Also, as Tama pointed out, we had set a precedent in Rambodia by not visiting Angkor Wat, arguably the greatest Buddhist temple in the world. Why would we go out of our way to visit a ratty monastery guaranteed to be rammed with disappointed tourists in a country most renowned for its *lack* of buildings? This motion was also passed unanimously, helped by the fact that it looked like an easy day's ride to Erdenet—just fifty or fifty-five kilometres.

We climbed gingerly onto our creaking steeds and cycled down to the Selenge *mörön*. Instead of a bridge there was another pontoon-on-a-wire. It was over at the far bank picking up a jeep.

'Another day, another *mörön*,' I said. Tama grunted. He was munted too.

I tried again. 'Be good to have a nice swim and a wash on the other side, huh?' Then I looked at the river: its murky brown waters were hammering past us, disturbed by a slow-motion boil of churning ripples that suggested dangerous undertows. The pontoon drifted towards us carrying the old grey jeep and what looked like an extended family taking their annual holiday. It was piloted by the dude from last night who had ruined our rice. We smiled awkwardly at the ferryman and waited for the family to disembark, but they didn't, so we wheeled our bikes on board. I was immediately accosted by a midget with the demeanour of a naughty carnie. He got me to check out the only female on the barge, a squat, unathletic, buck-toothed woman about my age who was dressed in an unfortunate sky-blue tracksuit.

'*Saikhan!*' I declared. The midget nodded enthusiastic-ally. I racked my brain for more words for 'beautiful'.

'*Soloitoi?*' I said. A barrage of laughter.

'Isn't that Mandarin?' Tama said.

'Damn. Maybe.'

While everyone else laughed at her or my expense, the poor woman in question half-hid behind the jeep, mortified. A squinty-eyed dude with a pencil moustache and a polo shirt that he'd rolled up to let his perky man boobs breathe found the whole thing particularly amusing. The midget kept pointing to the woman and giving me the thumbs-up; next he seemed to suggest that I should pay them money to have sex with Dumpy on the far side of the river, in the back of the jeep and/or the nearby bushes.

'Za, za, za,' I said dismissively, which seemed like the Mongolian equivalent to 'whatever'.

As we approached the far bank the midget stopped smiling. He gasped and pointed in abject terror to the loading ramp where a mountain of a man in very short shorts, all barrel chest and tree-trunk thighs, stood on the ramp. He shook his fist at me and punched said fist into palm with an audible *slap* before gesturing that he would beat me to the ground, then beat me while I lay on the ground. He was the epitome of the bad-guy wrestler.

'Bökh! Bökh!' I called out, hoping like hell that me and him would never actually *bökh*.

When we arrived on the other side, the wrestler had stopped grimacing and he shook my hand warmly. The carnies insisted on covering our ferry fares in return for our participation in that hilarious piece of analogue Mongolian *Candid Camera*. The midget was all smiles, laughing and calling me 'Shin Zeland soloitoi'. I checked the phrasebook; 'soloitoi' meant 'crazy', not 'pretty'.

The carnies wanted to give us a lift through Selenge and over the hill to Erdenet in their jeep. That morning it was particularly difficult to explain that we preferred to do it the slow, hard, painful way—we enjoyed it, apparently. We cycled up the path and they drove alongside us, shouting out all manner of presumably hilarious jokes until eventually they got bored and sped off.

'Those dudes would've appreciated my bodysuit,' I said. Tama stopped pedalling for a second. I could see him struggling to come up with a reply.

'You could've gone on tour with them,' he said finally.

An hour later we made it to Selenge—unless we'd taken a wrong turn and it was some scabhole five kilometres east or west of the real Selenge. Either way, the town we arrived in made Mörön seem like El Dorado.

Selenge had all the dust, disrepair and decay we had come to dread from Mongolia's one-goat towns, but without any of their rustic patchwork charm—and with a far higher concentration of mangy dogs. Apart from the canines the streets were utterly empty. We couldn't find any restaurants or canteens to order meaty soup at. It took ages to find a grocery store, and when we did we had to bang and bang on the door before a grumpy middle-aged woman opened up, wiping the sleep from her eyes. Our garbled demands for fresh tchtooork fell on confused ears. The closest thing we could see was a weird Albanian loaf in a plastic packet. Apparently there was no bread in the bread-basket of Mongolia. We bought two-and-a-half litres of sugary drink, a tub of chocolate ice-cream, eight Mars Bars, a big jar of peaches and some fake Pringles chips and sat outside in the alley beside our bikes, buzzing on sugar.

'Far out, that lady was surly,' I said, gobbling down sloppy peaches. 'What a Mongol!'

'*You're* the one who just—hee hee—burst into her store and shouted "bread, bread, bread" without saying hello,' Tama replied, lapsing into high-pitched giggles. 'Bread-bread-bread-bread-bread—breeeeeaaaaad!'

'All good points, Tama Pugsley, and duly noted. But it still doesn't solve our problem: where's the freakin *bread* at?'

'You should've harvested some wheat from that field before the—heh heh—hailstones got it,' Tama said.

We split up and went from one end of town to the other, down every single dusty alley looking for fresh bread or anything good. We failed. I did see a fence with D O G painted in letters tall enough that I could've stood between the o and G and made the fence spell D O I G, but I just couldn't be bothered. Eventually, reluctantly, I went and banged on the door of the first store again and bought the woman's scabby not-bread as well as some doughnuts. Tama deposited our last couple of days' worth of rubbish—three plastic bags full—in a little pile next to the store. I told him off, but when he asked me if I had a better suggestion, I didn't, so we left it there and rode out of town.

We plonked ourselves down to make some fish sandwiches in the first decent spot of shade we found. The only bread in Selenge turned out to be sweet, stale, crumbly and full of raisins. Tama drop-kicked it into the marijuana fields. We had fake Pringles and dry doughnuts for breakfast. I felt like a hangry ghost.

The path meandered through rogue plantations of almost-budding ganja, the plants taller than the day before's. I picked the tips and shoved them into my pockets as we cycled along. After a while the weed dropped away and we found ourselves stuck on another confounding and endless *faux plat*. My lungs were tattered sails that buffeted me haltingly upwards. I had to keep reminding myself that I was slowly gaining altitude, not losing my ability to pedal. It was a struggle to keep going, to keep *wanting* to keep going, and now that we were having a day off in Erdenet it was tempting to just crumple in a heap of self-pity then and there.

The scenery didn't help. It was still beautiful, with a sparkling stream meandering through an enormous valley and densely wooded ridges thinning out on the flat. But there were also lots of *gers* scattered about, five and ten at a time where before there was just one or two. It was hardly Calcutta, but for a country that averaged fewer than two people every square kilometre, it felt crowded. On closer inspection the 'sparse' pine forests on the plains were full of tree stumps, despite the odd rusted sign begging people to not hack down trees.

The meadows also had ominous patches of raw earth on the hillsides, which I recognised from New Zealand as little landslips, the surest sign of overgrazing. When the Soviet Union collapsed in 1991 the Mongolian economy went with it, leaving thousands of urban workers suddenly unemployed. This was followed by a 'goat rush' as folks headed for the hills, trying to cash in on a bull market for daggy cashmere jumpers in Canada and Japan. Those extra goats shouldn't have been there, perhaps, but what else were all those ex-Communists supposed to do—skip the flirtations with small-scale entrepreneurial capitalism and move straight to the sewer pipe?

The sun was out and it wasn't fooling around. Despite all my precautions, my right leg continued to get sunburnt. Meanwhile, the ligaments in my right knee felt like they needed replacing. My knee brace helped but it also chafed; it was giving me a saddle-sore halfway down my leg. My mood was dark and I couldn't wait to get to Erdenet. On the side of the road there was a savage smear of blood, intestines and fur. It took me a few seconds to piece it together as someone's ex-pet.

'I tought I taw a puddy-tat,' I said to Tama.

No response.

'Guess that's why you don't have pets in Mongolia, huh?'

'Dude, enough,' he said. He was bent over his handlebars and moving slowly.

Five hours after leaving Selenge we made it to the top of the pass. We pulled off the track into the shade of a stand of silver birches and lay down like corpses rolled off the back of a wagon.

'Man . . . I thought this was meant to be an easy day,' I groaned.

'It was,' Tama said. 'Maybe it's just hard cos yesterday was so epic.'

'Maybe.' I kicked my bike wheel. 'I dunno if there are many easy days on these things.'

Tama belched.

We cooked up our last tubs of instant noodles and stared unhappily at the results. I forced it down. By now my food fantasies had become quite baroque: *a whole roast chicken . . . no, roast duck. Turkey. What the hell, a whole motherfucken turducken, a chicken inside a duck inside a turkey. Wait—a Mongolian turducken! A marmot inside a goat inside a sheep in a cow in a horse—with hot sauce!* Tama wanted a sandwich, and not just an ordinary sandwich: 'a really really nice one'.

We had only two Mars Bars left, but since it was five kilometres to Erdenet and all of it downhill Tama suggested there was no point in saving them. It made sense to me.

We rolled down through a sweeping, empty valley. There were no *gers* on this side of the hill and that was a relief—it felt like wild nature again. There was a path to the right, curling up and over a random ridge, but who'd want to go that way? Erdenet was straight ahead, and close. I could practically smell the clean guesthouse sheets and packet soap.

'We should go and get a traditional Russian massage,'
Tama said. 'I've had one in New York, it's awesome. You go
to a sauna and lie on your back and after a while a fat lady
comes out and beats you with olive branches!'

'Cool. Does she have to be fat?'

'Yeah, the fat ones have more power.'

The path stretched out before us and we rode quickly
down the hill. After a few hundred metres the valley levelled
out. There were half a dozen *gers* scattered about, and a
couple of hundred goats grazing next to . . .

'What the fuck? This isn't on the map,' Tama said. 'Our
road—it's meant to go right through . . .'

It certainly *looked* like there was a huge lake filling the
valley. The closer we got, the lakier it looked: it was blue,
reflective of afternoon sun, and stretched mirror-flat for a
kilometre or more to the left. On the right it was pure lake
until a steep outcrop blocked our view.

'What the hell is that lake doing on top of our mountain?'
I demanded of no one in particular.

As always, we had a couple of choices. Cut left past
the goats and take a long and winding detour around the
lake, where there wasn't much sign of a path. Or cut right,
where a more substantial track reared up a horribly steep
hill. Neither of us mentioned biking back to the saddle and
taking that side trail. As we contemplated the killer hill, a
couple of young dudes on an old motorcycle came down
that way. We waved at them and they rode over. They
looked amused.

'Sigh binoo! We—' pointing to my chest, 'go Erdenet.
Erdenet?'

'*Za, za, za*, Erdenet,' the driver said. '*Ingeed*,' pointing back over the hill, 'ingeed, ingeed, ingeed,' making a roller-coaster with his hand, 'ingeed, ingeed, ingeed. Okay?'

'Does that mean there are six hills?' Tama asked me.

'Seven, I think.'

'What does 'ingeed' mean?'

'Faaaark.'

'Unadag dugui?' The motorcyclist pointed to our bikes.

'Za, za, dugui,' I said. 'Mörön Khövsgöl—dugui, dugui, dugui—' I made an earthquake with my hand, 'Mörön Khentii.'

'Khentii?! Soloitoi!' he said, and this time I remembered what it meant. They laughed and laughed. We didn't. The driver gunned the motorbike and they whizzed up the hill, without pedalling, just sitting there on that thing, laughing and burning dirty unregulated Russian petrol and destroying their precious environment.

'Man, I wish we had one of those,' Tama said.

'Me too.'

We tried to cycle up the hill but after a couple of wincing, stabbing minutes we had to get off and push. Luckily we were almost out of water so the bikes were a bit lighter than usual. From the top of the outcrop we could see the full expanse of the lake. It stretched for at least five kilometres across the valley floor. There was no way we could've got round it to the left—that was something—as beyond the blue of the lake there was a wide white shore of sand or salt, going for kilometres in places. The road we were on was smooth and flat, courtesy of a bulldozer manicure. Tama smashed down the first valley into a beautifully graded wide horseshoe bend, right then left; I didn't try to keep up, just watched him drift off over a rise and out of sight. On the far side I found Tama stopped in the middle of the road.

'What the hell?'

The road shot down a hill and bisected a corner of the lake in a ruler-straight line. Thousands of tonnes of rocks had been dug up from somewhere and crushed and dumped across the lake then rolled flat so people could drive over it. It was like a dam, except it didn't seem to be damming anything. After our long days in the untainted wilderness, suddenly all this taint—and no people, no machinery, no signage around to make it feel normal. In the orphaned right-hand corner of lake a group of horses licked dejectedly at the water. We rode past them over the scar of rubble. We rode past excavated dirt cliffs, holes in the ground, piles of rubbish, burnt things, more gloomy horses. It was the kind of place where Doctor Who hid from Daleks. Or Mongolian Death Worms.

Further on the water ended and dusty white sand covered a dead flat plain, slowly taking over the grass at its edges. Tama got me to ride out onto it and pose for some photos, but once I rode onto the sand and my tyres got stuck it became clear it wasn't sand. It was too . . . crunchy. It must've had something to do with Erdenet's copper mine, something scabby. I put my contaminated shoes on my pedals and biked out of it as quick as possible.

A few hundred metres later we came over a rise and saw a massive red pipe with the number 5 on it sticking out onto the not-sand it was probably responsible for. The road led towards the pipe and god-knows-what beyond it so we cut right and followed some bulldozer tracks up a hill away from the not-lake. It was going well until we almost rode over the edge of a ten-metre canyon gouged out of the hill. Tama swore and slammed on his brakes. I nearly rode into his panniers; if I had, I might have knocked him over the edge onto the fresh orange clay below.

'Good reflexes, bro,' I said quietly. Tama didn't reply.

We stood there clutching our brakes, staring down at the less-than-convenient construction road running perpendicular to us. We headed around the edge of the canyon and carried our bikes down a clay bank, then pushed them up the other side in the muddy ruts of a bulldozer. I could have murdered a Mars Bar. At the top of a small hill we came onto a random goat track and followed that. As we gained altitude I could see the fake lake and fake desert stretching out further, eating away at the hills. The number 5 pipe ploughed through the countryside, slicing through hills, filling up valleys; pipes 1 through 4 were nowhere to be seen. I felt like a medieval peasant getting his first terrifying glimpse of a Dickensian nightmare. From the sweaty top of the ridge we glimpsed the edge of what was hopefully the outskirts of Erdenet. Thunder cracked in the background. Storm clouds were massing to the north and east.

'We don't wanna be anywhere near this shit when the rain starts,' Tama said. At that moment the wind picked up, blowing tiny white granules across the hills. We cut across untracked paddock, making for the nearest buildings. They were not quite what I was expecting. Up close, the concrete warehouses seemed to be part of a decommissioned gulag. They were massive and had big numbers on the walls, long grass out front, the doors and windows boarded up, walls tinselled with rusty barbed wire. We pedalled hard through the empty dirt roads and turned a corner onto a paved street where we were confronted by a full platoon of Mongolian soldiers in drill formation goosestepping up the hill towards us. Tama glanced at me in alarm and swerved left down a side street and I pumped my brakes and followed him as thunder crackled overhead. The side street popped out in a subdivision of some demented Soviet suburban utopia or Potemkin village and we were surrounded by outsized retro bungalows crumbling to the ground behind white picket fences. In the sky there was a grey thunderhead shaped exactly like a mushroom cloud. The lightning started.

'Let's get a move on!' Tama yelled.

We raced around the corner and were confronted by a wide concrete motorway that was buzzing with traffic like I'd forgotten still existed. As we stopped to put on our helmets a thick, twisting pole of lightning zapped from the clouds to the ground and back again. Tama took off along the verge of the motorway, pedalling like a maniac. I struggled to keep up but couldn't—until he got a puncture. Tama did his quickest change-job yet as lightning sizzled around us to the left and right and straight ahead, the thunder louder and closer to the strikes. A police car drove by and slowed down to check us out but didn't stop. With a jolt I remembered the weed. I hurriedly emptied my pockets onto the roadside.

'What are you doing?'

'Getting rid of the drugs!'

'What if some cop stops to help me change my tyre? We'll be screwed!'

I clawed in the gravel to collect the pot then ran to a conveniently placed storm drain and threw it down. Tama had finished changing his tyre and he biked off ahead of me. I hustled to catch up. The sky darkened, cars and trucks beeped and flashed their lights at us. The fences and factories of Erdenet loomed to the right. It started raining, hard.

I couldn't catch up to Tama. I wanted to ride on the road where it was faster but I was scared to. I wanted to put on my jacket and my headtorch but there wasn't time. Up ahead Tama had stopped by the side of the road. As I got nearer he pointed down a driveway to a massive brick building. I nodded and followed as he zanged up the driveway, expecting to be struck by lightning any second, my skeleton shining through irradiated flesh. My heart hammered in my chest but I couldn't hear it over the hail now smashing down everywhere. We pedalled like crazy for what turned out to be the Erdenet carpet factory and lugged our bikes up the stairs to the front doors as the hail increased in volume. The doors were locked but we were under cover and safe from the lightning that was striking all around. Outside the sky was the colour of hail and the trees lining the driveway bent sideways in the screaming wind. We sat with our backs against the glass doors that led into an empty uncarpeted foyer and drank the last of our water.

When the storm finally passed we put on our helmets and headtorches and carried our bikes back down the steps. There was meant to be a couple of hotels along or off Erdenet's main street, Sükhbaatar Gudamj, which we may or may not have been on.

'It's getting dark,' Tama said. 'Gotta get a move on.'

'What difference does it make now?'

But Tama was in fight-or-flight mode, on the mission. I cursed and kicked hard to keep up. Tama turned right up a side street, which seemed crazy until we hit a major city street. It had pavement, it even had a traffic light, and its redness seemed a potent symbol of something. We followed the road, looking out in the dimness for hotels, potholes, broken glass. My tyres felt exposed and fragile. We rode past a building with a giant mural of Lenin on it and came to a grocery store.

'Let's stop here and drink some Cokes,' Tama said.

'I don't drink that shit.'

Tama stopped. 'Why do you have to be so *negative* about everything?'

'I'm not negative, I just don't drink Coca-Cola.'

'Whatever.' He stalked inside and got a Coke. I got a Fanta.

'Please, Tama, can we fucking *slow down* now? We *don't* need to get a move on!'

'If we hadn't got a move on back there we would've got smashed in that hailstorm.'

'Okay. Yes. Totally. But, we've made it. There are hotels everywhere.' I gestured vaguely.

'Like where?'

'Uh . . . like back there!' In our haste we'd rode half a block past a large, ugly Soviet-era hotel: the Selenge. Not the most auspicious of names, but at least it wasn't called The Lake and Effluent.

The walls and ceiling of the Selenge Hotel loomed over me in a *faux*-opulent vertigo of lacquered wood, buckled mirrors and fake gold trim. I expected the whole thing to collapse at the slightest provocation. Standing at reception waiting to be served, our bikes left defenceless outside, I was convinced that someone would steal everything, ruin our trip, bankrupt us.

One of the clerks wheeled our muddy, disgraceful steeds off into a storeroom and made an elaborate show of locking the door, but I still felt uneasy. We were taken up three flights of stairs and shown a room with scarlet fever wallpaper, two beds and a ceiling that was taller than a tent. We nodded and went downstairs to pay whatever it cost, then helped the porters lug our innumerable belongings upstairs. I made sure to carry my backpack with the half-ounce of yesterday's weed in it. With a huge sigh of relief Tama sat down on his bed—the mattress gave way beneath him, his knees jackknifed into his chest and his body disappeared. I laughed crazily and after a stunned second he joined in. I tested my bed: it only had three slats, positioned at shoulder, mid-back and buttock level. I sat on the bed at buttock level and caught a glimpse of myself in the mirror.

It was quite a sight. My hairy, dirty, dishevelled face was dominated by a pair of dinner-plate eyes, dilated and uncomprehending. It looked like a caveman that someone had dressed and trapped inside—it couldn't operate door handles—while they worked out what to do with it. Tama looked slightly less feral, but his eyes were ketamine-deep too and he was moving with the jerky, anxious motions of the hunted. He looked like a male model who'd just woken up in a dumpster.

'This isn't much of a holiday!' I said with a mix of outrage and pride. Tama sniggered.

'I was thinking that today,' he said. 'I had a thought of us sitting in a sauna, and I was like, "Oh yeah, *that's* what a holiday's like. . ."'

But this was a special kind of holiday. This was *misadventure tourism*, and us morons wanted plenty of suffering to go with our scenery. Tama went to the lobby to get some beers and I had a shower in the ensuite. The shower had a cold tap and a very cold tap, and it sprayed water from the faucets rather than the showerhead. There was no packet soap. Faced with a proper flush toilet for the first time since Ulaanbaatar, I did a gargantuan relief-poo that nearly blocked the bowl.

An hour or so later we ventured out for dinner. It was late by now, but Tama had a good feeling about a place called Casablanca Bar that promised 'huge leather couches' and was located inside a department store really close by. We wandered up the road, savouring the sensation of not riding. A lone horseman clomped his way down an otherwise empty main street. Quintessential image of old ways persisting in a brave new world—*tick*.

After ten minutes we hadn't seen any department stores. Walking back towards our hotel, baffled but not quite defeated, we cut across a potholed courtyard and asked some beggars huddled in the eaves of a condemned building where Casablanca Bar was. They pointed mutely behind them. Down a dark corridor we could make out a dim, intermittent light. Tama opened a heavy door onto the blare of Mongol pop, a haggard strobe light and an abject dancefloor. The joint was empty save for eight or nine girls in miniskirts propped up against the bar with bored work faces. No customers.

Tama and I had rocked some sub-par dancefloors in our time, but not now. I went to the cute bartender and shouted 'Casablanca', did she know where Casablanca was? She stared at me with unvarnished contempt. I tried again and after a gruesome pause she was kind enough to shake her head.

We walked back out to the courtyard and asked the beggars again. This time they were more specific: *next* to the nightclub, *züün, züün. Ingeed, ingeed.* Past the nightclub the corridor led into a flooded mini-plaza that was enclosed by empty shopfronts with broken windows. I stepped into a muddy puddle and swore, ready to give up, but Tama heard a noise down an even narrower corridor. We crept around a corner, wobbled across some planks laid over the muck and found ourselves at the entrance to Casablanca Bar.

Small groups of men were fondling cigars and drinking shots from bottles of Chinggis Gold in a dark, smoky room with a *Godfather* vibe. Zang. We were shown to some huge leather couches and collapsed happily into them, then ordered a couple of beers, a couple of soups and two of the most expensive item on the menu, figuring it was most likely to contain high-grade meat and lots of it.

We weren't disappointed. The most expensive item on the menu was twin mountains of tender beef chunks, piled on a thick bedrock of potato wedges and all mixed through with tangy gravy. In the low light I couldn't be more specific than that, but it tasted magnificent. I started at the top and worked my way steadily downward like an open-cut mining company with a fresh hill. I chewed only when absolutely necessary. When I finished my meal, plus a few of the chips Tama couldn't polish off, I felt happy and burpy and almost relaxed.

I was putting away the beers, getting ready to hit that

crummy discotheque, but Tama 2000 was uncharacter-istically munted. I bludged a cigarette off a table of big Mongolian lads and a couple of minutes later they called us over. There were three of them, our age or younger. They poured big shots of Chinggis all round and were very pleased when we knew how to drink vodka properly, with the finger-flick and all—unless they were laughing at us. The group's alpha male, a formidable dude called Bold—'Steel'—told us in good English that he was a basketball champion. He was certainly tall enough and he was dressed like a b-ball star, right down to the old-school Air Jordans. Bold trained every day; soon he would go to UB, then America, to play for the LA Lakers or even the Chicago Bulls. He loved the basket-ball heroes I had loved in my youth: Michael Jordan, Charles Barkley, Dennis Rodman ('He sexed Madonna!'). He poured out another round of shots.

'In day, we play basketball. In night—we drink!' We drank. I suggested we play basketball with them tomorrow. He smiled condescendingly.

'I am a big man,' he declared, 'a big man in a big country.' He pounded his chest. 'Big country—big history—big Chinggis!' He threw his shot down. We laughed and cheered. I scabbed another smoke, but the headrush was so intense I had to step out into the courtyard for some fresh air, Bold's words ringing in my ears.

As the one true father of Mongolia, I am like Captain Cook, Ned Kelly and Māui rolled into one. My number-one military innovation—my 'killer app'—is meritocracy. I promote people based on their ability, not their lineage, and it works . . . but I can't fully commit to it. On my deathbed I am faced with an impossible choice: which of my

10,000 sons should inherit my realm? In the end I go with my favou-
rite: Ögödei, the drunk. The rest is a stupefying orgy of fast horses,
beautiful slavegirls, decadence, genocide and mismanagement. My
unbeatable horsemen continue to surge over the unharvested steppe
in a tsunami of carnage that rolls from Vietnam to Poland, sure—
but then we rolled away again, and after a century or two it's like
it never happened. Like incompetent board members who failed to
follow a corporation's actually rather good mission statement, my
sons and daughters run my Mongol nation, the greatest land empire
the world has ever known, into the sandy ground.

I staggered back inside. Bold's friend had cornered Tama
and was talking passionately about something. Without
missing a beat, Bold told me that Mongolian girls were the
best, the absolute best, and that the girls in the countryside
had the best pussies in the world. I said I was sure he was
onto something, although Aussie girls were pretty filthy too.
He insisted that Australian women, even Kylie Minogue,
were nothing compared to his latest girlfriend, and I had
to concede the point. I told Bold that we had cycled from
Khantai to Selenge and found these huge fields of marijuana just growing wild, tonnes of it. Did Mongolians like
to smoke marijuana? He smiled.

'Mongolians like marijuana, yes.' His smile died. 'But we
do not like jail. In Mongolia, if you are catch with drugs, you
go to jail for many years.'

I said this sounded bad.

'You do not know. The main jail in Mongolia is in Ulaanbaatar, *under* Ulaanbaatar—it is like a dungeon. In winter,
many people freeze to death.'

I said this sounded very bad. He nodded seriously.

'I am a pro athlete. I have no time for drugs.' He reached for the vodka bottle. It was empty. He suggested that me and Tama buy the next one. I was all for this, but Tama was edgy and wanted to leave.

'Sorry, we must go home now, we are too tired,' I said.

'No problem! You buy the bottle—for us.'

Bold was still friendly but he was also very firm. His friends looked at me. Tama nodded quickly. We bought them a half-litre bottle of the bar's second-cheapest vodka and said our goodbyes before walking out of Casablanca into an ankle-deep puddle.

'What's the hurry, Tama 2000—can't you handle the jandal?' I punched him on the shoulder. He grimaced.

'That dude I was talking to, I think he might've been a gangster,' he said. 'He kept saying, "I have no gun, but government bad, shoot government! But I have three children, so—no shoot." His brother was in prison in UB, for drugs. It sounds fucken horrible in there.'

When we got back to the hotel I was determined to get rid of the weed. I couldn't find the bag at first and started to panic, but then I remembered I'd stashed it up behind the curtain rails. I emptied the bag into the toilet and pressed flush. The pot swirled happily around on the surface of the water. I flushed again: no luck. With a sigh I reached my hand into the bowl, scooped all the weed out and crammed it back into the shopping bag. I went to just throw it out the window but decided against it and sat down on my bed. My knees jack-knifed into my chest and my body disappeared into the sagging mattress and Tama howled with laughter and I howled and we both kept laughing until tears were rolling down our faces.

PART THREE

NOT MUCH OF A
HOLIDAY

REST DAY IN ERDENET

A giant sewing machine was drilling into my head. Tama groaned and pulled back the curtains.

'Concrete mixer,' he said. 'There's a big-arse building site down there.'

Below us was a big pile of orange bricks, mounds of dirty sand that workers were turning into grout and a large, smoke-spewing machine that might well have been a concrete mixer. Tama checked the clock on the GPS: it was 8.01 am.

I had been hoping to sleep in till early afternoon, but now that seemed pretty unlikely. We decided to cut our losses and track down a big cooked breakfast then find a plump *babushka* or two to thrash us with Russian shrubs.

We wandered back down the main street. In the light of day, Erdenet was even more concrete, permanent and inhabited. There were even cars. Compared to the towns we'd been rampaging through, it felt positively metropolitan. Something told me this was a town with bread—*and* cheese. We passed an imposing concrete edifice that called itself the спорт оpoн, which translated roughly to 'SPORTZ PALAZ'. It looked like a healthful tomb.

'Russian massage, bro,' Tama said knowledgeably. 'But first: American breakfast!'

We were looking out for the Sansar Hotel, which *Ronery Pranet* dobbed in as the best bet in Erdenet for a Western-style fry-up. The Sansar did indeed serve a Mongolian-style 'American breakfast' for the hotel's predominantly Korean clientele. Their ideas were approximately fifty per cent aligned with my own. There were eggs and bread, but the bread wasn't toasted, plus it was that disturbing sugary cake-bread popular in Asian countries that had missed out on decades of French oppression. There was sausage too, but it looked and tasted like plastic toy sausage. This didn't stop us getting through it all. Without missing a beat Tama said, 'Shall we go back to the main road and order some pizzas?'

'Hell yes.'

Our second breakfast was a paradise of melted cheese and minced piglet. I felt properly full for the first time in weeks, although I suspected I could inhale another extra-large pizza in half an hour. We were sitting next to a boothful of nattily dressed uni student types, on holiday from UB. They were well-spoken and polite, and after asking us where we were from and where were we going, they quickly lost interest in the boring backpackers and returned to their milkshakes.

We picked up our bathers and towels from the hotel and visited the Sportz Palaz. Inside it was large and empty and echoed like a defunct airport terminal in East Germany. The floor was covered with coarsely woven carpets depicting the Three Manly Sports in bright yellows, reds and greens while the walls were dotted with trophies and medals that sat neglected in dusty glass cabinets. Somehow we managed to ask about saunas and were directed down a flight of imposing granite stairs. Then we steamed ourselves. It was great, you just sat there and the sweat poured out of you, you didn't even have to pedal.

A light-headed hour later we wandered back out onto Erdenet's main street. There was probably a museum to visit, a desolate art gallery, a generic temple—not to mention the city's sole reason for existence, the copper mine. Erdenet means 'with treasure', and the town was built by the Soviets in 1974, literally overnight, after they discovered an entire mountain of copper nearby. The Cold War was still going strong when Erdenet was founded, so the Russians left it off all their maps (and our maps). The Erdenet Mining Corporation apparently arranged guided walks for tourists through the world's fourth largest copper mine, but seeing as how we'd spent yesterday afternoon on an unguided cycle tour through the arse-end of the whole enterprise, I was happy to consider that particular attraction 'done'.

Back at the hotel, I borrowed Tama's phone and texted my mum: 'still alive. halfway to moron. x.' Then I had a great chat to Laura. It was wonderful to hear her voice, tinny and distant though it was.

'How's Laura?' Tama asked when I was finished.

'Good, she's . . . actually, I dunno. Mainly I just talked about Mongolia.'

'Huh.'

Tama spread the maps out across his bed. According to our original plans, we should've been about one hundred kilometres to the northeast, on our way from Baruunbüren to Amarbayasgalant Khiid. We were still hoping to make it to Khentii province without having to deviate back through UB, but were abandoning our more ambitious/suicidal plans to trailblaze our way across the northern reaches of the Khan Khentii Strictly Protected Area. If we headed east and south from Erdenet we'd pass through Orkhon, Bayangol and Bornuur, then in a few days we'd be ready to stage a crossing into Terelj National Park from Batsumber, sixty-three kilometres north of UB. The only problem was, still, the lack of paths heading east–west through Terelj National Park.

We now knew what it was like to traverse Mongolia without the assistance of a dotted red line. We had travelled one heroic kilometre down to the shores of Khövsgöl *nuur* and back again, not to mention round and round in circles in the swamps of Tsagaan-Üür for two whole kilometres. Tama stared at Terelj, then Khövsgöl, then back at Terelj. He shook his head.

'Those Terelj mountains . . . they're way bigger than all the stuff we've been riding through.'

'What did the woman in the UB outdoor store say about them?'

'She said she'd never met anyone who'd gone up that way. Ever.'

'Oh.'

'And that no one lives there. No one.'

'Oh. Well, I bet Chinggis Khaan went there, all the time. How much bigger are they?'

'They're like . . . two thousand three hundred, two thousand four hundred metres—shit, there's a twenty-eight-hundred-metre peak just past Batsumber! The Tiger Mountain crossing was only nineteen, no, eighteen hundred metres. So, it's gonna be—'

'De-va-sta-ting?'

'Yeah.' Then, in a quiet, determined voice, 'It's all good.'

I groaned, then heard myself say, 'Sweet as.'
Neither of us smiled, or backed down.

Itinerary v2.0

(Erdenet, rest day) (today)

Day 14: To Orkhon, or close by: 106 km

Day 15: Camping out on way to Bornuur: 80 km

Day 16: To Bornuur: 100 km

Day 17: To Batsumber: short day—45 km (get advice about ways into Terelj?) (From WHO?)

Day 18: Camping out on way to Terelj: 60 km (?? 30+ km of bush-bashing over 2100-metre-high mountain??)

Day 19: To Terelj?: 50 km (??? eaten by bears and/or wolves?????)

Day 20: Camping out, on way to Möngönmorit: 40–60 km

Day 21: To Möngönmorit: 40–60 km

Day 22: To Baganuur: 64 km

Day 23: To Tsenkhermandal (or Jargaltkhaan): 67 km (or 112 km)

Day 24: Camping out on Mörön *gol*: 40–70 km (or 90–120 km)

Day 25: To Mörön Khenti: whatever it takes

Itinerary v2.0 was notably lacking in rest days. It also had us arriving in Mörön the day before our flight from Ulaanbaatar to Beijing. That meant we'd have to hitch back that night or first thing the next morning—or miss our plane, overstay our one-month visa and end up camping on the floor of the New Zealand embassy, if there even was one. The next fortnight was going to be hard. Really hard. The trip was *already* bloody hard, so this shit ... its hardness was scarcely imaginable. Well, if it got too much we could always—actually, no, we'd be on our own out there. We were going to have to deal with it.

We did a big shop at Erdenet's only supermarket. Tama found some rough-n-ready muesli, and over in the far corner, its golden glow emanating from an antique refrigerator, I saw a dozen stacked-up bars of cheese. Cheddar, no less. Booya. We bought two whole kilograms of the stuff as well as the only sunscreen we could find, which seemed to contain not insignificant amounts of bleach. Then we trudged off to the nearest internet cafe and spent the next six hours drinking beers and updating the blog. I did the words and Tama did the pictures and the complaining about slow upload speeds and Cyrillic keyboards.

As the sentences fell out of me, I realised that so far Mongolia had been everything I'd hoped for, and heaps more. It was bigger, friendlier, prettier, more random, wilder. It was also much harder—the cycling, the eating, the communicating, the pooing—all of it. When we left the internet cafe I was exhausted but also tipsy and a bit wired. Tama was subdued. Just before I fell asleep that night a plaintive mumble carried across the room.

'What?' I asked.

'I said, there's no real reason why we can't go through Ulaanbaatar. I know we said we weren't going to—but, sheeeeit . . .'

'I guess . . .'

'It'd still be Mörön to Mörön, wouldn't it?' His voice was tense. 'I mean, we'll still be biking to Mörön, and it'll still be fucking hard . . . I just don't know about bush-bashing over those crazy hills.'

'Me neither, bro.'

'Maybe if we didn't have the bikes . . .'

'Yeah, we could tramp it for sure . . .'

'So, fuck it—let's just go to UB,' he said.

'. . . Okay.'

'It's not, like, cheating or anything.'

'Course not.' I tried to laugh off that absurd notion.

'We could have a rest day. Drop off some of our cold-weather gear. Do some more blogging.'

'True. Yeah, I reckon we need to.'

'Okay, sweet. G'night, bro.'

'G'night.'

Soon Tama was fake-snoring. I lay there staring into the blackness, a manic smile of relief pulling at my cheeks.

DAY 14: AN UNEVENTFUL DAY

The next morning Tama returned to the internet cafe to back up his photos. I found myself alone in the hotel room twiddling my thumbs. After this it would be back to that tiny tent for two weeks, living in each other's scabby pockets, no privacy, no lockable doors . . . I decided to seize my chance.

I peeled off my sticky, vaguely beer-smelling MORON T-shirt and let it fall to the floor, then I slid my saggy, once-white briefs off. Under the shower's just-warm-enough dribble I put the money in the slot and fired up a greatest hits of my sex life past and present . . . *Laura's upturned eyes, deep and serious, her lips inches from my crotch . . . Fondling Rosanna in that drunken elevator, then Rosanna on her back on the carpet, knees by her ears . . . Kate on her back, ears by her knees . . . Fiona staggering into my bedroom, my voice loud: 'Keep your boots on'* . . . *Fiona keeping her boots on* . . . Man, we've got a long way to ride today. *Finger-banging that girl—Nina? Nancy?—on that balcony, Nancina breathless in the night: 'Fuck me'* . . . Here we go, more soap. *Laura bent over in the Cambodian night, full moon shining on her triumphant arse* . . . Remember to dump the weed before we leave. *Laura reverse cowgirl in my tent that*

first time, my hands on her tits . . . That Mongolian maiden in the
tent, my hands on her tits, Tama's hands on her arse, Tama's—
Wait. Tama can wait outside. What if it's raining? In the
vestibule. What about the bikes? The cheese. What?

My cock sagged a bit. I kept trying.

That British girl on the train sucking me off in the dining
car . . . Drew Barrymore twenty years ago, masturbating in a spa
bath, a whole movie theatre full of 22-year-old cheerleaders dressed
as Russian schoolgirls watching a porno of me fucking Drew
Barrymore in a spa bath and they're all masturbating over it,
dildo-ing themselves and panting and moaning—don't forget the
cheese—*my cock bursting through the screen, the girls all come*
in screaming unison, a United Nations-style, all-female bukkake
party of masturbating girls squirting into my face splayed twitch-
ing pink brown pussy everywhere a cacophony of mons and moans
me coming all over it FUCK—

I ejaculated against the bathroom wall. There wasn't
much of it. A savage pounding in my lower back made me
crouch in the shower feeling dizzy, self-violated. Maybe I
should've saved those precious vitamins and minerals for
the ride.

We pedalled slowly out of Erdenet down grim cobblestone
streets, past half-hearted signs for TATTOO and BEST URBAN
STYLE tacked to sagging Soviet apartment blocks that were
surely built long before 1974, but no, before 1974 Erdenet
didn't exist. A derelict bus shelter said ERD NE, ERDE T,
R N ET over and over in flaking paint. Erdenet's industrial
zone began before its residential zone had properly ended.

On the roadside, ominous white pipes with disintegrating cladding crept past shops for half a kilometre to a nightmare factory that towered above us spewing black smoke into the sky, a huge number painted on its smokestacks: not '1984' but '1986'. Tama got a puncture and had to stop and fix it in a carpark with no cars but plenty of cows, the cows sniffing at broken glass and chewing on plastic bags.

Just past the city limits we slowed down at the sight of a nomad who was berating a motorist in a BMW stopped in the middle of the road. The horseman pointed at the Beemer's bent and bloody fender then at a horse lying dying in a ditch with its back leg bent at a gruesome angle. The poor nomad had just become a lot less nomadic.

In the surrounding fields, *gers* sat next to sickly-looking streams I was glad to not be drinking from. On the left, hills led up to the bleakness of the Erdenet copper mine. I squinted, trying to imagine the mountain that had been there forty years ago, but I couldn't see it. We rode hard to get clear of the industrial skank.

Twenty kilometres down the road Tama stopped and turned to me.

'Where my cheese at?'

'Oh! It's—in the hotel fridge.'

'Damn, bro, that was your one errand while I was at the internet cafe! What were you doing?'

'I was, uh, making powdered milk. Sorry, dude.'

We cycled on in cheeseless silence. After a couple of hours I noticed something strange: I wasn't getting tired. The road was sealed, smooth and easy, and likely to stay that way for a while. We were flying along the main trunk line that connected Erdenet with Darkhan, another industrial town that lay about halfway between UB to the south and Russia's Ulan-Ude to the north. There was much more traffic now, but only relative to deepest Khövsgöl, with one car or truck every five minutes rather than every five hours. The main road had another morale-boosting feature: kilometre markers counting our progress out of Erdenet. On the flats we could manage close to twenty kilometres an hour, which meant one encouragement-pole every three minutes. There were still plenty of hills, grinding hours of them, but on the big-arse downhills our speed would punch past fifty kilometres an hour—Tama maxed out at fifty-nine—and then the distance markers fair whizzed by.

After four hours we stopped for lunch by a stream, already sixty-five kilometres away from the garbage-munching cows of Erdenet. We pushed our bikes over a lumpy field and collapsed in the grass where we were instantly savaged by sandflies.

'It's good being mumble again,' Tama mumbled.

'What?'

'It's good being on THE ROAD again.'

I nodded in agreement, even though Tama had his cowboy hat over his face. I was glad for the corrupting smoothness of tarseal. Also I was happy just to be moving again. That rest day, although physically necessary, was hard on the mind. It raised tricky questions, like, *why*? Why do this to yourself? But now that we were back on the mission, panting and sweating and chewing up those white lines, the pain was its own reward. We watched Mongolian holiday-makers bathe in the Baruunbüren stream. Their car stereos provided tinny yet soothing background music and despite the insect bites I nodded off for twenty minutes.

A couple of kilometre markers later, we passed the turn-off to Amarbayasgalant Khiid. The Lamaist monastery was fifty kilometres up the road. It was hard to know what all this yellow-hatted Tibetan Buddhism was doing so far north of the Himalayas.

'Hey Tama, it's a *Lama*-ist monastery!' I said. He shrugged and kept riding.

It was cloudy but still the sun hammered and nailed my legs. I sweated through my shirt until it was a sodden disgrace with salty white high-tide lines showing through against the blue. At an afternoon piss stop I convinced Tama to let me film a 360-degree pan of the steppes that culminated in a close-up of Tama's urine, in profile, streaming across the frame in a shonky golden arc. It would've been perfect except I accidentally filmed the end of his knob and ruined the shot.

In a couple of hours the kilometre markers ticked over to one hundred, the most I'd ever ridden in a day, and by the time we reached 106 we were in Orkhon. It was still light. I could've easily ridden another twenty kilometres and collapsed in a heap after that, but instead we pulled up at a truck stop with some picnic tables on a balcony and a commanding view of the Orkhon *gol*.

While I waited for my beer I did yoga in the carpark: eagle pose, Zoolander pose, marmot pose. I felt fit, healthy and, most importantly, capable. A big-eyed boy from the truck stop wanted to have a go on my bike so I unclipped all the bags and helped him on. He was just able to straddle the crossbar and he rode around the carpark in slow, crooked orbits, his face set in a determined grin as he dreamed of growing up to be a moron.

We had a look through the menu but couldn't make head or tail of it. I decided to take matters into my own hands. When a couple of cripplingly shy teenage waitresses came to take our orders I got out the phrasebook and pointed to the words for 'noodle' (гурпнптан), 'mutton' (хоннны мах) and 'soup' (won) over and over again while Tama said helpful things like 'What do *you* recommend?' and 'I'll eat *anything*—whatever *you* think is good.' This charade went on for ten minutes, accompanied by lots of good-natured shoulder-shrugging and smiling from us and deepening frowns from the girls.

Ages later we were presented with two sticky lumps of wheat noodle in bowls of hot water with some undercooked mutton floating on the side. It seemed our performance had scared the waitresses off adding any other ingredients to our dinners. It was by far the blandest meal we had eaten in Mongolia, even with the addition of pickled ginger and too much tabasco sauce.

Afterwards the truck-stop owner came and sat with us while we tucked into some beers. He was a nice man with a kind, acne-scarred face and the blue-and-white-striped shirt of an overgrown cabin boy. He asked if we wanted a room for the night. We pointed to our bags, our summer tent, and gestured that we were going to *maikhan* by the *mörön*. He frowned and picked up the phrasebook. It took him a while but finally he pointed to the Mongolian word for 'mosquito'.

It was nearly dark by the time we drunkenly pushed our bikes through a confusing landscape of sand dunes and tussock to a flattish spot near the river. We stumbled down for a wash, but up close the water had the sweet stink of rotting grass and cow manure. The river mud got thicker and it felt like there were bones underneath it. We decided to abandon that project. Four hundred kilometres and eight hundred years upstream, Chinggis's son Ögödei had founded the first Mongol capital of Karakorum; I could see why he hadn't built it here.

Back at the tent we found the truck-stop owner was right about that mosquito. It was a bastard.

DAY 15: A KIWI SHORTCUT

The day began with a good solid yoga and mosquito-bite-scratching session (filmed it), then we chowed down on big bowls of muesli with powdered milk and water (filmed it). As we packed up our campsite a herd of wild horses thundered by just twenty metres away (filmed it, yes!).

Biking back to the main road through the sand, we had an argument about me filming too much stuff (thought about filming it). Tama said we needed to save the camera memory in case we ended up bush-bashing through Terelj National Park.

'Aren't we going to UB instead?' I said, alarmed. 'I thought we decided yesterday—'

'We might, and we might not,' Tama said gruffly. 'We just might . . . change our minds.'

Tama's use of the royal 'we' made me want to punch us/him in our/his royal mouth. I wasn't about to just *change my mind* about meeting a muddy death in the trackless wilds. Then I got a fucking puncture, and Tama didn't offer to help fix it.

Back at the truck stop we asked the owner for directions through to Bayangol. The main road headed east to

Khotol (20 km), veered northeast up to Darkhan (53 km), then backtracked due south (73 km) before finally arriving in Bayangol. Surely there was a shortcut for the main route from Khotol to Bayangol—a shortcut that would save us, like, 90 kilometres, almost a whole day's riding?

The truck-stop owner frowned at our maps. He seemed to know of a 'short' (or '*shuud*', meaning, who knows—'dead end'?), but the short/*shuud* was very complicated. He also appeared to have something against a town that sounded like 'Sashket', a name he spat out with religious disapproval and that we couldn't find on our map. Eventually he gave up and just pointed down the road, so we bought ten litres of *tom us* off his son and crossed the Orkhon *gol* on a bridge that had thankfully not been washed away.

On the east side of the river Mongols were smoking fish over fires and drying them on the walls of their huts. The fish skins were a sickly burnt-yellow colour but despite their ugliness they were oddly appealing, plus you could order by pointing. I asked Tama if we should buy some.

'Nah, those are river fish—you don't wanna eat that filth.'

'Actually, I reckon I *do* wanna eat that filth.'

'Even though they come from that scabby river?'

'Yeah, and?'

'The river you were totally grossed out by last night?'

'. . . Okay, maybe I *don't* wanna eat that filth. But still.'

I rode east in a disgruntled silence, the flesh of those smoked river fish melting in the mouth of my mind like the tenderest salmon, the most succulent pork. Somehow it was already late morning. The sun was roasting fish and humans both and we were behind schedule, again.

On the left side of the road the townspeople of Orkhon had built a striking concrete tableau and painted the shit out of it. The rising sun sent lemon yellow rays into a baby blue sky and urged on the excessive growth of two massive, steroidal stalks of golden wheat, while in the centre of the sun there stood a muscular, patriotic sheep. It was Socialist Realism meets *Sesame Street*, and it cheered me up a bit.

Half an hour down the road a couple of shabby dirt paths curled off to the right in a southeasterly fashion. This might've been our 'short' to Bayangol—or it might've been a dusty wild-goose chase. There was a large farmhouse at the junction and we went to ask for directions. At the front gate we were welcomed by a ferocious dog who tried to bite his way through his chain.

We met a farmer with no shirt on and a gut that in certain Pacific Island cultures would be indicative of great wealth. He led us into his farmhouse, insisted we have some salty Mongol tea, tried to feed us lunch even though it was 10.45 am, demanded we stay the night even though it was 10.45 am, stared at our maps blankly, got out some maps of his own and stared at them blankly, then took Tama's pen and started ruling lines from Orkhon straight to Ulaanbaatar irrespective of topography, townships or tracks.

Fifteen minutes later we staggered outside with our defaced map, determined to ignore the dude's advice. This was easily done since we couldn't understand a word of it.

A smoky factory on the horizon grew larger and smokier. Two thousand pedal strokes later we reached a town called Saikhan, which of course meant 'beautiful'. It wasn't. We pulled over in a hot, dusty carpark with views past power pylons and heroin-addiction-inducing apartment blocks to the factory's smokestacks. A young dude in a baseball cap was slouched on a motorcycle. We asked him for directions to Bayangol, pointing past the factory. He nodded, but noncommittally, and this put me off since I didn't want to spend another afternoon riding through toxic waste. Neither did Tama.

We decided to stick to the main road and try for a crossing a bit further up. Before we left Saikhan Tama went into a grocery store for sugary drink and came out with a couple of strawberry frozen yoghurts in plastic cups. They had the potential to be delicious, but were diabolically hard to eat. I had gnawed off the top layer and was trying to access more yoghurt when I squeezed the cup too hard. My dairy treat flew into the air and hung there for a tantalising instant, before landing a couple of metres away in the dust. The kid from the grocery store and his squinty little brother were watching from the doorway, and while Tama laughed they took pity on me and got me another on the house. I did exactly the same thing. Tama gave me the rest of his. I was nibbling at it very carefully when I heard a loud click. The grocery store kid had his mobile phone out to take a photo of the unkempt hairy sunburnt yuppy peasant who couldn't handle his yoghurt.

A few kilometres on the road started bending to the north, as we feared it would. We were now riding away from Bayangol, and every kilometre we travelled would have to be paid back in full later on. To our right a stately old steam train chugged slowly southwest across the fields, pulling a long line of carriages.

'I wonder if there's a path alongside the train tracks,' Tama said.

'Surely. For access!'

We approached a tiny town with a sign saying но7мон, not pronounced 'ho-seven-mo'. On the outskirts were a couple of farmers, one fat and one skinny, both topless in the heat. We thrust the map at them and told them there was a 'short' across to Bayangol. They nodded, pointing up the road, then right. Somehow Tama got the impression they said 'two kilometres'. We thanked them and cycled on and soon came to a thin trail heading right, east, the way we wanted to go. We bumped into the fields following a narrow path that quickly became a semi-path, then a joke of a path, overgrown with useless low-grade ganja and our tyres slipping in the sandy soil. It was slow-going, with plenty of tipping and cursing. When Tama got off his bike and pushed I did the same.

The train tracks ran along the top of a three-metre-high berm, but there was no sign of the access road we had hoped for. Instead we came to a rusty old barbed-wire fence. It was the first fence we'd seen in rural Mongolia, presumably there to stop wild horses and stray Mongolian Death Worms from wandering up the berm and getting unravelled by a coal train. We hefted our bikes over the fence, then scrambled up the berm.

Selenge province unrolled before us: low green hills, an occasional tree in a semi-cultivated field, blue-brown peaks in the background, all under a sweltering sky. No access road. We could struggle on through the lumpy, sandy, horrid paddock, or ride our bikes along the train line. There couldn't be more than one or two trains between Darkhan and Erdenet per day (so we reasoned), and we had just seen a train go past, so the tracks should be clear for a few hours.

We saddled up and juddered over smashed rock and the rotting wood of the sleepers. I was having a grand old time hollering the chorus of 'Stand By Me' when Tama hollered, 'Train!'

A big red train was indeed hurtling towards us. I slammed on the brakes, leapt off my seat and dragged my bike down the berm, water bottles bouncing from their holders. From the safety of the paddock I looked up and realised the train wasn't exactly *hurtling*. Tama and I laughed sheepishly while we waited for the train to pass by at no more than twenty-five kilometres an hour.

We continued on our way, looking back over our shoulders every few seconds. It was slow and jolty going and seemed to be getting worse, plus the novelty factor was wearing off. About two kilometres to the west we could see the main road to Darkhan. We were travelling directly parallel to that road, much slower than before our shortcut.

After fifty chiropractic minutes we were forced to admit that riding along the train tracks wasn't any better than riding through the field. We heaved the bikes over the barbed-wire fence and struggled along through cannabis, scrub and thistle. We hit a sandy path, and made okay time until the sand thickened. Before long, we were in a mini-desert, surrounded by low sand dunes. My front wheel dug into the sand. This is what they mean by 'hell on wheels', I thought, then I fishtailed and toppled off my bike. Even Tama couldn't plough his way through.

I dragged my bike slowly through the burning sand, utterly dejected, expecting a vulture to land on my shoulder and start nibbling my face. Finally the ground became firmer and we could ride again. A couple of bends on we rode into a stand of dense and incongruous pine trees. We pulled off the trail, grateful for the shade, gulped down some fish sandwiches and collapsed on the tarp in a dead snore.

I woke up slowly and reluctantly. At first I thought I was back in New Zealand on the Kapiti Coast, and half-fancied I could hear the roar of the ocean over the dunes. But the roar got louder and turned into a Land Cruiser that drove right by without seeing us.

On the other side of the pine grove there was a shallow river. The water looked marvellously clear and clean. We were about to strip off for a swim when we heard cries from upstream and saw about thirty teenage Mongol boys swimming in their underpants. They yelled and waved, then ran to pose for photographs with us. The teens had asymmetrical haircuts and the boiled-egg musculature of aspiring bodybuilders. Surrounded by these wannabe-beefcakes, wearing my sunglasses and bike gloves and an idiot grin, I made Gary Glitter look like Mother Teresa. We decided not to join them in the river.

'Where are all the girls?' Tama said wistfully.

'Dunno. Maybe this is, like, a metrosexual boy scout camp?'

Fifty metres upstream we came to a second swimming hole, populated entirely by teenage girls in bikinis. None of them offered to pose with us. We rode through a clump of pines and on the other side could see the edge of a small town dug into the sandy hillside with a train line running through the centre of it. We had a look on the map. There was a little yellow road from Nomgon (HO7MOH) which terminated at Salkhit, possibly pronounced 'Sashket' and the scene of some primal trauma for the truck-stop owner.

This was most likely our current destination. It had been five hours since we left Saikhan; I was amazed by how lost you could get in a pretty much flat field. Meanwhile, the road we wanted to be on, the big red main road to UB, was still five kilometres to the east. Five admittedly hilly kilometres. What to do?

'We could've biked to Darkhan in three hours and be halfway to Bayangol by now,' I said quietly.

'I know.'

Silence, broken by Tama's sigh.

'The train must go to UB as well as Erdenet from here, that's why all those metro teens are here,' he said hopefully. 'Maybe we could wait a few hours and hop a train to UB, hobo-style.'

'It'd probably take us back to Erdenet.'

'You reckon?'

'Dunno, but—fuck that. Let's just try to find the shortcut.'

We rolled through Salkhit, speeding up when we glimpsed a pack of wild children coming for us with jars of strawberries. We found a dirt track leading out of town. It was rutted and dusty and after a few minutes it was clear it was heading not east but due north, straight for Darkhan, forty kilometres in exactly the wrong direction. By now it was a matter of principle to avoid Darkhan at all costs, even though it would have guesthouses, restaurants, desolation, beer.

A vehicle came up behind us and we flagged it down and tried once more to get directions for a shortcut to Bayangol. After a minute of unbridled confusion, the driver crowed, '*Shuud! Shuud!*' and got us to follow him as he turned around and drove back through town then out into some sandy fields littered with broken glass.

'Bayangol! *Shuud!*' he said triumphantly, pointing up a hill with no path on it. He used his hand to evoke a trail that went up and down one big hill, then over a second steeper hill, then up a long slow incline, *ingeed, ingeed, ingeed* all the way to the *tom zam* (main road). We thanked the man profusely and gave him a pack of smokes, then another, while his wife looked at us like we were mildly retarded.

We slogged our way up a rugged hill with the faintest of paths on it. I was sweating like a seahorse. Tama stripped off his sodden riding shirt.

'Ingot, ingot, ingot, fucken ingot!' I said.

From the top of the hill twin trails rollercoasted sharply down, up, and down out of sight. I went first. It was hair-raising even before I noticed the little chunks of barbed wire sticking out of the ground. I pointed to the path and heard Tama yell in surprise and when I looked back he was a couple of metres off the track, recovering from a swerve. For the next half hour we rode with our eyes locked just ahead of our front wheels, weaving back and forth around half-buried barbed wire, teeth gritted for the dramatic pop-and-burst. The valley to the right was a chaos of berms and trenches. Massive man-made corrugations and scarifications stretched for over a kilometre in some cryptic, illegible pattern. We stopped and stared.

'What the hell?'

'It must be so animals can shelter,' Tama said. 'Like, if the wind's coming from the north, they hang out on the south side.'

I thought about this for a second.

'What kind of herder has access to that kind of earth-moving equipment?'

'Good call. Maybe it's an old Russian military base. Or a nuclear test site.'

'Are you sure we're going in the right direction?'

The sun was behind one of many clouds. I had no idea were east was. We could've been heading back to Darkhan, or Orkhon, or anywhere.

Tama checked his compass.

'We're kinda heading north again,' he said quietly. 'Hopefully we'll go right in a second.'

I groaned and mounted my bike and we rode feebly up a long hard hill. I was not cut out for this. The pain took over and all I could think about was spreading it evenly over both legs, making sure my calves got it as well as my thighs. I cursed the heat, prayed for some wind, some rain.

Up a valley to our left was a white fullstop of a *ger* and a faint snarling that grew louder as two frenzied *ger* dogs streaked towards us, barking horribly. Tama and I snarled and barked back, loud and genuinely savage. I was so fucked off at those mutts for choosing *now* of all times to make a fuss that in my exhaustion I imagined them getting close enough to attack. I'd jump off my bike, unclip the metal fuel bottle from my pannier and as the dogs flew at me I'd swing the bottle baseball-style with a hard hearty *thunk* into one mutt's skull and then the other, I'd knock those rabies bags out of the air and as they lay whimpering and twitching on the ground I'd pound that fuel bottle into their heads and their dog-faces would come apart like rotten jellymeat, I'd smear their infected canine brains across the grass and I'd realise I was still barking and I'd stop, my satisfaction replaced by remorse and horror, I'd hastily jam a rolled-up 10,000-tugrug note into the collapsed skull of each animal as compensation to their owner and ride, ride away as fast as I could . . .

Luckily the dogs backed off. If animals really can smell fear, perhaps they can smell other things.

We were out of chocolate and running low on water, but there was no shortage of hills. We decided to drink the half-litre we had left, but first Tama dug around in his front pannier for some sachets of electrolytes he'd been saving for this kind of situation. In his black helmet and aviators, topless, greasy and dust-stained, Tama reminded me of a Vietnam War chopper pilot with post-traumatic stress disorder.

We drank down the electrolytes. My body cried out in gratitude. It was possible again.

At the top of the next hill the view was unnecessarily gorgeous, almost pornographic: soft downy flanks of gold and apple-green grass undulating in every direction, goosebump mounds quivering in the lightest of breezes. No factories, no farms, no roads, no humans—just us and the wild wheat. It could've been centuries either side of 2010, the highway from Darkhan to Ulaanbaatar long gone or as yet undreamed of. The sweat cooled on my back. I pushed on, wondering why it didn't hurt anymore. I gazed up the ridgeline at the cockroaches scuttling along the lopsided horizon. I gazed at the cars, the main road. The main road—zang!

To the left at the top of the rise there was a stately three-storey manor of a truck stop. Mutton soup zang!

We cycled across the empty forecourt past derelict fuel bowsers to a front door that was boarded up and cornered with cobwebs. It looked like it had been abandoned for years. As I turned to leave, there was a flicker of shadow behind a broken window. I called out for *tom us*. A silent hand reached through a gap in the boards. I passed one empty bottle through, then three more. The hand disappeared and a short while later it returned the bottles, full. We had stumbled into Dr Seuss' *Lorax*, and I had just met the Once-ler. I pushed a packet of Marlboros through the gap. The hand took them in silence.

We put on our headtorches in the fading light and wobbled off down the road, drinking deeply from our bottles. I sucked the road into my eyeballs, and that was enough to pull me forward. To the right the ridges dropped away now and then, affording brief glimpses into the afternoon's grim gulches. With a jolt I realised it was Saturday night: 9 pm over here, that would make it about seven o'clock in Melbourne . . . Laura would be having dinner, at home or out with friends, at a good, affordable, probably Asian restaurant, getting ready for a party, taping on fake limbs for a fancy-dress party with some ironic hipster theme, 'underwater space perverts' or like 'ghosts on drugs'. She'd be cycling around the tarsealed steppes of Melbourne, queueing up for theatre tickets, something weird in a warehouse, data projectors in a dumpster, a 'devised work-in-progress developmental performance showing' utterly lacking in content called, working title, *Underwater Space Perverts and the Ghosts on Drugs* . . .

Foreign, all impossibly foreign.

We rode south in the deepening greyness, hugging the clay verge as the occasional bus whizzed by. There was no sign of Bayangol. The GPS reckoned it was at least another twenty kilometres, so we started looking out for a nice flat sheltered place to stop. After fifteen minutes we gave up on 'nice'. With trucks rumbling by in the background I pitched the tent on a rakish angle in a marmot hole-infested paddock swarming with midges then collapsed on the ground and watched with pathetic gratitude as Tama cooked up instant noodles followed by fishy rice.

'You're a good man, Tama Pugsley,' I croaked. He looked up and grinned.

'All good, bro! Have a rest. Big day tomorrow.'

To keep the legions of biting midges at bay, Tama wedged a dozen crumpled cigarettes into his back bicycle wheel and fired them up like foul incense sticks. I sucked feebly at the smoke. We ate our dinner in the dark and the rain started, slowly at first. We crawled into the stuffy tent. It was Tama's turn on the rainy side: that was something. Before I passed out it was agreed that under no circumstances should we attempt another Kiwi shortcut in Mongolia.

DAYS 16–17:
SOME GARDEN-VARIETY SUFFERING

It was still raining when I woke up. The air was crisp and refreshing as I took an underwhelming morning crap in a marmot-hole. We ate quiet bowls of muesli in the red-and-grey nylon vestibule, gazing out into the murk.

We took to the tarseal with our jackets on but not zipped up. It was a nice change to be cold instead of sweating and to not have to worry about sunburn.

'Just a bit of garden-variety suffering,' I told myself. 'Just like summer in Invercargill.'

After twenty-five kilometres we climbed a hill and careened down the far side into the fences and forecourts of Bayangol. The existence of this place made more sense than the towns up north; it was like any shabby service town a couple of hundred of kilometres from any capital city.

Bayangol had a couple of good general stores and we loaded up on water, juice, fresh yoghurt and cylindrical meat. I found and enthusiastically purchased a framed picture of a Chinese child wearing an orange hat and yellow dungarees. The kid had mad, bulging eyes and was grinning wickedly as he bit into an oversized and clearly fake plastic carrot.

'What are you going to do with that?' Tama asked as

I struggled to cram it into my backpack next to the wet tent and the broken novelty riding visors we were yet to wear.

'Lug it a few hundred k's across Mongolia then break it, or lose it the day before we leave.'

'Cool.'

From Bayangol there were two routes to Bornuur. Back in Erdenet we had opted for 86 kilometres of dotted red line down a detour valley that would give us more of a chance to see the 'real' Mongolia and avoid the 'hellish' main road. But since then we had discovered that the main road wasn't so hellish, and this morning, what with the rain and the gradual yet unrelenting depletion of my morale and motivation, we opted to stay on the main drag for a 57-kilometre blast due south. Our entire focus was now on avoiding any and all unnecessary adventures. We wanted to get to Ulaanbaatar and the comforts of LG Guesthouse two days distant as quickly and painlessly as possible. Today we'd make Bornuur for a late lunch, then it was only 28 kilometres to the town of Bayanchandmani. Too easy.

The rain picked up as we headed out of Bayangol. I stopped and zipped my jacket up then put my hood on and my helmet over the hood. The hood pressed in on my ears and made me feel like I was in my own head, rather than the middle of nowhere. The legs went up-down-up, up-down-up. The head swivelled left, right, left. The eyes took in the wet fields on the left, the wet fields on the right. Laura parachuted out of the sky in a billowing Mary Poppins dress and no undies, drifting nearer and nearer but never quite landing. *The Graduate* played at full volume on a big-arse screen in my parents' living room while I sucked on a badly rolled joint. The road began to climb up a long gentle hill and just kept climbing; half an hour later we were still inching up that same hill. My jacket stopped me getting wet from the rain, but it also captured and concentrated all my sweat on the inside, where it gathered and pooled at my elbows and streamed in thick rivulets down my back.

From a saddle near the top of the hill we could see the line of the road dip into a long shallow valley then rise again on the other side, getting thinner and higher until it left the green behind and merged seamlessly with the grey of the sky. Cars drove by. Sometimes they beeped. The odd eagle circled in the murk.

It was boring, I realised; cycling all the time was boring.

We stopped for a breather at the top of the pass and were buffeted by gusts from both sides as we munched on a big bag of salted peanuts bought in Bayangol. A car pulled up and the driver ran through the rain towards us not wearing a jacket. He clutched a bottle of vodka and a single plastic cup and poured me a triple measure—I nodded and slammed it down, then Tama did likewise. I offered the nice man some peanuts. He nodded, grabbed the whole bag and ran back to his car and drove off. We were stunned and a little outraged, but that whole thing was Mongolian hospitality, sort of.

We wobbled down the hill in top gear, nutless and tipsy. All was buzzing well until the road tilted up again, then it was back to struggletown. There was a large, rusted Soviet-era billboard on the side of the road with a picture of a skeleton driving a car: scythe in one hand, vodka bottle in the other, no hands on the wheel, car and skeleton sailing gracefully off a cliff.

We came to a valley with a sheer drop on the left that was perfect for sailing down. On the far side of the valley a hill had been scalped, its green skin peeled back to reveal a uniform dark grey. We saw a roadside information sign, the kind of useless thing First World countries are littered with, and pulled over to check it out. This one consisted of a large piece of unlaminated paper that had been stapled to a flat piece of wood. The paper was sodden and ripped. In the bottom left corner, barely legible but in English, it read: 'Reclamation Area'. It was unclear what they were reclaiming, and who from, and who 'they' were.

I was getting hungry, bicycle-seat-eating hungry, but it was raining harder than ever and there was nowhere to shelter. If the tent hadn't already been drenched when I'd packed it up, it'd be well drenched now. Meanwhile the meaty soups of Bornuur beckoned so we rode on, helped up the hill by a freshening tailwind. Sporadic shooting pains in my right hip, left hand, right shoulder. Kilometres of wet asphalt. I expected Bornuur around every new turn and was disappointed again and again. I wanted to unfold the maps and properly suss out our position but we couldn't do that without ruining them in the rain. Five hours from Bayangol I'd had enough and told Tama as much.

'So what do you wanna do?' he asked, nonplussed.

'Eat.'

'Where?'

'Here.'

'Under the tarp?'

'Sure.'

'Noodles?'

'Anything.'

'Not in a restaurant?'

'What restaurant?'

Tama sighed and gave in. We pushed our creaking bikes off the road and leaned them against a drooping power-pole. Our cycles formed two-thirds of a triangle, then we draped the tarp over the top and sat down on the sodden grass to make the final side: a Kiwi *ger*. I made salami-ish sandwiches while Tama boiled up some instant noodles. It was one of the quietest lunches I have ever had.

Bornuur was around the next corner.

We pulled into a busy truck stop and queued up to buy all eleven of the store's Mars Bars, dripping all over the linoleum and getting funny looks from the motorists who were hunched over their steaming meaty soups. We went outside and as we were snorting a couple of chocolate bars a convoy of mud-spattered Nissan Pathfinder rally cars screeched to a halt in the carpark. The cars had matching decal maps of Mongolia on their sides. It showed a route zigzagging from Ulaanbaatar to Mörön Khövsgöl, then Khatgal and the lake, east through the taiga forest, down through Erdenet and back east to UB. It was almost exactly the route we had taken, except these guys were probably doing the whole loop in a day. One of the rally drivers, a white guy in a yellow-and-green race suit, got out of his Pathfinder and strutted towards the truck stop. When he saw us and our bicycles he stopped strutting for a second—then he laughed, long and hard. As we pedalled away the oversized oblong snout of a TV-grade video camera poked out a Pathfinder's window and followed our slow progress down the road.

The rain slowly cleared, then returned, then properly stopped. An hour later we rode into Mongolia's premiere alcoholic horse-milk district (disclaimer: might not actually be Mongolia's premiere alcoholic horse-milk district). It was a sight to behold: dozens of little wooden *airag* stands peppering both sides of the road for a boozy Mongolian miracle mile, some flying the tattered flag of smuggler-bag shadecloth, some with stools and some strictly drive-through, all these stands manned and womanned by impassive vendors who gestured mutely to stockpiles of 1.25-litre plastic bottles, emptied of sugary drink and filled with off-white alcoholic horse milk. Motorbikes and jeeps, buses and horses were pulled over onto the grass and nomads and housewives were buying *airag* by the bottle, by the box. Some of the fancier *airag* stands had rickety billboards depicting healthy, shiny, vaguely obscene mares frolicking in irradiated meadows, their distended horse teats glistening moistly under the studio lights. As tempting as an authentic cultural experience likely to end in dysentery was, me and Tama decided we had 'done the ay-rag thing' back in Snake Valley. We slogged on towards the warm beer of Bayanchandmani.

We biked over a ridge and passed a large *ger* village on our left.

'That might be Bayanchandmani. We'll have to sleep in a *ger*,' Tama shout-mumbled over his shoulder. He kept cycling past it.

'Dude! Are we gonna stop there or what?'

'Nah, we're going to Bayanchandmani.'

'But—isn't *that* Bayanchandmani?'

'Maybe. Probably not.'

'Well shouldn't we go and *ask*?!'

'Dude, you don't have to yell at me.' Tama sounded genuinely hurt.

'Sorry, it's just—I'm just tired. You navigate. Let's keep going.'

'I thought you wanted to stop.'

'I want to stop at *Bayanchandmani*.'

Tama looked back. 'That's not it,' he said quietly.

'Fine. Great. *Awesome*. Let's keep *going* then!'

Tama turned away. He was quiet for a bit, then he said, 'You should see how angry you look.'

Seven hours after we left Bayangol we got our first glimpse of Bayanchandmani. The shimmer of concrete and coal smoke on the horizon would usually fill me with hippie angst and make Tama bike at top speed in the opposite direction, but this time it was a relief. The only thing was, it didn't get any closer. I cranked and creaked across the plain, dragging my pain along the road. I changed up and pushed harder, but Bayanchandmani remained defiantly out of reach. I stopped, panted, swore.

'Just a little further bro, we're almost there,' Tama said.

I rode a bit further, but it didn't make any difference: the town came closer, then drifted further away again. I stopped and bleated in exasperation at whichever goat would listen. For a little while Tama rode beside me with his right hand on my back, pushing me on. Finally the road flattened out—fuck it, we'd been riding up another *faux plat*.

Bayanchandmani finally wrapped its powerlines and fences around us in a gritty embrace. We had covered 110 kilometres since breakfast.

After a litre of red sugary drink I felt less bad and was ready to suss out a room for the night. The tent wasn't an option—it was still saturated, and bound to stay that way until we could dry it out somewhere. I asked at the grocery store for a *zochid buudal*, hotel, because our phrasebook didn't have words for 'motel' or 'hostel'—even 'gulag', a gulag would've been fine for one night. The store owner replied with an emphatic *'baixgui'*, pronounced 'buko': 'don't have'.

I gestured around, taking in the whole town. Buko. I insisted, we were on the main street, it was here or nowhere, surely Bayanchandmani must have . . . Buko.

Then an old man who had been sitting in the shadows of the store got up and led me outside and pointed down the road to a building with a faded numberplate of a sign that looked like 304NA 6YYAAN. This roughly matched the phrasebook Cyrillic for 'hotel'.

I thanked the man profusely, told Tama to guard the bikes and ran to the hotel. Inside there was a dingy bar that lacked customers but was staffed by an entire extended family group, geriatrics to infants, who answered my request for a room with a ragged chorus of *'baixgui'*.

'But, it says "zogin burdang" on the wall outside,' I insisted. They looked at me.

'We could just sleep on the floor.' I pointed to the floorboards and mimed curling up in a ball. The father shook his head angrily.

'Well, where then?' I spat out, indignant. '*Where*?!' No reply, not even a 'buko'.

I walked slowly back to Tama, who was finishing off a can of beer.

'Man, flag this place—let's just hitch a ride in a truck back to UB,' he said. 'We could stay at LG, have a shower, get some burgers . . . watch a DVD . . . sleep in an actual bed . . .'

I shook my head. I wasn't ready to admit defeat quite yet. I also wasn't convinced that hitching at dusk with two bicycles and sixty kilograms of luggage would be any easier than finding a room for the night.

'Five more minutes,' I said.

After pleading with my fourth uninterested shopkeeper, a woman customer sighed before grabbing my arm and dragging me up the road.

'Guard the bikes!' I called to Tama, who rolled his eyes.

The lady led me a half a kilometre to a grocery store identical to the one we'd just been in. We went inside then she disappeared out a back door, leaving me alone with a heavyset shopkeeper lady who appraised me coolly.

'Zogin burdang?' I whimpered. She nodded, deadpan. A few seconds later a zangy young woman carrying a small child entered the store and stood behind me. She didn't look at me or say anything. I didn't say anything. The shopkeeper didn't say anything. While no one was saying anything, a third woman arrived and motioned for me and the young woman to follow her upstairs. I hesitated, and for a panicked moment I thought I had blundered into a brothel. I knew the warning signs: if there was a topless preadolescent boy sitting cross-legged on a mat in a windowless room and the ambient stench of corruption, *run*.

But the women led me upstairs to a large room that was empty except for three single beds. The beds didn't have mattresses, they were just wood platforms that the younger woman hastily threw some blankets over—but it was better than pitching our sodden tent on a forecourt, and far better than a buko.

'*Zochid buudal*,' she said, with the faintest trace of a smirk.

'*Za, tiin, mash sain*—Zang!'

I skipped down the road to tell Tama. He was standing

out by the road, his thumb pointed forlornly at an empty street.

'Nah bro—this is Mörön to Mörön,' I said. 'Come on.'

'Wow, an actual bed,' Tama said when I showed him the room. He sat down with a thump.

We put away a few beers, then Tama went off to take a crap.

'Good poo?' I asked upon his return.

'Yeah, another massive one.'

'Shit, man.'

'I know. I don't know where you put it all.'

'You know, I think what happens is, I go to do a poo and I can't, and my body somehow reabsorbs all that waste matter, and processes it, desperate to get some form of—nutrient . . .'

'But dude, if I captured the amount I poo every day and put it next to you, it'd be like—'

'*Please* don't do that.'

'—it'd be the size of your head.'

We wandered out in search of more food for me to digest but not excrete. The first canteen we found had a lovely MILF proprietress, no customers, a ship's steering wheel on the wall—god knows where from—and a long and complex menu although in practice it only sold *huushuur*. This was fine, for a first course.

Six *huushuur* and four beers later we hit a place next door with a grand pool table, a single pool ball, no cues and no customers. Our table was next to a wall of dirty mirror. There was a dude sitting opposite me in a green army jumper with hair all over his face, a pink and flaking nose and a big red crack in the middle of his bottom lip, laughing and throwing the beers back while spilling mutton soup down his top. I filmed him.

Later when we lurched out into the dusk Tama saw some kids and dug around in his bag for a toy koala to give them. He found one but its head had come off. Tama stood staring at the decapitated marsupial humping a plastic boomerang and laughed a strangled, delirious laugh.

Back at the hotel I pretended I needed to go for a crap and snuck outside for a smoke. I was through with fooling myself that this 'holiday' was any kind of healthful experience. We were riding ourselves into the ground, literally, carrying on like yuppy ironmen without the protein bars or angina medicine. If the odd cancer stick helped get me through this, so be it. I lit up and inhaled greedily, sucking the smoke deep into my lungs and holding it there till my vision clouded over. My head lolled forward and I sat down heavily against the fence. Cymbals crashed underwater; it was the hotel dog having a bark.

You'll get through it, a quiet voice said, just stop for a bit. I giggled.

Tama came lumbering down the outside stairs.

'Hey Tama,' I slurred, 'I'm . . . smoking.'

'Do what you gotta do, bro,' he said. 'I'm shitting.'

'Cool,' I said, then under my breath: 'Lucky bastard.'

At 6 am Tama's iPhone alarm blasted us awake with a MIDI version of 'Bad to the Bone'. Out the window, all was light brown, light grey: the wooden fences of Bayanchandmani were dunked in fog. I struggled out of bed with creaking knee joints and checked the tent, which I had draped over the spare bed. It was still wet.

'How are you feeling, bro?' I asked.

'I feel . . . good, actually,' Tama said, sounding pleasantly surprised. 'I've got a few saddle sores on my arse, probably what haemorrhoids feels like, and my thighs are a bit tired. But other than that I feel pretty good.'

'Great. I feel fucked.'

'Not long now, man—hot shower, cold beer and some DVDs to take us far, far away from here . . .'

We chowed down on monster bowls of muesli and splashed out with a cup of tea. When I went to wash our bowls at the tap outside I noticed that the washing-up sponge, the chopping board, every utensil in the utensil bag and the utensil bag itself all reeked of horsemeat salami. I threw away the sponge and bag and soaked everything else in water for as long as I could, which wasn't long because it was only 66 kilometres to Ulaanbaatar and we were keen to get there as soon as possible and supersize our rest day into a rest-day-and-a-half.

Tama 'fixed' one of his broken bicycle spokes with duct tape, then we climbed back on those bikes. On our way out, the guard dog who had been so territorial and barky all night long whimpered when it saw us and tried to hide behind the door against a fence that served as its kennel. Tama threw a headless koala at it. We rolled out of Bayanchandmani with that bittersweet feeling I got when leaving a place I didn't necessarily like but would probably never return to.

As we inched southwards, the sun burned the fog off and started in on my leg. We were definitely in the hinterland of

Mongolia's biggest city now: there was more traffic on the road, actual road signs and an increasing concentration of billboards, even if many of the billboards were only advertising emptiness and rust. Up on the ridges by the tree line there were elephantine log cabins and sprawling fenced-off estates: the holiday houses of the rich, or tourist resorts for foreigners. Crawling up a long gradual incline, we gaped at a particularly monstrous red-roofed estate with a paramilitary fence and what looked like a watchtower. On the far side of the rise we were whizzing down towards the plains when a dog started barking urgently. It ran across the field towards the road, hoping to cut us off at the pass, but we were travelling at close to forty kilometres per hour and we whizzed right by it.

A few minutes later we were on the flat when a couple more dogs tore out of a *ger* camp and came snarling for us. The first mutt was a mangy little thing but it was followed, then overtaken, by a formidable wolf-dog with gleaming yellow fangs. I barked at them as gruffly as possible, but maybe they could tell my heart wasn't in it because they kept coming for me—not Tama ten metres behind. Just me. I yelped and tried to pedal faster, but they kept coming until they were snapping at my back wheel. I kicked out at the wolf-dog, but since it was behind me that mainly just made me wobble all over the road.

Luckily Tama still had a stash of rocks in his handlebar bag, which he started pegging at the dogs. His first shot was way wide but his second shot bounced off my back pannier into the mangy dog's face; it whimpered and slowed to a trot. The wolf-dog kept coming for me, a growl deep in its throat. I howled and lashed out with both legs. An oncoming

truck blasted its horn, I swerved to avoid it, Tama threw
a rock that whizzed past my leg, I yelped again. His next
throw bounced off the road into the wolf-dog's belly. It leapt
whining in the air, then slowed down too, still barking but
more feebly now. Tama gave me a mega thumbs-up.

'I owe you a Mars Bar, bro!' I shouted.

'Sweet dog!'

Composure partially regained, we discussed the logistics
of swinging a length of chain with a padlock on the end at
erratic rabid canines while pedalling a mountain bike down
a potholed road in top gear, and concluded it would likely
end badly.

I pulled over and filled my pockets with nice pointy rocks
for the next mutt that tried it on. In the distance we could
see a small town and agreed to stop for some fake Fanta.
A thirsty Tama biked ahead, his jumbo thighs working
like merciless pistons. When I got to the 'town' Tama was
standing next to a pile of pungent bloodstained sheep pelts,
half-drying and half-rotting in the sun. No shops.

'This isn't a sugary drink place—it's a scabhole,' Tama
said and rode off.

Half an hour later we made it to a sugary drink place
where I accidentally purchased two litres of plum iced tea
that was disgusting, but not disgusting enough to waste.
Sitting at a rather genteel picnic table under a sun umbrella,
I realised I had never got around to having my final rabies
shot in Beijing. Rocks it is, I thought, patting my lumpy
pockets to reassure myself.

Down the road a ways we had to stop while a couple of
hundred sheep ambled across the asphalt, driven from one
poor pasture to another by modern nomads in baseball caps

and cargo pants. Once they finished crossing we came over a small rise and there it was: a pall of smog covering the outskirts of the city, the unfortunate result of Soviet masters building massive coal power stations at the western end of a long valley with prevailing westerly breezes.

We passed through a large red-and-white-striped tollgate that proclaimed ULAANBAATAR loudly in Roman script and didn't have to pay the vehicle tax as our bicycles weren't considered vehicles. Billboards captured and confounded my eyeballs, offering me ΑΠΑΤΑΠΗ 3ΑΜ ΧΚ, 50 ΤΟΓΡΟΓ and вогх. Lego-bright petrol stations pushed бензин onto willing customers. One billboard with a naked orange bulldozer reclining on a pile of flattened dirt aggressively declared, in English, PROGRESS CREATES SUCCESS. Train tracks crossed and recrossed the road while powerlines tangled in the sky. Grass was replaced by gravel, by dust. At the edge of a dusty forecourt there was a squat circular building with a sloping roof—a concrete mockery of a *ger*.

We turned a corner and rode into a traffic jam. Cars, jeeps and trucks, all backed up for miles. We squeezed past in the gutter, on the verge, in and out of potholes, passing everyone.

'Two wheels good, four wheels bad,' I thought to myself, not for the first time.

As the streets widened and the traffic thickened I thought I saw something sneak into my peripheral vision, then drop back, then sneak up again. We were overtaken by a Mongol lycra warrior on an unnecessarily expensive road bike. He was wearing a sports utility belt with a drink bottle on each hip and a mysterious blue aluminium object, possibly a spanner, dangling from his arse like a misplaced tail. He was pedalling hard and when I 'sigh binoo!'d he ignored me. I perked up, and even though we were in heavy traffic I changed up, edged past Tama and swung past the outside of the outside lane into the middle of the road and nearly got taken out by an oncoming taxi.

'Careful!' Tama yelled, but I was on the mission, determined to catch that yuppy. I raced down that no-man's-land. After a couple of hundred metres I passed him, but he fought back and gained a few bike lengths. I pedalled hard to close the gap. It went on like this for a couple of kilometres with both of us weaving through the traffic. Tama was unimpressed but determined to keep up. The spandex bandit swerved onto the pavement—there was pavement now—and tried to pull ahead that way, but we kept at him. A couple more hectic minutes and he stopped at a murky fountain, panting heavily. I surged ahead, shouting and pointing to my luggage, victorious.

Suddenly there was a scene of startling familiarity: Dragon bus station, the place from whence we had sallied forth seeking the first Mörön!

Even though it was just a carpark, it was extraordinarily comforting. For once we weren't lost—and even better, we weren't exploring! Not needing to ask for directions, practically locals, we homing-pigeoned our way towards the LG Guesthouse. Past the two-storey apartment blocks, past the giant roundabout where the buildings dropped away and the slums on northern UB's hills reared up in a patchwork technicolour tsunami. Past the graffiti'd swastikas, past the train station, along Narny Gudamj (Narny Street) then across the boulevard and down the back alley. Past the dilapidated basketball court hemmed in by brown-and-white high-rise towers and into the underground garage where cycle tourists could store their bikes.

The LG staff checked us into the same twin room we'd stayed in eighteen days earlier. Eighteen days?! Jesus Chainsaw. Any one of those days had been stuffed full of at least a week's worth of mishap, epiphany and photo-op.

I lay on the soft, forgiving LG sheets listening to Tama have a disco shower, which is not code for a wank but a shower with an in-built radio that blasted out Mongol pop classics to help you wash, a feature that more than made up for the shower roof being slightly below head height. Then we headed out for lunch. Tama hummed a song from his Canadian childhood:

Hungry, hungry, yadda yadda,
I could eat a goose-moose burger
Fifteen pickles and a purple plum!

We went back to Ikh Mongol, a steak-and-beer house catering for wealthy gluttons we had discovered two weeks earlier. We sat at the same table, on a balcony with a view of a busy street dominated by a lopsided high-rise, its south wing two storeys taller than its north wing. Tama ordered a 500-gram beef steak, rare, with country potatoes, 'red and white sauce' and salad. I asked for lamb shish kebabs with rice and salad, and we both ordered extra garden salads plus two pints of boutique Mongolian lager.

We can't keep this up, I thought as I gulped down my beer and sweated gently in the heat, waiting for my meal. Riding so much, eating so little—eating a shitload, sure, but still not enough. We could do ourselves some permanent damage, and for what? Because it's there?

These thoughts were hastily cleared away to make room for lunch. Everything was drenched in flavour: salt, vinegar, olive oil, pepper, chilli, tomato sauce, mayonnaise. The lamb chunks were ... they were ... god, they were good. Juicy, succulent and ever so slightly bloody, a veritable mouth-orgy of baby sheep. The side salad contained exotic vegetables such as carrot and beetroot, things I could hardly remember the taste of, and the salad dressing alone was worth drinking from a martini glass. The rice was much better without Tama adding raisins and milk powder to it. Bellies full, minds empty, we gazed at the pedestrians walking up and down Seoul Street, happy that the local zangers emulated Russian sluttishness rather than Chinese modesty.

We staggered out of Ikh Mongol in a food coma and wandered around downtown UB until we found a DVD store. We wanted to rent or buy a copy of the film *Mongol*, which had come out a couple of years before. Neither of us had seen it, and it seemed the perfect symbiosis: a trashy escapist action version of the Chinggis Khan story with plenty of killing that would nonetheless be relevant and educational, like watching *Mad Max II* in the middle of the outback.

The DVD store had all sorts of random rubbish on its shelves, but no *Mongol*. I asked the clerk about it and he shook his head and buko'd angrily. It turned out that the Mongolian response to *Mongol* was comparable to the Kazakh response to *Borat*. Many people deemed the script insufficiently patriotic, even though young Chinggis did do a lot of patriotic staring into space. Some Mongolian bloggers also insisted that Mongolia's greatest warrior was never captured and held as a slave, and that to suggest such a thing was deeply offensive. Finally, and least forgivably, the beloved Chinggis was played by a *Japanese* actor. This was like casting Barry Humphries to play Sir Edmund Hillary.

I wandered into the music CD section and my eyes alighted on a guy called something like бурхана хэнэх зовного, whose close-cropped hair was photographed in statesmanlike black and white. хэнэх was standing on a distinctly Mongolian steppe wearing black combat fatigues and casually holding a large, bright red (colourised) flag. The edge of a swastika armband was just visible. On the back cover хэнэх was standing behind a lectern, his armband more prominent, orating from a little black book—and it didn't look like he was reading out phone numbers. This was the cultural output of Dayar Mongol, Mongolia's version of the One Nation Party, whose anti-Chinese racism was spruced up with retrograde Nazi iconography. I couldn't bring myself to buy it, but if I'd been a thirteen-year-old Mongol boy I would've thought it was awesome.

We couldn't agree on a movie. I refused to watch *Toy Story 3* because it was probably a devious and idiotic toy ad; Tama refused to watch the new *A-Team* because 'It's gonna be shit', even though that was the point; he was apparently unable to ironically appreciate said shit-ness like *moi*. After an inordinate amount of dither and faff we eventually settled on a Matt Damon film set in Iraq, which promised plenty of killing and little to no educational content.

Back at the guesthouse Tama convinced the reception staff to let him unscrew the common-room DVD player from the wall and take it up to our room. When Tama put the disc in it booted up to the main menu, but we needed an 'enter' button to make it play, and the DVD player didn't have such a thing. We needed the remote control, which we didn't have, and nor did an apologetic reception staff.

'You've got an iPhone, can't you like download a remote control app or something?'

Tama ignored me. He ejected the DVD then reinserted it, and as the tray shut he pressed 'play' four times in quick succession.

'What are you doing?'

'Trying to make it work.'

He pressed 'eject' again then shoved the tray and as it closed he mashed the 'skip' button six or eight times. The DVD started playing.

'What the—what did you just do?'

'Dunno, but it works,' he said with a laugh.

'Tama 2000, hacker extraordinaire! He's half MacGyver— half Charlie Sheen! He's James Bond—at a titty bar!'

'Thanks. I think.'

The movie did its job of taking us far, far away from our bodies and bicycles for a bit. After Maaaatt Daaaamon had snapped everyone's spines and united the warring tribes of Iraq and the closing credits had rolled, we just lay there sweating. The balcony doors were open onto a sweltering heatwave of an endless summer twilight. In theory it was time for dinner but I'd put away two bags of potato chips and four beers and for the first time in weeks I didn't feel even slightly hungry.

Tama was asleep, snoring softly. I went and stood on the balcony and looked out at UlaanBaltimore. As the light slowly bled from the sky, the sounds of children playing basketball slowly crossfaded into the noise of drunken men arguing and smashing Chinggis bottles in the playground.

REST DAY IN ULAANBAATAR

The twenty-seventh of July, 2010, unfolded in strictly administrative fashion. We visited the Seven Summits outdoor store and tried, unsuccessfully, to get Tama some replacement spokes. We popped into a roadside sex shop looking for local porno playing cards, but all they had was inflatable pussy-mouth-and-arsehole dolls and contraband 'Australian Brand' Viagra. We carbo-loaded, hard. We stocked up on muesli, salami and cheese—lots of cheese. At the Minii Delguur market we met a man called Batbot, another one, who was very excited to meet white people and wanted Tama's mobile number. We updated our Facebook statuses from 'In Mongolia!' to 'Still in Mongolia.'

Tama called Ami. I called Laura. She said I sounded a long way away. I didn't know what to say except, 'I am.'

In the afternoon I wandered into the LG common room, which was empty as usual, and stopped in front of a large, faded map of Mongolia. I'd glanced at it the last time we'd stayed here, but I hadn't noticed all the little radioactive symbols. There was one of those heart-stopping broken triangle-circles on the eastern shore of Lake Khövsgöl just north of where we'd camped; another one a couple of hundred kilometres east of Ulaanbaatar, near Mörön Khentii. I called out to Odval, a general helper around LG and a very patient woman, who was about to start cleaning the bathroom.

'These nuclear symbols,' I said, pointing to the map. 'What do they mean?'

'The lake name? Khövsgöl,' she said. 'Very beautiful.'

'No, are these—test sites?' I tapped the radioactive symbol.

'Oh, no. This is, uh, in Mongolian we say *uran*.'

'We slept right by that top one, without knowing.' I was becoming anxious. 'Is it a bomb site?'

'This *uran*—is metal. In the garden.'

'Oh—like uranium?'

'Yeah, yeah.' She pointed to another symbol. 'This is *alt*, gold.'

'But this uranium, this *uran*,' I persisted, 'it's a very bad poison, the worst. People use it to make nuclear weapons. Do you understand?' She looked at me blankly. 'You know Chernobyl? Hiroshima?'

Odval shrugged. 'Sorry, I must . . .' She gestured to the bathroom. I let her go.

We had to move out of our twin room into a six-bed dorm that afternoon, due to prior bookings. There we met an emaciated Australian man in his late thirties who had manky dreadlocks, a gaunt skull face and a spectacular skin condition I was relieved not to know the name of.

Collapsed on a bottom bunk, Skullface gave the impression he'd been parlaying his sickness benefit into an extended

Third World drug holiday for at least a decade. He wasn't particularly impressed by Mongolia so far, but nonetheless he was planning to stay for at least a month.

'I've been everywhere else,' he told me gloomily.

I recommended Lake Khövsgöl, and he seemed interested—until I described the bus ride. Then I began telling him about our cycle trip and, against the odds, Skullface managed to turn paler. He left the room muttering and shaking his head. Like in an audition, he was instantly replaced by a couple of fresh-faced, excitable young lads from Germany. Sebastian and Erik were fresh off the Trans-Mongolian express, straight from Moscow, and were extremely happy to be here.

'Finally, after all these years ...' Sebastian's voice trailed off.

'We are in bloody Mongolia! Woo!' Erik bellowed from the bathroom, where he was shaving 'for the last time in a month'.

Erik and Sebastian had a dream—a crazy, irresponsible dream. They were going to ride horses across the great Gobi Desert. They had never ridden horses before, but they were happy-go-lucky dudes who weren't going to let little details like experience or common sense stand in their way. They were headed to Karakorum tomorrow. The plan was to buy a couple of fine Mongol steeds there and hit the untamed steppe.

'And the best thing is,' Sebastian said, 'we even have a blog! So friends back home can share our Mongolian adventures!'

'It's called *Mongolian Hoof Prints*,' Erik said proudly.

'What blogging site do you use?' Tama asked.

'Live Journal.'

Tama snorted in disgust. 'Their content management system's a shambles,' he said darkly.

'We would love to stay and chat,' Sebastian said, pushing Erik towards the door, 'but we must gather supplies for our long journey to come.'

'We have heard that Mongolians love to drink vodka—is this true?' Erik asked.

'Uh, sure,' I said. 'I guess.'

'If someone offers you vodka, you must drink it, yes?'

'Not really.'

'I wonder if we will have to get drunk, just walking to the markets and back!' Sebastian cried. 'Who knows what will happen—in Mongolia!'

They galloped out of the dorm. There was an awkward silence. Finally Tama said, 'Fuck riding horses across this country—especially if you've never done it before. That sounds like hell.'

'Yeah. Hey, um . . .'

'What's up?'

'Nothing, we should just . . . update our blog.'

We spent the next few hours monopolising the hostel's free internet, eating dinner at the computer, ignoring greasy looks from the other guests and receiving texts from our new Mongolian friend.

5.58 pm   BATBOT: How do you do good evening
            tomatom name bat

6.09 pm	BATBOT: I am glad to meet you nice to meet you what can i do for you leave it to me i don t doubt it okay
7.21 pm	BATBOT: What is your purpose tomatom in visiting come to mongolia
7.25 pm	TOMATOM: No comment
7.31 pm	BATBOT: I m so happy to meet you what a pleasure it is you made me overjoyed that is sheer luck
8.54 pm	BATBOT: It is said that if you have friends you are like an open steppe
8.57 pm	TOMATOM: Are you drunk like a winding river?
9.03 pm	BATBOT: I am tond of travelling okay
10.40 pm	BATBOT: I have get heaties is the countryside
10.51 pm	BATBOT: My friend has got a car
11.18 pm	BATBOT: I talked with you do you have anythin to say don t go without me

I finished my beer. 'Man, that was an epic blogging session, but we smashed it,' I said. 'I gotta hand it to you, Tama Pugsley—you really go the extra mile.'

Tama sighed. 'You too, Doig—you go the extra *kilometre*.'

'. . . Thanks.'

Before we turned in for the night I tracked down the long-suffering Odval and tried to explain our situation.

'We want to have breakfast tomorrow, but we want to leave at six, to avoid traffic. Is this possible?'

'Yes—but sorry, kitchen is not open until seven o'clock, sorry.' She stifled a yawn.

'Well, could we have our breakfasts early? It's included in the cost of the room, so . . .'

'Sorry, kitchen is not open.'

'Okay, look, couldn't you just leave some bread and jam out for us—and the toaster? We can make it ourselves.' She sighed.

'Okay, let me . . . I will make you.'

'Thanks! See you tomorrow!'

I went back up to our bunk room. There was no sign of Skullface, just Tama on the top bunk. He was using his iPhone to fix some Javascript problems on www.jewca-noodle.com, a dating site he'd built for one of his enigmatic New York colleagues.

'Have you sorted out breakfast?' Tama asked without looking up.

'I think so. She's going to get up early and make it for us.'

'Really? Damn.'

'Yeah, I feel a bit bad, but—oh well! Any more texts from Batbot?'

'Four. I told you you shouldn't've given him my number.'

There was a knock on the door. I got out of bed and opened it, expecting the Galloping Germans or whatever they called themselves, but there was no one there. As I closed the door I noticed a tray on the floor with a plate on it and a plastic bag on the plate. The bag contained butter, jam and Nutella sachets and eight little slices of toast, already cold. I was still staring at tomorrow's breakfast when Sebastian and Erik reeled down the hallway, flushed and triumphant.

'The rumours are true!' Sebastian panted. 'Mongolia makes you drunk! Mongolia makes you *so drunk!*'

'What happened?' I asked, dreading the answer.

'A man was playing the pool outside. He offered us a shot of vodka. We had to drink!' Erik mimed throwing back one shot after the other.

'Was he called Batbot?' I asked.

'That's crazy—how did you know?'

I had to laugh. Hopefully it was a different Batbot.

'Did you get your shopping done?' Tama asked.

'Yes—drunk!' Erik said, and high-fived Sebastian. 'I love this crazy country!'

I was in Poland a few years ago with my friend Paulina. We were on the morning train from Krakow to Oswiecim, known to English speakers by its German name, Auschwitz. We ended up stuck sharing a carriage with a couple of dorky young lads from Britain. Paul and Richard were staying in the same hostel as us and had tied up the communal bathroom all morning using matching hair-straighteners to get their fringes just so before visiting the world's most notorious concentration camp. They were telling us how hungover they were, about the crazy nightclubs they'd been to the night before. Then the conversation took that grim, inevitable turn to the one subject you could never escape in Poland: the distinction between tourists and travellers.

'Lots of our mates are on like package tours, Contiki and that,' Paul said, 'but we didn't want to be like stuck in a bus, know whamean? We didn't want everything to be like planned in advance and stuff. We're not *tourists*.' He brushed his fringe out of his eyes.

'Yeah, we're not tourists—we're *travellers*, innit!' Richard said and nodded enthusiastically. 'We're here to have authentic experiences, know whamean? After this we might go to *Prague*!'

Paulina and I had been giving each other knowing glances when I caught an unwelcome glimpse of my blood-shot eyes and greasy stubble in the train window. An awful realisation dawned on me: I looked like I'd been out clubbing till five in the morning too—because I had! Paulina as well. We'd been at Klub Taboo Go-Go the night before, swilling down Zywiec lager and Bison Grass vodka. In fact, we'd been kicked out of Go-Go for dancing on the tables. We'd stumbled back to the hostel as it was getting light, knowing full well that in five hours we'd be catching a tourist train to the gas chambers. I had to admit that, yes, I *did* know exactly whamean.

On the walk from Oswiecim train station Richard and Paul stuck close to us, probably because Paulina spoke fluent Polish and they wanted their Auschwitz experience to be as authentic as possible. There was a snack bar on the edge of the camp and the lads wanted to grab some hot chips before heading into the barracks, innit? Paulina and I reluctantly waited in line with them, looking for a chance to slip away. Ahead of us some sweaty Americans were complaining about the queue, how long it was, how *starving* they were, didn't have to wait like this at the Killing Fields. Paulina freaked and ran out of the compound faster than I could chase her. I found her sitting on a fence on the edge of a field, doing her best not to cry.

DAY 19: HARD RUBBISH

B-b-b-b-b-b-bad—

Tama groaned and swatted his phone. In the early morning light I wrenched myself out of bed and reheated our toast on the gas stove in the tiny communal kitchen outside our dorm. I speared the bread with a fork and held it campfire-style over the flame, trying not to scorch it, and when I did I covered the scorchy bits with Nutella and gave them to Tama. Tama was having a grumpy bear morning. He had stayed up crunching code until 1 am and now he wanted to rest, but I could hear the traffic building outside. It was time for us to get a move on. A couple of blocks from LG we stopped outside a corner store and I raced in to grab eight bottles of *tom us*, one of vodka and a dozen chocolate bars. Tama waited with the bikes, doing some last-minute coding.

When I came out he was squinty-eyed and pale, not a happy camper.

'Doxycycline?' I asked.

He nodded weakly. 'I'm not looking forward to this traffic.'

'C'mon bro, you'll be right—and if it's shit, you can film the shitness on your GoPro.'

Tama grumbled but he got the camera going. I rode lead. We set off eastwards through heavy traffic, dodging potholes, buses, frantic commuters. The burning-sweet taste of leaded petrol lined the back of my throat. Downtown UB stretched much further east than I'd realised. We'd never bothered walking further than the Seven Summits outdoor store, but there was this whole consular bit with pretentious fences and gates and bored security guards. From UB there was a main highway heading all the way to Moron Khentii, a sweet 318 kilometres of fresh-laid bitumen. But to the northeast there was still Gorkhi-Terelj National Park, which had rivers and wildflowers and would be our last chance to soak up the Mongolian wilderness on this trip, and possibly ever. So we decided to take a 'long cut'.

Sixty or seventy kilometres away, most of it uphill, lay our destination for the night: the Ecotourism Ger Camp, or 'Bert's House of Cheese'. I merged at a nightmare round-about and took a left at what was meant to be the turn-off to Gachuurt, which would take us through to Terelj township and then to Bert's. I pedalled into a big, empty carpark where there should've been a road. When I looked back, Tama was shaking his head at me.

'Too soon?'

'Still five more k's of this shit.'

'Sheeeit.'

As the sun rose into the sky and struggled to burn off the bus fumes, concrete buildings were replaced with wooden shacks, dirty gers and lean-tos and, under bridges, piles of rubbish that might actually have been dwellings. It was dire, but at least grimly photogenic.

Tama checked his GoPro; it was malfunctioning and had

recorded nothing. Tama got back on his bike and had a mobile sulk. We found the turn-off to Gachuurt and headed left.

Just under twenty kilometres from downtown, the valley of Gachuurt was where the moneyed set of Ulaanbaatar got away from it all, erecting two- and three-storey McMansions with chain-link fences, triple garages and prominent security cameras. They must've been a coal-mining executive's dream to heat on minus-35-degree nights. On the right there was a massive hotel-and-leisure centre with fortified walls topped by ugly statues. It was a Vegas version of Karakorum, as if Ögödei Khaan's pleasure-city wasn't depraved enough the first time round, and its parking lot was filled with shiny tour buses. The hill on the left was covered with a large, glamorous cemetery with blinged-out gravestones that glinted in the sun.

At the top of the road a little dirt track busted out of the suburbs and suddenly we found ourselves next to a clear, bubbly stream. We stopped to admire some attractive Mongolian hipsters fishing and sunbathing downstream. I convinced Tama to wait while I set up the tripod for him to do a ride-through with stream and hipsters in the background—but when he tried to get riding, his chain jolted off the front gears, his foot slipped off the pedal and his shin grated down the pedal's metal edge.

'CUNT!'

'Woah bro, are you okay?'

'Nah . . . yeah. Motherfuck. Imagine if we had to stop now, because I fucked my leg on the pedal. What a way for it all to end.'

Tama rubbed his leg. There was a long pink scrape and a little blood, but we weren't getting off the hook that easily. We made our way up a gently sloping but relentless valley, passing pockets of holidaying city folk and derelict *gers* until the hills opened out like gigantic elevator doors and we found ourselves on a bleak, deforested and slightly lopsided plain.

'Man, if I don't get my eight hours' sleep, I'm fucked,' Tama mumbled. 'I'm like . . . Tama 1500.'

'Bro, today you're about Tama . . . 500. Approximately.'

'Hey—Tama 1000, at least!'

'Okay, four figures—just.'

Left foot, right foot; left foot, right foot: push, push, push.

'So, you really partied on with Bret and Jemaine in New York, yeah?'

'Why?'

'Just—y'know, curious.'

'Sort of . . . not really. My flatmate was good mates with Bret, so she hung out with him heaps. I went out boozing with them one time.'

'Yeah, and?'

'And heaps of drunk Scottish guys came up to Bret and hugged him. One of them tried to pick him up off the ground, like in the show. Everyone thought it was really funny—except Bret.'

'Yeah cool—so what was he *like*?'

Tama thought about this for a few seconds. 'He was heaps like in the TV show, actually. Only, he was less . . . interesting.'

'Oh.'

Left foot, right foot. Push. I emptied my pockets of dog-rocks. Anything to make it easier.

'Tama bro, remember that Kiwi Experience mission you talked about us doing? Catching that nasty bus around New Zealand with a bunch of 22-year-old zangers and filming it all—me pretending to be an Aussie tourist, you pretending to be, like, Icelandic or whatever? Seeing New Zealand through tourist eyes—and banging as many Dutch girls as possible?'

'What about it?'

'Just, it's an awesome idea. It'd be hilarious.'

Tama frowned. 'Yeah, but we've both got girlfriends now, so, not such a good idea.'

'Dude, I was just trying to—forget it.'

We huffed and puffed our way through a hamlet not marked on our maps and with no sign of life except a solitary goat that stopped eating a fence just long enough to bleat at us. The track headed right and got steeper, rougher. My pedal clips scraped on the ground, but if I tried to get my feet into them I'd grind to a halt and tip over. I was thirsty but if I reached for my drink bottle, same deal, so I licked the sweat from my upper lip and dealt with it. There were long steep patches where riding became impossible and we had to push, almost carry those bikes uphill, feet slipping in the loose rock. My thighs were solid rods of dark red pain from hip to knee. But five hours and 500 vertical metres after turning off to Gachuurt we made it to the top of a 1859-metre pass and were rewarded with lush conifers, highlighter-yellow wildflowers and a view of soft blue hills stretching for miles in all directions. Gorkhi-Terelj National Park. It was like being back in Khövsgöl again, and I almost felt nostalgic.

After some extremely generous salami and cheese sandwiches, Tama cheered up and all was well with the world again. We whizzed down a few excellent kilometres of winding tree-lined trail, whooping and sucking in that good air. We rounded a corner and started down into a wide sweeping valley. There was thick forest to the right and a tan-coloured ridge, exposed and grassless, to the left. Beyond the ridge we could make out the first tourist *gers* of Terelj. We zigged and zanged down the hill. As we approached the ridge, a buzzard rose into the air, then several more. They flapped slowly away from a long white scar on the ground that it took us a while to identify as landfill.

Plastic bags, plastic bottles and discarded building materials stretched up an unlucky gully for one hundred metres or so, while patches of churned up dirt suggested that some folks bothered to bury their waste, however shallowly. The ridge conveniently hid all that filth from the holidaymakers just around the corner. Presumably the plan was to fill up the gully until just before it became visible from the *gers*, then move on to the next gully. At the bottom of the dump there was a pile of asbestos cladding. It was covered in bird shit and looked well pecked.

Apparently Mongolia wasn't exempt from one of tourism's central ironies: the best places get ruined first. Apart from the fake lake of copper runoff on the way to Erdenet, this sneaky corner of Mongolia's most popular national park was by far the worst pollution we'd seen. To sort it all out, Mongolia would need proper rubbish trucks. But the trucks would need proper sealed roads, millions of kilometres of roads—and that would cost billions of tugrugs. Meanwhile, the asphalt would wreak havoc with the migratory patterns of animals and humans alike. It would be a mountain-biking tragedy.

Five minutes later we were rattling down the dusty, potholed streets of Terelj township, and three minutes after that we were on the banks of the Terelj *gol*. Wealthy Mongolian families had parked their SUVs along the riverbank and were frying up slabs of meat on coal-fired barbecues. This should've been the nicest stretch of water since Khövsgöl *nuur*, but there was rubbish under every third tree, and the grass of the riverbank was sprinkled with broken grass and gouged by all-terrain tyres.

'Gross,' I said.

Tama smiled grimly. 'It kind of sums up Mongolia, hey— lots of beautiful places, and lots of Mongolians running around smashing Chinggis bottles, filling the place with rubbish.'

'Yeah. And then there's us.'

'. . . Yeah.'

We dismounted and pushed our bikes across the river, which came up to our knees and was frosty cold. There were more trees on the far side and the piles of rubbish were smaller, but pristine it was not. Further down the track we saw a figure walking, almost floating towards us from out of a massive valley to the northwest. He was young and had blond Jesus Cobain hair and was topless and recently pale but now there were big chunks of pink skin peeling off his shoulders, nose and cheeks. He waved us down. He was French.

'I have been . . . north,' he said uncertainly in a thick accent. 'This is big valley, I walk and walk. There is no human, no animal, no sound—just this river, and the voice in my head . . . I see many strange thing.' He frowned. 'Or maybe—I am not sure. I see the mountain, I go towards it, but the mountain, it does not come close . . .' He looked wistfully at our mountain bikes. 'I wish for a bike,' he said, adjusting his backpack. 'This walking, it is so slow . . .'

We gave the Gen Y saint a slug from our water and he trudged on. Tama stared up the valley, then looked away.

'D'ya wanna do it?' I asked.

'Nah, fuck that. Let's go eat some cheese.'

The further we went downstream, the more the river-bank felt like a riverbank and not a squat party. After a couple of kilometres we found a spot where it was glass-free and safe to swim without gumboots. I fell into the water and the cool sting of it converted the ache of my muscles into a delicious all over skin-tingle. The water lapped at my face; I gasped and coughed and was happy.

Thanks to the twin miracles of GPS and *Ronery Pranet*, we were able to blunder through the forest pretty much straight to Bert's House of Cheese. Located at precisely N47° 58.702', E107° 29.837', Bert's House of Cheese was a *ger* camp in a healthy field framed by the ever-present placid wooded ridges, with not a smashed Chinggis bottle for miles. It was run by an eccentric gouda-making Dutchman who had come to Mongolia for a few months and—you guessed it—shacked up with a local zanger and never left. When we arrived there was no sign of Bert, but in the middle of the *ger*s there was a little wooden shack, and through the windows we could see stacked wheels of damn fine cheese. A precocious ten-year-old boy with a round face and piercing blue eyes came up and told us in passable English that Bert was away in Ulaanbaatar, but his mother, Kana, was shopping for dinner in Terelj and would be back soon. The kid showed us to a *ger*. Then he hooked us up with some cheese.

We lounged in the sun munching chunks of cumin Gouda. It was soft and fresh and—what's the word?—*piquant*. Tama's mood was a hundred per cent improved, especially after I took it upon myself to head back into town single-handedly to get food and petrol so we didn't have to worry about it in the morning. On my way to Terelj I stopped under some trees for a cheeky Marlboro, then proceeded dizzily down a path I didn't recognise straight into a swamp. All hope was lost until I realised I could navigate my way back to Terelj by following the faint then increasingly solid thumps of a PA system that had started pumping out detuned Mongolian disco hits for some mining baron's overpriced wedding.

There were no petrol stations in Terelj, although one woman encouraged me to go 'three *kilometr*' away without specifying the direction. I saw a tall dude chilling on his back porch and I asked him about *benzin*. He laughed and said, 'No problem.' I followed the man, another Batbot, around town for a while, collecting his friends. After a few minutes there were eight of us and still no *benzin*. It took the whole gang one unhurried hour to find someone willing to siphon a litre of fuel from their car into my bottle. In the meantime I made seven new friends, let five of those friends have a go on my bike, and had a reluctant ride on a big horse. Climbing onto its back was okay, although much higher than my bike seat, but then it started moving without me even pedalling. I made them stop it and I jumped off in a hurry and they all laughed at me. The horse was owned by a guy called Nergüi.

'Nergüi doesn't drink Chinggis,' Batbot explained. 'He is Muslim—he is crazy!'

After Nergüi did a blockie on my bike his friends made

an elaborate show of searching my bike for me, patting down the frame and tyres looking for improvised explosive devices, making cracks about 'Taliban' and 'Al-Qaeda' that already seemed like relics from a bygone age, like jokes about secretaries and Irish Catholics.

'You American, you—BOOM!' Batbot said, and everyone had a laugh.

'No—*bi Shin Zelandaas irsen*,' I said.

'*Shin Zeland*? It is very small.'

'Yes, but *Shin Zeland* has many sheep!' I said, proud of this fact for the first time in my life.

'How many?' he asked.

'Forty million.'

The group whistled appreciatively.

'And how many people?'

'Four million.'

'*Za, Shin Zeland* is same as Mongolia—*mash sain!*'

I made it back to Bert's House of Cheese in the last of the light. Tama was sitting in an open-air food tent lit by candles, surrounded by half a dozen tourists and the same number of empty plates. They were mainly Dutch and all back from a day of horse-trekking. A middle-aged woman and her henpecked husband were telling the group about their experiences, in English for Tama's and now my benefit.

'I think . . . I do not like this horseriding,' she said. 'Horses are stupid animals.'

Apparently her horse had thought the same thing about her, spending most of the day trying to toss her out of her saddle and trample her to *huushuur* under its hooves. The woman's husband nodded sadly, like the whole thing was his idea.

'Did you think of having riding lessons before you came to Mongolia?' Tama asked 'politely'. The lady looked at him like he was impertinent, possibly retarded.

'I came here to have *holiday*,' she said. 'This horseriding is meant to be *relaxing*.' She shot her husband an icy look.

'Yeah maybe,' I chipped in, 'but if I didn't know how to ride a bike, I dunno if I'd come to Mongolia and do a five-day bike ride.'

She snorted. '*Everyone* in Holland knows how to ride bicycles,' she said dismissively. 'This country just needs some better horses, with softer backs.'

Kana served me up a groaning plateful of steak, potatoes and cauliflower drenched in heart-stoppingly good cheese sauce. While I munched, Tama told some war stories from our last thousand kilometres. The tourists were impressed, especially a pair of young Dutchwomen who kept wriggling closer to Tama like he was an oversized hunk of ladybait. But hearing Tama relate our exploits from the comfort of a relatively normal setting made me feel weird. It all sounded fantastical, fraudulent. I kept wanting to cough 'bullshit' under my breath—even though I had been there next to him hiding from lightning under that tarp, restraining that drunken motorcyclist, confusing those teenage waitresses. More than that, it felt wrong to hear our escapades shunted into the past tense already, like the whole thing was over—it was breaking the spell, and I wasn't quite ready for that.

I excused myself and went back to our *ger* where I poured myself a generous mug of Chinggis Gold. I sat out on the grass, taking in the stars and the distorted wedding music. I had a ciggie, and the sky exploded with fireworks. They were from the wedding upstream—garish puffs of pink and green, the extravagant thrill of sodium and strontium, barium and charcoal, copper and tugrugs burning holes in the sky. Each eyeful was followed by a thunderous boom that echoed across the valley. It was the perfect gift for the national park that had everything: noise pollution, light pollution. Tama ambled over and watched the fireworks with me. They were impressive but nothing we hadn't seen before. After ten minutes we lost interest and went inside the *ger* and lay on our beds drinking Chinggis.

'Man, this is the life,' Tama mumbled. 'All I need now is my beautiful Ami and a hot bisexual Mongol girl and I'm sorted. Oh yeah . . .'

'And a soundproof *ger* to yourself,' I added.

There was no reply.

'That's cool bro, you don't need your own *ger*. I'll just get some earplugs . . . Tama?'

But Tama had fallen asleep, still half-sitting up, mug of vodka balanced on his chest. I tiptoed over and put the cup on the floor. He mumbled but didn't wake up.

'G'night, bro,' I whispered and snuck outside for a smoke.

DAY 20: ALMOST LIKE A HOLIDAY

Under a shadecloth, Kana was serving up a spectacular array of breakfast cheeses: gouda, cumin gouda, chilli gouda, a fried-up soft cheese called quark, eggs poached with cheese and cheesy grilled tomatoes on cheese bread, plus non-cheese items such as cucumber, tomato and homemade pâté, all chased down with bone-strengthening glasses of warm, fresh, non-fermented, non-horsey milk. The Dutch equestrian champs were finishing their coffees and about to hit the trail. We wished them luck, and the girls gave Tama their email addresses on a scrap of paper he left on the table.

Kana cleared the plates away then sat with us and we asked her about the country to the north and east. In theory we were going to follow whatever paths we could—or, failing that, blunder our way through the taiga forest—until we reached the remote Dungeons-and-Drag-ons town of Möngönmorit. We expected this to take us the best part of two days. Kana said we could head up the valley we were in, following the Tuul *gol*, and be sure to cross the only bridge we come to and follow the river's east bank to the northeast. After about thirty kilometres the river would head north, but there would be a break in the hills and we needed to cut east here onto a 'big plain'. Further east, we would find some cold springs. It was fifty or sixty kilometres from the cold springs to Möngönmorit, including a 1934-metre pass.

'You can camp at the cold springs,' she continued. 'After springs, there are no people—just bear.' Something about the way Kana said it made her bears sound more substantial than other people's bears. She wished us a safe journey and good luck; we thanked her for her hospitality and advice, and especially for her cheese, then bought some more cheese and departed.

There were wildflowers, there were pines. The Tuul *gol* gurgled away on our right. The sun shone down, wispy clouds chased each other across the sky, a light breeze took the sting out of the sun. It was a bit of an uphill grind but today I didn't mind it. This was one of our last chances to appreciate this landscape, mountain-sized warts and all; in a couple of days we would be on the plains, then gone, like the whole thing never happened.

I rode with my salt-encrusted shirt unbuttoned and flapping around me and felt suffused with a lazy sense of wellbeing. *This* was what it was all about. This was why Dennis Hopper and Peter Fonda had sold that cocaine to those Mexicans in *Easy Rider*—so they could buy a couple of hogs and cruise around rocking out to 'Born to be Wild' by Steppenwolf, a band who took their name from Herman Hesse's 1927 novel about an eccentric gentleman who loved 'to trot alone over the Steppes and now and then to gorge himself with blood or to pursue a female wolf'—which was of course inspired by me and Tama.

We slobbered and bared our canines to the blue sky; we howled with joy.

A couple of hours up the Tuul *gol* valley we came to a little bridge. It was solid and well-made and completely out of place, probably built by a private tour company to ensure Dutch horseriders could make it to their competitively priced, authentic luxury pleasure *gers*. On the other side of the bridge we lost sight of the river but kept cycling north into a blank landscape and a thickening silence that pressed in from all sides, crushing the words in my head. What was there to say, or think, about the smoothed-off ancient hills that surrounded us? I kept my head down and focused on pedalling.

After half an hour the stillness was broken by a jeep driving up behind us. We slowed down to let it pass; it slowed down too. We stopped; the jeep stopped. Two young men got out and gestured that we should follow them back to their *ger* and have an ay-rag party.

'*Bayarllaa,* but no,' we said. 'We must—*dugui, dugui, dugui.*'

One of the men was wearing an old T-shirt that said NEW ZEALAND over and over in faded and cracking print.

'*Shin Zeland,*' Tama said, pointing to the T-shirt then himself and giving a thumbs-up. The dude looked blankly at Tama, then gestured again that we should come and *uukh airag*—drink then vomit fermented horse milk. We shook our heads again and pointed up the valley towards the silence. Finally they got back in their jeep, did a U-turn and drove back the way they'd come.

Our path slowly rejoined the Tuul *gol*, which was snaking lazily across the plains, fringed by a thick band of trees and bushes. When we got close we stopped and stashed our bikes in the bushes then stomped our way through the undergrowth until we popped out on the rocky shores of the *mörön*. It took a while to find a spot that was more than knee-deep, but after a bit of wandering downstream I found a bend where the water came up to my waist. I looked around to show Tama but he was fifty metres upstream, almost out of sight, submerged in a hole of his own. I dunked myself in the water and savoured the soft rippling of the water on the rocks, the diamonds of sun on the surface of the stream, the buzzing black flies in my mouth. It was marvellous to be on my own and doing almost nothing.

We hiked a little way up a hill and had a picnic in the shade of a larch tree. There was a great view of the river and beyond it the acne-scarred hills. Not a pile of rubbish in sight. We had real salami and gourmet cheese—it almost felt like a proper holiday. As I lay in the dappled half-shade dissolving my sandwiches in stomach acid, I spied a Mongol guide on horseback leading a party of westerners up the valley. They hadn't noticed us.

'Shhh,' I whispered to Tama, 'wait until they're a bit . . . SIGH BINOO!'

The horses bucked—one of them reared up, nearly tossing a woman out of her saddle. She cursed, possibly in Dutch.

'*Sain, sain bainuu!*' the guide called back, laughing.

Climbing back onto that bike seat was tough. The weather was still promotional-brochure clear, the scenery pixel-perfect, and I was deeply lethargic. I could've slept the week away. Also I was getting concerned about exactly where we would camp that night. Meanwhile, Tama was in great spirits. Too great.

'. . . New York is so awesome—there are all these Haitian and like Rwandan restaurants, and my friends know about some amazing underground clubs that are only open on a Monday, and only if you know the password . . .'

'Uh-huh.'

'. . . One time we were at this awesome hip-hop night, really boozed, and Prince came into the club with his bouncers and all his entourage—he was sitting like five metres away from me. It was amazing, he was even shorter in real life . . .'

'Mmm-hmm.'

'. . . I've got this awesome uncle in England, he wants to set me up with an offshore tax haven so I don't have to keep paying New Zealand tax when I'm not living there . . .'

'Oh, yeah, sure . . .'

All that amazing awesomeness was making me depressed. I began to suspect that New York had chipped away the shell of crippling yet protective self-effacement with which New Zealand coated its young. Was there some secret ingredient in the bagels, or the cocaine, that made New Yoickers relentlessly positive—to a fault?

Tama had always been an optimistic guy; that was one of the reasons I liked him so much. It made a nice change from my depressive German philosopher-reading friends. Recently, though, Tama's sunny disposition was a bit— brighter. Bloody Yanks . . .

. . . thought the bloody Aussie. After all, *I* had escaped from Wellington years ago because I was desperate for a slice or two of amazing awesome, and once I had a nibble of Melbourne, I was hooked. I fell in love with Australia's brash, arrogant, twangy ways, not to mention its robust economy. I began to Aussify myself, accent and all, to the point where my Kiwi mates begged me to turn it down and put some flamin' pants on. All of them except Tama, who wanted more noise, less pants. So who was I, some wannabe-kangaroo-fancier, to begrudge my best friend for moving to the fully sickest city on earth and having an amazing awesome when he got there? New York *did* sound great, it really did. It was just—a bit much. I took a gulp from my water bottle, tensed and untensed my shoulders. Perhaps the pot was calling the kettle 'awesome'.

The hills on the right dropped away. Tama checked the GPS.

'This is it—awesome!'

We headed over a low rise, away from the afternoon sun. Half an hour later we came into a vast flat emptiness bordered by distant hills. The springs were somewhere up that way, and beyond that—nothing. Sunburnt Frenchmen, hungry bears. A flock of birds flew over our heads, headed west.

'Whaddya reckon, bro?' Tama said.

'Sheeeit . . . how long you reckon to the springs?'

'Dunno. Couple of hours? Four?'

I sighed. 'Y'know, Kana said they weren't *hot* springs . . . and that there were *bears* . . .'

We peered at the map. The plain stretched south as well as north, south for a good twenty kilometres before it folded into a mess of valleys and ridges. It was about sixty kilometres to the main road that zanged east straight to Mörön; too far for today, but we could get halfway there at least.

On the other hand, if we charged north towards the not-hot springs, we'd make it to Möngönmorit—bloodthirsty bears and uranium mines notwithstanding—by the following afternoon at the earliest. We wouldn't reach the road to Mörön until the day after that.

Tama sighed. 'Maybe we should camp at the south end of the plain, then bust out to Erdene for sugary drink and rock the highway?' he suggested.

'Bro, that sounds—yes, please.'

Our shadows lengthened beside us as we rode south. My knee creaked and each one of my vertebrae made its presence felt. In the late afternoon light the wild grass on the plains took on an unbearable crispness. The occasional stunted tree or triangular rock looked monumental, iconic. There were whopping marmot holes next to and in the middle of the track, and just once we glimpsed something disappearing into its burrow, big as a beaver but far from any river.

The path got rockier and pebbles churned under my tyres. We came across a holidaying family whose car had broken down in huge puddle. They gave us a slug of rancid *airag* then a bowlful of vodka to take the edge off. I gulped it down; sparks flashed. I loved this crazy country.

I rode on in the failing light, not feeling my legs. A few kilometres down the road we approached a stand of trees that could have been pines, but it was hard to tell.

'Let's stop and camp in those trees,' I said.

'Uh, how 'bout we stop and camp here? Bears like trees.'

Kana hadn't said anything about bears in the southern part of the park, but we hadn't asked her. I pitched a wobbly tent on the least Swiss-cheesed piece of ground I could find—only seven marmot holes, five on Tama's side—and

Tama got gourmet on the *benzin* cooker. Terelj had yielded cabbage and potatoes and when they were fried in oil and combined with canned fish, rice, chicken stock and plenty of cheese they made for an outstanding dinner. After we'd eaten two colossal servings and put away a surprising amount of Chinggis vodka Tama packed all of our food into a single pannier bag, tied a rope around it and hoisted it into a nearby pine tree, downwind of us, like he'd learnt as a child in Canada. I rolled the best spliff I could with a few pinches of half-dry leaf I'd found in the bottom of my bag, like I'd learnt as a teenager in New Zealand. We smoked it in the dark wearing our headtorches.

'Man, it's so sweet how you can just camp anywhere you like,' Tama said, 'and you don't have to worry about getting in trouble or anything.'

'Iwasjustthinkingthat,' I said through held breath. 'Bro, remember when we camped out at Foster? The night befooooore'—I exhaled in a long gust—'Wilsons Prom?'

Tama stifled a giggle. 'Yeah. We went to that scabby pub and got boozed—I went to the jukebox and put on 50 Cent and all the locals left!'

'Yeah! And we didn't know if there was a campsite so we pitched my tent behind the bushes just off the main road . . . I didn't sleep all night cos I was paranoid about cops finding us . . . and when we got up in the morning, we were opposite the Foster Police Station!' I sniggered and reached for the roach.

'Shit yeah, that was classic. We hitched a ride with that redneck who told us his girlfriend was okay in the sack—but her *mum* was amazing!'

'Yeah—a wild Wilsons Prom cougar-zanger!'

We joked about Yogi Bear's cousin, Gobi Bear, trying to steal picky-nick panniers from pine trees, Boo-Boo, then the wind picked up and it got cold, really cold, even with all my wool on. We retreated into the tent and Tama fell asleep straight away. I lay there in the dark wanting to talk, not paranoid exactly but definitely alert. Every nylon rustle was a swiping Gobi Bear paw.

DAY 21: DRIED FERMENTED MILK OF A HORSE

We woke up the next morning, which was a pretty good sign we hadn't been eaten. Tama's Ortlieb was still hanging unmolested from the tree. While Tama wandered up the hill to snap some shots of the Barbie-pink wildflower meadow in the pines, I did some morning bike yoga—mainly knee and hip maintenance, too little too late, probably better to just cut my kneecaps open and tip the bike lube straight in.

Tama came back sooner than I expected with pictures of tree trunks noughts-and-crossed with claw scrape and surrounded by fresh faeces. Those bears might be small, but they left disturbingly large droppings—unless it was just Tama, but he swore they weren't his. We decided to leave immediately and worry about breakfast later.

I felt fresh and strong on the hills, and fast, especially when the conifers closed in around us. Riding lead I roared and whooped over a thickly wooded ridge. On the other side the hills abruptly lost their foliage and their colour and a bleached yellow replaced the morning's greens. We had probably just left Gorkhi-Terelj National Park. Ahead of us the sky was flat and grey. A couple of valleys on, a horseman appeared on top of a hill and cantered towards us. Or rather, a horse*boy* in an oversized *deel*: the kid was no more than twelve. The kid confirmed that *tiin*, yes, we were on the right track to reach the *tom zam* ('big road'). He reached into his robe and offered us a handful of *aarts*, sour milk curds; more specifically, the dried fermented milk of a horse. The *aarts* looked like lumps of congealed washing powder. It was not hugely appealing, but it was bad manners not to accept gifts from locals, so we both grabbed some, *bayarllaa*, thanks. I popped a big chunk of the stuff in my mouth and crunched it between my teeth. It was pungent, curdled, almost fizzy, a mockery of everything that dairy stood for. At the same time, the stuff was strangely moreish.

I nodded and smiled. '*Mash sain!*'

We shook the cowboy's grubby hand and then he galloped away over a ridge. As we rode I chewed hungrily on piece after piece, marvelling at the unpredictable waves of disgust and enjoyment sweeping through my mouth. The name was remarkably apt: it *did* taste like arse. And yet, just one more . . .

'Do you like that shit?' Tama asked, incredulous.

'No. Yeah! Kinda. It's . . . interesting. Like wrong yoghurt.'

'Do you want mine?'

'What, haven't you eaten it?'

'No way—when he wasn't looking I hid it in my sock. I didn't want to be rude.' Still pedalling, Tama pulled half a dozen grey-white lumps out of his grey-brown sock and thrust them at me.

'Sure. Your sock might have . . . sterilised it,' I said hopefully.

Tama rolled his eyes and rode ahead. I chowed down on

the brittle shards of authentic cultural experience, dreading yet also savouring that final tangy wrong note.

Our track split in two, each trail as obscure as the other. We heard the barking before we saw the dogs. I patted my pockets: no rocks.

'Come on!' Tama yelled and caned it down the left-hand path, trying to steer and unzip his handlebar bag at the same time. While I howled as fearsomely as I was able, Tama lobbed a couple of stones at the dogs but they didn't slow down. I threw my final piece of *aarts* with all my might at the closest dog, a horrid custard-coloured fleabag, scoring a direct hit in its left eye. The dog yelped and jumped in the air. Both mutts stopped and sniffed the *aarts* then ran whimpering back to their *ger* with their mangy tails between their legs.

'Zang!'

'Nice one, geezer! You shouldn't've eaten all that *aarts*— it's the perfect dog repellent!'

We continued down the dusty track, eyes peeled for more scabdogs. A couple of kilometres on we came to a fenced-in enclosure containing an obscene three-storey brick house in the ostentatious style of Gachuurt. Forty metres away, a solitary builder was perched atop the oversized wooden ribcage of a second half-built mansion. Surely they weren't holiday houses. When most of Mongolia was meant to be public property—everyone's, yet no one's—it was a mystery how people could build yuppy enclaves like this, and why *here* rather than *there*.

Half an hour later there was the low rumble and dust trail of a motorbike. A boy, again not more than twelve, rode up astride a flash red motorcycle with a cheetah decal on the fuel tank. When the boy stopped, his toes only just reached the ground, but he managed to keep upright. He was wearing red tracksuit pants with a thick gold stripe, an ace black-and-white leather jacket and fancy leather boots. He was smiley but very shy, and when we asked him the way to the *tom zam* he just smiled and nodded.

'Do you live in that massive house?' I asked him. 'That, ah, *tom* . . .' I looked in the phrasebook. '. . . *tom baishin*?'

He smiled and nodded. This was inconclusive.

Further south the path petered out into a random scatter of rocks, low shrubs and clumps of grass clinging feebly to the sand. It was slow, wobbly, arse-jolting terrain. We dismounted and pushed our bikes over and around rocks that were red and volcanic-looking. Behind a waist-high igneous cube we found a couple of goat carcasses rotting in the scrub.

'Warning: this track sucks,' I said.

'What track?'

After some more floundering Tama saw what he thought was a path fifty metres to the right, and even though I couldn't see anything, I followed him onto the subtlest of trails that was narrow and lumpy but much, much better than nothing. Quarter of an hour later the valley flattened out and we caught sight of the flat grey stripe of the main road. Even better, there was a distance marker: 230 kilometres to ОНАОРХААН (Öndörkhaan). We didn't want to go to Öndörkhaan, but Mörön was twenty-seven kilometres before Öndörkhaan, so—zang!

Back on tarseal we slid across the scenery in a daze, looking but not seeing. We experienced the benefits of one of the few completed sections of Mongolia's 'Millennium Road', a public works project the Mongolian People's Revolutionary Party government began in January 2001 with the grand plan of linking the country's westernmost town of Ulaanbaishint with the Halhïn *gol* on the eastern border, via Ulaanbaatar. When, or possibly if, the Millennium Road is finished, it will be 2640 kilometres long and effectively connect nothing with nothing, since the lion's share of traffic to and from UB head due north to Ulan-Ude in Russia, or south-east to Erlian, Höhhöt and Beijing. It was a long, skinny and futile symbolic gesture, but one that nonetheless assisted us immensely with our own pointless symbolic gesture.

We stopped for sugary drink at a little town that turned out to be Bayandelger, not Erdene. The map confirmed it: we were twenty kilometres further east than we were expecting and had spent the last couple of hours rock-hopping down a completely different valley from what we had intended.

'An accidental Kiwi shortcut!' I said.

'Yeah, and for once it paid off!' Tama was amused, even though he'd got it wrong.

'Maybe it's a sign.'

'Of what?'

'Dunno—that, Mongolia wants us to hurry up and get to Mörön?'

'Nah, if Mongolia was serious about it, she'd give us a proper tailwind.'

'And a travelator!'

Even without a mechanised walkway we made good time along that flat grey road under that flat grey sky. The hills were still beautiful, sort of, but after a fortnight of gaping it was getting harder and harder to really *see* the landscape. In my fifteenth year of Third World sight-seeing, I needed larger and more outrageous spectacles to be truly astounded: not just nomads on horseback but bigger nomads, better nomads—Chinggis Khaan himself, thirty metres tall and shining in the sunlight. Kinda thing.

The asphalt turned sharply to the left and suddenly we were heading due north. This didn't make sense until we realised that the 'town' of Baganuur was actually a massive open-cut coalmine. Our road made a discreet twenty-kilometre detour around what we could only glimpse as a darker grey on the horizon, endless piles and drifts of it, offset by the lighter grey of smoke plumes. Baganuur's coal was apparently responsible for the heating and smogification of UB for the duration of its nine-month winter.

'I love *Mine*-gol-ia,' Tama said in his Governator voice. 'I dig its big gaa-ping holes.'

'Ha, Minegolia—you make that up?'

'Nah.' Tama had read an article about Mongolia's resources boom, which was apparently even boomier than Australia's.

'The mining industry's going mental, the economy's growing like fifteen, twenty per cent a year. Apparently there are gold mines in the Gobi Desert that make Erdenet look like a kid's sandpit—and they're all run by Aussies.'

'Jesus.'

'Yeah, it's crazy—these wanker mining executives are all saying that in a few years, Mongolia is gonna get rich like Australia.'

'Really?'

'Apparently.'

'I'll believe it when I see it.'

On the far side of Baganuur we pulled into a rest stop with a great view of the coal pits and a stone plaque with a picture of Mongolia and a man in a hat labelled мnуnn нутаг, no doubt Mongolia's Gina Rinehart. A group of five Mongol couples were crowded around a small stone picnic table. One of the men got up to give us the obligatory shot of vodka and we were away again, my face tingling, riding into Khentii, the final *aimag* (province) of our adventure.

A few kilometres down the road we came to our fourth Naadam. There was a *huushuur* stand right by the road. We watched a short teenage girl with a TOKYO BURGER cap pulled low over her eyes smear minced mutton into one half of a circle of dough, fold the other half over then dunk it in a deep-fryer and sell it to us for twenty cents a pop. Neither of us suggested heading across the field to check out the 'festivities'. I realised with a hint of sadness that I'd lost the urge to treat Mongolia's national sport like shonky performance art.

It was a long, smooth, uneventful sepia-tone afternoon. We rolled across a sturdy concrete bridge spanning a flood-plain that I couldn't imagine seeing in flood. On the far side of the bridge there was a large blue-and-white road sign with some very good news: it was 199 kilometres to оhаорх-аан, and a mere 172 to морон. I shimmied up the pole and kissed the sign with grateful cracked lips. We were out of the woods now, figuratively and literally. From here it was all plain tarsealed sailing, no more shortcuts and no surprises. If we didn't bother camping out on the Mörön *gol* we'd be in Mörön in two days max: by tomorrow night if we really smashed it.

As we pushed further east the cloud thinned and the hills turned from brown to a dirty gold. After three weeks in the saddle my bike practically rode itself—not fast, but fast enough. We rode in single file, close together, taking turns tailing each other like Tour de France riders, taking advantage of the reduced air resistance in the wind shadow. I hardly needed to pedal at all as I sat on Tama's back wheel while he slogged it out and broke the wind. The downside of following someone that closely was that you couldn't admire the scenery so much. You had to concentrate on the stroboscopic black band whirring half a metre in front of you without getting hypnotised and riding into it. We trundled along at close to twenty kilometres an hour, 'Born to be Wild' playing on repeat in my head, which made a nice change from 'Total Eclipse of the Heart'. As the distance markers slid by it was almost like being on a travelator.

When we were nearly 100 kilometres east of our morning campsite but still thirty away from Tsenkherman-dal, our destination for the night, the road tilted up just a little and stayed that way. I wasn't on a travelator anymore; I was on a hill and for some fool reason I was cycling. Half a wheezy, knee-destroying hour later we started running out of steam. Tama's shirt was slick with sweat; mine was probably worse.

A red van pulled over and a middle-aged Mongol dude waved us down. He was friendly and spoke decent English. He proposed that we stop our 'slow' and 'dangerous' cycling immediately and put our bikes in his van, and for a 'small fee' he would be our tour guide, driving us to 'all the best places of Khentii', including a swimming hole 'where the water reaches to your neck' (Tama's chest), followed by a visit to Dadal, the birthplace of Chinggis Khaan, located 200 kilometres north-west of here—'so beautiful', apparently, and much too far for us to ride without blowing out our itinerary and missing our flight. For 'a little bit extra', our entrepreneurial acquaintance suggested he could rent a jeep and we would blaze a trail into the Khan Khentii Strictly Protected Area north of Möngön-morit on a pilgrimage to the 'most powerful mountain in Mongolia', Burkhan Khaldun. Chinggis Khaan was buried there, the man assured us. It was 'a place of great wisdom' and the mountain 'will answer all your questions', even if you didn't know what they were. Did we want to go, now?

Tama and I conferred quickly in whispers then turned back to our presumptive tour guide.

'No,' I said.

'Thanks, though,' Tama added.

The man laughed loudly, showing a mouthful of strong yellow teeth.

'Okay, okay, you don't come with me this time. But next time you are in Mongolia—I will show you all the wonders of Khentii!'

'Cool. Um, would you mind telling us the way to that nice swimming hole?' I asked.

The man stopped smiling and looked me right in the eye. 'No,' he said, then burst into laughter again. He shook our hands warmly, jumped in his van and roared off. We had a Mars Bar. After this it was still fifteen kilometres to Tsenkhermandal and before that another pass, Bor Hujirïn *davaa*. This was a 400-metre vertical climb to a saddle at 1890 metres, as high as we'd climbed in Mongolia. Too high for today. We scaled down our plans to just making it to the top of this pass and finding somewhere to camp, even though that would mean delaying our arrival in Mörön from tomorrow night to the day after.

There were a couple of *gers* sitting in a grassy valley on the right, quite a way back from the road. I asked Tama if he wanted to go and stay with some nice peasants. He told me not to call them that. We had been planning to spend every second night in a different *ger*, but it hadn't worked out like that. Tonight, I was up for it.

'Man, I'd love to—but I'm buggered,' Tama said. 'I can't be arsed making small talk out of that crappy phrasebook for like five hours. I just want to have a good dinner, enjoy the view, drink some Chinggis and have a good sleep.' He stared into the distance, grumpy and determined.

'I know, but this is one of our last chances—tonight and tomorrow, then we're outta here!' I tried to keep the whinge out of my voice.

'If we weren't doing so much riding every day, I'd be happy to struggle through an "authentic experience",' Tama said, clawing the air with quote fingers. 'But bro, I'm all struggled out.' He was silent for a few seconds. 'Besides, we had that awesome night in the construction hut—doesn't that count?'

I didn't have the energy for an argument I wouldn't win, so I left it. Tama got on his bike and I followed the back of his helmet up the hill. Near the top of the pass, a majestic vulture was sitting on the side of the road, sunk talon-deep into the remains of a sheep's back, which it had scooped out in a neat semi-circle. The vulture was gulping down intestines like it was spaghetti bolognese. This seemed as good a sign as any to stop for dinner. We pulled off to the left-hand side of the road, away from the vulture, and pushed then carried our bikes across a field of thick grass, up a bank and over a little ridge. On the other side the sky was ten times bigger. The hill dropped away into a vast bleak valley. The brown grass rolled off in a dusty, uninhabited carpet before bunching at the horizon into a couple of dozen little mountains, their wind-blasted smoothness punctured from within by exclamations of rock. Beyond the first range: more mountains, blue and hazy ones. If I wasn't out of breath already it would've been breathtaking. I was reminded of the drunk basketballer from Erdenet: 'Big country—big history—big Chinggis!'

This was Chinggis Khaan country, right here—I could sense it. I could almost see a dashing young Chinggis urging his horsey battalion over the distant hills and across this very steppe, a legendary ghost army with attendant plume of ghost dust, raping and pillaging and reforming the Mongolian taxation system . . .

Apart from that guy in the van, no one knew where the *Washington Post*'s Man of the Millennium was buried. Rumour has it that a royal burial guard rode to a remote and top-secret location, slaughtering every human and animal they met along the way. Once at Mystery Place they diverted an entire wide and fast-flowing river, buried Chinggis and forty of his hottest concubines plus concubine bling in the riverbed before redirecting the river, concealing his grave forever. Or he was buried on the steppe before thousands of horses trampled the burial site to mush. Or he was buried on Mt Burkhan Khaldun. (I back the '*mörön* burial massacre' theory, but I'm biased.) Either way, Chinggis's burial guard is then meant to have reported back to a platoon of 800 soldiers, who slaughtered them on the spot. The platoon hightailed it back to Karakorum and was promptly massacred in its entirety.

After Chinggis's death, his descendants sealed off a million-hectare wedge of forest, river, mountain and steppe around the Tuul *gol* and declared it off-limits. Ögödei Khaan and co. called this region *Ikh Khorig*—the Great Taboo. Its borders were patrolled by warriors trained to kill intruders on sight. Centuries passed; trespassers were prosecuted. Then in the early 1920s Mongolia fell under Soviet influence. Anxious to discourage counter-revolutionary Chinggis-worship, the Communists changed the area's name from 'the Great Taboo' to the only slightly less intriguing 'Highly Restricted Area'. The Soviets surrounded the Highly Restricted Area with another one million hectares of plain old 'Restricted Area', which they peppered with artillery ranges, tank bases, cheeky air fields and most likely a top-secret stash or two of nuclear warheads. But no roads, no bridges or towns. People had no good reason to venture in there and lots of reasons to stay away. Then the USSR collapsed and the Restricted and Highly Resticted Areas were abandoned pretty much overnight.

A few years later, untamed-wilderness-craving western-ers started exploring the place. This is what anthropologist Jack Weatherford found:

> . . . *the Soviets left behind a surreal landscape of artillery craters strewn with the metal carcasses of tanks, wrecked trucks, cannibalized airplanes, spent shells, and unexploded duds. Strange vapors filled the air and peculiar fogs came and went. Twisted metal sculptures rose several stories high, strange remnants from structures of unknown purpose. Collapsed buildings, which once housed secret electronic equipment, now squatted empty among lifeless dunes of oil-drenched sand. Equipment from old weapons programs*

lay abandoned across the scarred steppe. Dark and mysterious ponds of unidentified chemicals shimmered eerily in the bright sun. Blackened debris of unknown origin floated in the stagnant liquid, and animal bones, dried carcasses, swatches of fur, and clumps of feathers littered the edges of the ponds.

The Restricted and Highly Restricted Areas have been rebranded by the Mongolian government as the 'Khan Khentii Strictly Protected Area'. This makes it sound like a national park rather than an irradiated wasteland. The heart of the Khan Khentii is apparently a regular Garden of Eden—the only catch being, you have to pass through half a dozen circles of hell to get there.

This was why there weren't any roads going east–west from Selenge province to Khentii province. This was what we didn't know when we sat down in Khatgal a couple of weeks ago to plot our itinerary, trying to keep north to avoid the pollution of the cities. This is what we missed out on because we didn't have the balls to go bush-bashing across those 2300-metre peaks. Not just impenetrable forests and killer bears: poison forests, glow-in-the-dark bears.

I wolfed down my cabbagey rice with tabasco sauce and plenty of pickled ginger, not pausing to chew. Tama wandered down the ridgeline to photograph the sunset and I crawled into the tent feeling a trifle bloated. I dozed on and off, disturbed by half-dreams about needing to comply with an endless litany of Tsenkhermandal Council Nocturnal By-laws. As a foreigner I needed to get permission to go to sleep properly, but the flapping of the tent was an endless series of forms that needed filling out and the loose guy ropes were all strings that needed pulling. I wasted a few hours trying to bribe my bedroll until at some point in the dead of night I woke with a sickening urgency. Dinner was a greasy cannonball lodged in my guts. As I struggled with the tent's zipper, Tama stirred.

'What're you doing?' he mumbled.

'Think I'm—throwing up.'

'It's cos of that filthy shit you ate,' he replied blithely and rolled over.

Oh yeah, I thought to myself. All that filthy shit. Not the cabbagey rice, not the mutton pancakes, but the dried fermented milk of a horse: *aarts*.

I yanked the zip down and with my legs still inside the tent I vomited. And vomited. Like a storm cloud emptying itself of hailstones, like a factory pipe gushing copper effluent, like a fifteen-year-old sprawled in a park after too much rocketfuel, I puked my guts out.

It was astounding that so many litres of barely digested rice and cabbage could come hosing back up my throat and pour out onto the freezing moonlit ridgeline. Next came the stabbing pains in my bowels, phase two in the old gastric pincer movement. I wriggled into my jacket for warmth but put it on back-to-front by mistake. The hood flapped in my face and I tried not to fill it with vomit juice. I staggered outside onto grass made fluorescent grey by the full moon and took cover behind a stack of rocks, clutching at my guts like a ham-acting Shakespearean stab victim. I pulled down my pants and squatted, waiting for the dreaded rush from both ends . . . but only cabbage strands came, and only from the top. At the moment of truth I was still too constipated from the doxycycline. I dragged myself back to the tent, groaning. Tama sat up and looked at me.

'I dreamt that me and Ami were train barons,' he said, and fell back into a dead snore.

I felt wrong all over, but especially in the head. And guts. I lay on my back and played dead.

I was wrenched from my delirium by an obscene slurping sound in my ear. At first I thought it was Tama, abusing himself in his sleep with visions of Ami's caboose. But I realised the noise was coming from outside the tent. *Wolf? Bear?. . . Chinggis?!*

A loud neigh was followed by a tremendous gush of horse urine slamming into the side of the tent. That narrowed the options down. I screamed and banged on the nylon but the piss kept coming. I unzipped the tent and found myself staring at a bad-arse black stallion complete with a fire hose of a horse cock and a muzzle stained with the remains of my dinner.

'Bugger off!' I screamed ineffectually. Then, 'Giddy up!'

The horse snorted in derision and turned towards me, sending a blast of scalding urine into my face. It burned my eyes and when I spluttered in outrage it filled my mouth.

'D-dirty horse,' I gargled. 'I hope you get hit by a bus— mashed into dog meat! I hope your whole fucking family dies in a *dzud*!'

The stallion whinnied and kicked his forelegs to the moon. His mighty stream sailed over me in a pungent glittering rainbow.

Stupid tourist, he neighed, shaking his mane and galloping off into the night.

DAY 22: RUNNING ON EMPTY

There was no spew outside the tent that morning, no hoof marks either. Surely it wasn't all just a dream? Then I became acutely aware of the rank burnt-grass odour of horse piss in my hair, the carpet burn in my throat and the vomit stains on my T-shirt—my last clean T-shirt. I let out a low, distressed moan. I felt like I was poisoned. Which was pretty much accurate.

It was a glorious morning on our spectacular ridge-line—according to Tama. He was tucking into a saucepan full of muesli; the sight of it made me retch. I sat on the other side of the tent until he finished, unsure of what to do with myself. My body felt so wretched that I had somehow disconnected from it. I could still perceive the pain but it was from far away, like I was staring down at myself through the wrong end of a telescope. Tama strolled over and patted me on the back.

'Bro, your spew stinks like horse piss. D'ya want some barley sugars and electrolyte drink?'

I crunched a few barley sugars. They stayed down, just. Tama mixed up a couple of sachets of electrolytes with the last of our water. I managed to drink half of it.

'Man, I feel like . . .'

'Like *aarts*?'

'Pretty much.'

Convalescing on an exposed ridge without any water wasn't an option that would end well. We had to keep moving. There was no way of washing the tent so we just packed it up with the rest of our stuff and hit the road, like we did every morning. I'd lost my protective calf-sock and the sun was beating down, but I couldn't be bothered putting on any sunscreen. Coming down off the pass the pedalling added new layers of hurt to my punctured stomach and scorched throat.

At the bottom of the hill we rolled into Tsenkhermandal. There wasn't a 400-metre hill climb still to come, because we had accidentally camped out on top of the Bor Hujirïn *davaa* last night. Tama said at least that meant we were slightly ahead of schedule, but I wasn't interested. We loaded up on water and Tama got some chocolate then we rolled on. East of Tsenkhermandal the landscape was dry and hot and empty. 'Empty' might not be quite right—like colonial explorers calling Australia 'empty' because they couldn't see any Anglican churches—but I wasn't a nomad, I didn't know how to read those withered grasslands.

Meanwhile, my mind was as featureless as the road ahead. All my awareness was focused on not vomiting. Tama rode lead and I followed him, sort of. I tried to stay in his slipstream, but after a couple of kilometres I'd drop behind and couldn't see the point in catching up. The smaller he got, the slower I'd go. Tama would cycle ahead for a quarter of an hour or twenty minutes then stop and wait for me, munching on a Mars Bar. I couldn't bear to watch. I drank water until I felt queasy, then got on with it. A speck on the horizon turned into a smudge, then a blot, then a town, which was marked by a surprising little sign: УЗНХАРМАНАан.

'What the hell—I thought we just went through Tsenkhermandal!'

Tama checked the maps.

'Nah man, this is Tsen*khar*mandal, not Tsen*kher*mandal. Important difference,' he said with a smirk.

I didn't want to stop but Tama popped into a scabby-looking grocery store and came out waving a mysterious package.

'Fried eggs for dinner, bro!' he called cheerfully.

The thought turned my stomach. It was a shame—they were the first and last eggs we saw on sale in rural Mongolia.

'Not for me. Where the hell are the chickens at anyway?' I looked around for roaming packs of steppe-fowl, angry at their absence.

'Well you're not vomming anymore, so, that's pretty cool.' Tama grinned.

'Yeah—it's *amazingly awesome*,' I replied.

'Don't sweat it, Doiggus. It'll be all over tomorrow. Let's get a move on, eh?'

It was one hundred kilometres to the final Mörön. I got my motor running, headed out on the highway. I wasn't looking for adventure, or whatever came my way—I just really, really wanted to get it over with. I felt like that Irishman in the joke who's asked why he's hitting himself in the head with a hammer. He replies, 'Because it feels so good when I stop.'

I rode lead for a bit, then Tama took over. In my head, Jay-Z kept telling me that he had ninety-nine problems blah blah blah.

Ninety-nine problems? Try mountain-biking across Mongolia with horse-curd poisoning, be-atch. Every five or ten minutes a truck drove by, and each time I fantasised about hitching a ride back to LG Guesthouse, even though all the trucks were going the wrong way. Finally a massive blue truck came rumbling westwards: it was towing three huge trailers, each overflowing with a mountain of dirty cashmere that was taller than the last and all held in place— just—by tarpaulins made of smuggler bags. What I wouldn't give to curl up under one of those . . .

Tama was pulled over twenty metres up the road.

'You ride in front, bro,' he said.

'Thanks Tama bro, but, nah. You're faster, you'd have to wait for me all the time.'

'I have to wait for you anyway. And I worked it out: if you ride lead you go about two kilometres faster than if you're following me.'

'Really? You worked that out?'

'Yeah man, I've been timing you on the GPS. It's 18.5 k's an hour when you're in front, 16.3 k's when you're behind.'

I guess it was a psychological thing. When I was in front, I was—in front. I didn't want Tama to get frustrated and overtake me so I'd push it a bit, even though I felt ruined. But when Tama was in the lead and I had to pedal hard just to keep up, even in his slipstream, the whole thing depressed me and I just wanted to pull off the road and crawl into a sheep carcass. So I rode lead, and it worked—we went slightly faster.

Even so the afternoon scraped by excruciatingly slowly. To keep my morale up, Tama cycled next to me and regaled me with tales of drunkenness and shonk from the Big Apple.

'So one Saturday night I was in Manhattan at my friend Allie's penthouse apartment, drinking with all her cute friends. I got a text from Allie saying come to the lobby and let her in, she'd gone out for beer and forgotten her keys, but when I got down there was another text, someone else had let her in, so I got back in the elevator and two girls got in with me. They were really cheesy but kind of hot, nineteen or twenty max, total frathouse skanks. They were all, "Where are *you* goin', boy?" And I said, "My friend's penthouse," but they were like, "No you're not, you're comin' with *us*."'

'Did they?'

'Yeah, bro. Next thing I'm sitting on their couch, pashing one of the girls' faces off and feeling her up. She was pretty saucy but a bit wack, at one point she like pulled my beanie off then put it back on again. I said, "What are you doing?" and she said, "Just checkin' you're not bald," and kept kissing me. She was pretty hellish. I could've probably banged her right there on the couch—maybe her friend, too—but then I thought, Fuck this, this girl is actually pretty rank, I'd prefer to be drinking beer with my mates, so I got off the couch and put my T-shirt on. She was all, "Don't go, you don't know *what* you're missin'," and I was like, "Yeah, I reckon I do," and left.'

'Oh.'

'Yeah. Allie and her mates are way cooler . . . The only thing was, after a couple more hours drinking I was really boozed, and I started thinking about that girl and her couch again. Y'know? So I went down in the elevator to look for her apartment, but I was too drunk, I couldn't remember what floor they were on.'

Tama pedalled on.

'Did you, um, do . . . something?' I forced myself to ask.

'Oh yeah, nah I just stumbled around for ages without finding it, so I went out and had a shawarma and went home. You can get these awesome shawarmas in Manhattan for like four bucks, it's awesome.'

We rode on in silence. Tama had a bit of a chuckle.

'Bro, what about that foursome you tried to have? That was hilarious.'

I shuddered. Before I could go to my happy place I was back at that fateful poetry gig, defaming a freshly ex-girlfriend to the tune of 'Summer Lovin''. Afterwards I got drunk and drunker and ended up at a house party in Collingwood full of trashed poets swilling goon from a fruit bowl. I was getting somewhere with this girl called, I think, Lucy; we were dancing and having a bit of a kiss. The only thing was, this other guy, Ezra or Pablo or something, and his girlfriend Jessica, they had their eyes on Lucy too. For a while it was all good—I was grinding Lucy, Pablo was grinding Jessica, then the girls were grinding each other and pashing on while me and Pablo danced behind them and made sure we didn't accidentally touch hands. Then as if an alarm had gone off in his pants Pablo grabbed both the girls' hands and pulled them up the stairs. I wasn't going to miss out on this so I ran up behind them. Someone yelled, 'Use the room on the right! NOT MY ROOM!'

We burst through a door and both the girls fell onto someone's bed and started going for it. Pablo sat down in an armchair and unlaced his twelve-hole Doc Marten boots one eyelet at a time without smiling or taking his eyes off the girls for even a second. He had dark eyes and a dark beard and looked increasingly satanic. I tried to get in on the action, but it was all moving so fast—before I had time to get undressed and hard, Lucy was already spread-eagled on the bed with Jessica licking at her pussy, Pablo naked and engorged and preparing to mount Jessica from behind. His cock was larger than mine in every way. He thrust into her and Jessica moaned and moved forward to pash Lucy, knocking me off Lucy's tits. I moved down the bed, trying to get my head between Jessica and Lucy's crotches so I could get at Lucy's pussy. I had just started licking when Pablo must've banged Jessica extra hard because she slammed forward and squashed my head between her and Lucy's bushes like a grapefruit in a nutcracker. My head popped out the side, Jessica tumbled squealing onto Lucy and Pablo thrust forward with a fearsome bellow, his cock missing Jessica's pussy and slamming with all its might into the side of my head. I was momentarily blinded. Pablo peeled it off me with a *schlupp* and slammed it back into Jessica without missing a beat.

That cock was kryptonite to my libido, and at that moment I realised I wasn't going to be able to get an erection that night, possibly not for the rest of my life. I should've run for it then and there but I was very drunk and what was happening around me was unprecedented. I'd never seen other people hard fucking at such close quarters, so I stuck around, and spent most of the next couple of hours slumped against the wall, chipping in with a bit of a lukewarm finger-bang now and then, but mainly just watching Pablo fuck his girlfriend from every conceivable angle, then ignore her and move on to Lucy. This made Jessica quite upset, but when she crawled over and tried to get me hard so she could be part of a proper orgy, not just a bystander to her boyfriend's wayward urges, it was no use. No matter how she slobbered over my flaccid member, no matter how desperately she stared into my eyes as she yanked and wanked my balls, there was no movement at the station. Eventually she turned her back on me and tried to get in on some of her boyfriend's cock action. I finally admitted defeat, put on my pants and shoes and crept out. No one noticed.

We stopped for a late lunch at a broken-down truck stop in Jargaltkhaan, a tiny town whose main and only attraction was a road leading north to Dadal and the Onon *gol*, via the Mörön *gol*. The place could've done with some tumble-weeds to liven it up. Jargaltkhaan was the last town before Mörön. According to the road markers we had seventy-two kilometres to go; if I wasn't sick we could've been there that night. I had lost track of the actual date weeks ago, but I did know that in Mörön-to-Mörön-time it was day . . . twenty-three? Twenty-two? Meanwhile, I had grown used to the feeling of being behind schedule *all the time*.

Tama called the waitress over, and after a gruelling game of charades she disappeared and came back with a ragged calendar and pointed to 31 July. We didn't have to be back in UB until 3 August. We were way the fuck ahead of schedule.

'I don't understand,' Tama said. 'We had that rest day in UB and everything . . . we must've just fucked up that schedule that we did in Erdenent, cos we were so stressed out about it, and now we've still got two days up our sleeve if we want it . . .'

I looked at Tama in alarm. 'Do *you* want it?'

'What?'

'Another . . . shortcut?'

'Maybe. I'm not fussed. Nah.'

'Good. Let's just get to Mörön and go home.'

Tama had a beer. I ordered a bowl of beef or mutton or possibly horse soup that came out lukewarm but I was still able to eat half of it.

'Dude, you're keeping it down—awesome!'

'Shut up or I'll vomit on you.' I smiled despite myself and went to have a sip of salty tea then thought better of it. 'So whaddya reckon the final Mörön will be like?'

Tama thought for a moment. 'Some dusty streets, with some alcoholics. Maybe some scraggly dogs, and a shop that sells Chinggis. That would be my optimistic expectation.'

'And what's your pessimistic expectation?'

He laughed. 'Pretty much the same—just no Chinggis.'

Outside in the parking lot we met a motorcyclist-monk who blessed Tama by putting his hands on each side of Tama's face, breathing onto his forehead then running his hands down over his head and shoulders, before doing the same to me. The monk's breath was soft and warm, and as his rough hands flicked off my shoulders I felt my head clear, as if he'd sucked the poison out of me. We thanked him and Tama offered him some cigarettes, which he declined with a silent laugh.

After the monk went inside the diner, a drunken Mongol stumbled up to us saying he was a monk, too. The drunk demanded cigarettes, and money, lots of money. We tried to leave in a hurry but I got a puncture in the broken glass, so I had to hang out with the drunk while Tama fixed my tyre.

He hassled me until I asked him for some money, then he walked off in a huff. A couple of kilometres out of Jargalt-khaan a motorcycle slowed down as it passed us but the rider didn't wave.

'That was a cop,' Tama said, 'I saw his CB radio. Mongolian *C*H*I*P*S*, bro!'

The police officer must've done a U-turn because half a minute later he pulled up alongside us and waved us over. He was riding a shabby old motorbike that looked close to death, but his uniform was immaculate. Tama shot me a glance: *where's the weed at?* I shrugged and looked away. The cop explained that we should follow him to his *ger*, drink vodka with his family and stay the night. We declined, hopefully politely. He nodded sadly, wished us *sain yavaarai* (safe journey), got on his bike and rattled away.

'You still got it?' Tama asked.

'Yeah man.'

'Is it well hidden?'

'I'm not actually sure where it is, so, yes. Gotta have something to look forward to back in UB, right?'

'True. Just don't get us arrested before then.'

We took off again, me riding lead. The plan was to ride a little bit further, another thirty kilometres, making it a 95-kilometre day and just forty to Mörön the next morning. There was a catch, as always: soon we had to climb a couple of hundred vertical metres to make it over a 1400-metre saddle. I did my best to keep a respectable pace, and I was doing okay until we hit the hill. Then it was like going the wrong way on a travelator. I had to pedal just to stay in the same place. There was a hideous groaning behind me—not Tama, but an ancient military truck grinding up the hill surrounded by a foul halo of diesel fumes. Tama pulled alongside me.

'I don't wanna breathe that shit in,' he said. 'I'm outta here!' He changed down and pedalled faster, trying to outrun the troop carrier or whatever it was. I wanted to keep up with Tama and for a few pedal strokes I could but then I couldn't. I felt like I was trying to pedal a boulder. The truck got louder, the smell fouler. It overtook me and made me cough. I slowed down, trying to give it some space, but the vehicle slowed down too. I pushed harder, trying desperately to overtake it—and it sped up again. I was stuck in its filthy slipstream, gulping down exhaust. My calf buzzed with sunburn; my knee twinged and clicked; my thighs, my poor overworked thighs, never again, not like this. My stomach, a bubbling lake of queasy; my lungs, they burned; my throat was now lined with lead; metronome icepicks stabbed through both temples. I coughed up a piece of undigested something. My head slumped forward; I let it hang there. The saying 'chin up' made a lot more sense now that I actually couldn't hold my chin up. I took a deep, dirty breath.

'FUCKING CUNT!' I screamed, as loud as I could—at the hill, at the truck, at Mongolia, at myself. It felt kind of good, so I did it again. When I looked up the truck was ten metres ahead of me. I tried to overtake it, but I couldn't. I wanted to stop, but I didn't. I put one foot over the other, again and again and again. I kept plugging away at this horrible chore I'd set myself months ago when I thought it'd be more fun. Every inch of my body screamed in protest—except for a tiny spark, an ember hidden deep in my guts, that was loving every second of it. Unless that was just the food poisoning.

Tama was waiting at the top of the pass with his camera out to capture my triumph, or whatever it actually was.

'Smile!'

I managed a lopsided grimace.

'Nothing a bit of Photoshop can't fix,' he said.

I lay down on a stone bench and didn't move. I had a view back down the valley and could see the road we'd just come up as it took a ninety-degree left turn for a couple of kilometres and held that grim line for maybe another three, then ninety degrees right and off to the horizon in a dead straight line. That far edge of the afternoon where the blue sky hammered down into the land, that was lunch; we'd ridden twice that far today. All told, we'd cycled across one-third of Mongolia. Tama and I had survived twenty-two days of the Sisyphus workout, *sans* nutritional supplements. From here it was all downhill to Mörön—literally.

We coasted down the east side of the pass, not needing to pedal. Just before we ran out of hill we pulled off the road and pushed our bikes up a rise towards a clump of rocks that looked like good cover for a campsite. It was a gorgeous spot: rusty yellow tussock grass, a scattering of dark red rocks with vibrant orange lichen on them, and a view of the road to Mörön. Back up the hill we spotted a couple of stray dogs, one tan-coloured and the other a dirty brown. They were loping along the road, feeding on what scraps they could as they headed east to Mörön. That would be me and Tama in our next lives. We hid behind the rocks and hoped the dogs couldn't smell us.

Once the dogs had gone Tama cooked up some rice then put a few eggs on to fry. The yolks were a rich gold colour and as I stared at them, saliva welling up in my mouth,

I realised that for the first time all day I was hungry. I must've been feeling a bit better.

'Laura's gonna pick me up from the airport, I can't wait! I'm gonna email her and get her to park her Micra in a dark corner of long-term parking—heh heh heh—and ride me in the back seat, reverse cowgirl style!'

'Yeah, Ami's picking me up from the airport too.' Tama lay back on the tussock and stared at the sky. 'She's gonna take a week off work, we're gonna spend it *all* in bed. And in the spa. And on the kitchen bench.'

'Laura said she'll cook me any meal I want. I can't wait—maybe some kangaroo spag bol, with like asparagus and rocket salad, or . . .'

'Ami told me to send her a shopping list of *all* the food I wanna eat, she's gonna fill our fridge with it the night before,' Tama said. 'She's gonna make a special food platter for me to eat in the car, scallops and oysters and meatballs and shit.'

We tried to high-five but we were lying too far apart.

'Hey Pugs, do you ever feel . . . like a bit of a cliché?'

'What kind of cliché?'

'Dunno . . . an awesome cliché?'

'Damn straight.'

We both stared into space.

'You know what one of the best things about Laura is?'

'Apart from the cat food fetish?'

'Apart from our *performance art connection*. No, and it's not all the awesome jumpsuits she owns, or that she'll write all day and then, like, read me JD Salinger stories while I make us dinner. It's that she's *not fussy*. She's really, really—not fussy.'

Tama nodded slowly. 'Ami's not fussy either. She's totally cool about stuff. I'm not used to it.'

'Maybe that's it! A girl who doesn't complain—that's a marrier, hey?'

Tama frowned. 'I guess—as long as she's a dirty bitch in bed. And into travelling. And mountain biking. And weed.'

The air smelt funny, like wood smoke.

'Hey bro, d'ya reckon the eggs are ready?'

'THE EGGS!'

Tama scrambled over to the pan, but it was too late—the pan was smoking and the eggs were dried out and blackened at the edges. Tama hacked at them with his spork, cursing as ruined egg yolk mixed with rancid charcoal.

'Stink. Shall I chuck it out? Or d'ya still want to eat this shit?' Tama pried a burnt grey lump out of the pan.

'Do you?'

'Nah . . . yeah. It'll be sweet with some bread and butter and chilli sauce. I'm not fussed.'

I looked at the eggs, then at Tama.

'Me neither.'

. . . *Eight centuries on, my legacy endures around the globe. The championing of free-trade zones? That was me. The wearing of trousers and cowboy hats? Me first. The drinking of the fermented alcoholic milk of a horse? Me me me. But my proudest achievement is the mode of tourism I invented: storm into Southeast Asia and / or Eastern Europe, disregard local customs, rape, pillage, blog, return home with souvenirs. Massacre, Contiki, call it what you will— Chinggis-travel has become the pre-eminent mode of experiencing the world. Little wonder I am celebrated by in-flight magazines everywhere as 'the Richard Branson of the Dark Ages'* . . .

DAY 23: THE FINAL MÖRÖN

I was awake before sunrise, happy not to be vomiting. The pre-dawn light was exciting enough to make me crawl out of the tent, set up the tripod and attempt a few shaky 360-degree pans of our campsite. Above a ring of jagged black hills the tiny white dot of an airplane drifted like an ember through a light blue sky smeared with thick streaks of peach and silver. I was really glad I wasn't colourblind. In the shadows below, a thin grey line led east towards the horizon—to the final Mörön.

There was no traffic on the Millennium Road that morning, no birds in the sky. It was unreasonably peaceful. Months later I found out the reason for the morning's excessive beauty: on 1 August 2010, southern Russia started to burn. A July heatwave brought temperatures a nutsack-roasting eight degrees Celsius hotter than normal. Then half a million hectares of taiga forest and wheat field—about 100,000 hectares more than Victoria's 2009 Black Saturday bushfires—went up in smoke. Western Siberia burned, and Buryatia, just north of Khövsgöl, and the eastern Siberian town of Boryza, a few hundred kilometres northeast of our campsite. People died. Vladimir Putin visited the charred remains of a village that he said looked like 'something from a horror film'. And as the worst wildfires in Russian history sent smoke and soot and billions of little embers drifting lazily over Mongolia, I got to savour a once-in-a-lifetime sunrise on the steppes by clambering up to the ridgeline and singing Mongolian opera at the top of my haggard lungs.

We had muesli with powdered milk for hopefully the last time, then packed up the dirty tent, loaded up our panniers and hit the road once more. I was ready to cycle the final forty kilometres to Mörön. The hill we'd slept on turned out to be the last significant topographical feature between us and our destination. It was flat, ocean-flat; I knew that already from the lack of altitude lines on the map, but now we got a palpable sense of it. The land stayed like that all the way east to Chinese Manchuria, 500 kilometres distant.

'Ninety-nine bottles of Chinggis on the wall, ninety-nine bottles of Chinggis, if one of those bottles should happen to fall, ninety-eight bottles of Chinggis for me . . .'

The cycling was a breeze. I felt like I could keep on riding, for days, weeks, months . . . On one level I knew this was because the end was almost in sight, but another part of me was piping up, saying it was a shame to stop now. We'd only just begun . . .

I counted the power poles as they trundled slowly by: exactly eleven per kilometre. Twenty-two. Fifty-five. I lost track around seventy when we disturbed a congregation of at least 500 goats that were bleating around on both sides of the road and across the middle. It was by far the largest flock of anything I'd ever seen.

We rode slowly. We didn't really talk about it, but I got the sense that Tama was feeling a bit weird about reaching the end too. He started taking photographs of things he would've biked right past a few days ago, like the power poles, anything. There was a hint of a creekbed on the left. This was the Mörön *gol*, which meant, as far as I could tell, 'River river'. According to the map the Mörön *gol* followed the road for a little under ten kilometres until they both reached Mörön town. We considered jumping off our bikes and running over to the *mörön* to do . . . something, but there was nothing there, just a distant dried-up ditch. Tama snapped a couple of photos then we pedalled on in silence.

The final Mörön came into sight just before midday. We both stopped when we saw it. I shot a glance at Tama; he seemed a little nervous, then he got his camera out. The town sprawled over a flat dusty plain for about a kilometre. Sunlight glinted off its unpainted tin roofs. Rising up behind Mörön there was a quintessentially Mongolian hill, no longer steep or craggy, its edges smoothed away by millions of years of sandblasting wind. We kept riding. About a kilometre before town we came to a nice bold МОРОН road sign where we stopped and changed into our Ami-designed MORON T-shirts and spent half an hour filming ourselves riding past the sign from a variety of angles, with and without high-fives. Then we rode on, as slow as we'd ever ridden in Mongolia, relishing the sensation of not having to get a move on. Tama's *Mongol tug* hung limply from its flagpole.

The first building we reached was a green-walled truck stop set back from the main road with fifty metres of dust for a carpark. A massive sign above the front door said БУУЗ. Beyond the truck stop there was a band of patchy grass split by a dirt track. It led to low fences, peaked roofs. There were wonky wooden power poles everywhere and near the 'centre' of town a grand total of seven trees. That was it.

I don't really know what I was expecting—fireworks? A heap of broken Chinggis bottles? Naadam? But there was nothing in the sky except a few white scrapes of cloud and there were no drunk Mongols to wrestle. I had known, in the abstract at least, that Mörön number two was going to be a whopping anticlimax—and it was. But somehow this was worse, much worse. This Mörön was too flat to even have an *ovoo*.

Tama rang Ami and after a few seconds I could hear her cheering at the other end. I stared at a road that went forever in both directions, from nowhere to nowhere.

'You wanna call Laura?' Tama thrust the phone at me.

'Oh—yeah, of course.'

I called Laura. It rang for ages.

'Laura! Babe, we're here. We made it.'

'CONGRATULATIO—*Sorry, you don't have enough credit to make this call. Please visit the Virgin website to top up . . .*'

I handed the phone back.

'So shall we hitch out of here?' Tama said. He wasn't joking.

'Tama, we've just biked halfway across—don't you want to check out downtown Mörön?'

'Not really.'

'Are you *serious*?'

'Dude, this place is exactly like every other town we've been to. It's the same shit as Khutag-Öndör, Selenge, Khatgal, fucken, Bayanchandmani . . . it's the same as the first scabby

Mörön. Just more dust.' He kicked the ground. 'Let's go to UB and have a burger.'

'Don't you at least wanna go and get some sugary drink—and some Chinggis? For the hitch back? C'mon, bro. We've got to.'

I started pushing my bike towards the ramshackle fences. Tama stayed where he was, but after a few seconds he sighed and followed me. We headed up that dusty path into that dusty town. There were hardly any scraggly dogs, and not even a single alcoholic. Eventually we found an open shop staffed by a grumpy middle-aged woman in a beige jumper with her hair pulled back in a severe bun. The shop had silver tinfoil stuff covering the walls and a picture of an astronaut landing on the moon above a shelf stacked with vodka bottles. I pointed to the top shelf.

'Chinggis Gold. *Alt.*'

'*Baixgui.*'

'Chinggis.'

'*Baixgui.*'

I brandished a fistful of crumpled thousand-tugrug notes, the last of our money till we got back to the ATMs of UB. This didn't help.

'Uh . . . Chin-jis? King-gis?'

'*Baix-gui.*'

'VODKA,' Tama said.

'*BAIXGUI.*'

We stared at her; she stared right back.

'Fanta?' I said.

Grudgingly she went over to a fridge and got us a bottle of green sugary drink, then counted out 1500 on an old wooden abacus. I handed over the money. She handed over the sugary drink. It was warm. As we left she hurried to lock the door behind us.

'What the fuck, man?'

'Maybe . . . maybe there's another shop?'

'Do you really think so?'

'No. But shall we check? Get some footage and stuff?'

'Fuck that. Let's just go to the truck stop, have some lunch and some beers, and get out of here.'

A Mongol woman walked through the dust towards the stop, surrounded by four young kids and trailed by a cowboy in dusty boots. The headless koalas! I rummaged in my panniers and found the plastic bag full of stuff we had failed to generously bestow upon Mongolian children in all the gers we didn't stay in. I pulled out one notepad and texta and put it in my pocket, then ran over to the lady and gave her everything else. She was suspicious at first, but when she looked in the bag she gasped and called to her kids. As I walked back to my bike the kids were swarming around her, and they seemed happy.

'Bayarllaa!' she called out.

We gave them a thumbs-up and resisted begging for vodka.

A big van was parked outside the truck stop when we returned. Inside, a corner table was packed with loud sunburnt Germans who were washing down their mutton soup with plenty of beer. They scowled at us when we walked in, as if we were single-handedly ruining their tourist-free Mongolian experience. We sat in the opposite corner. When the waitress came we ordered a couple of ухрннн мах (beef) somethings and asked for two large купер beers.

'Sorry, no alcohol today,' our waitress said apologetically.

'But—what about those guys?' I gestured to the corner table. 'They've got, like, heaps of beers!'

The waitress looked over at the Germans, who were noisily demanding another round. She looked back at us sadly.

'Please. *Saryn ekhnii udur arikhdaltgui udur.*'

'Uh . . . can you . . . in English?'

'New government law. First of month is No Alcohol Day. I'm sorry.'

'No Alcohol Day? But . . .'

'Please.' She was kind of cute.

I looked at Tama. He looked back at me, eyebrows raised in a pained question mark. If we'd ever earned ourselves a beer *ever*, in our short, shonky, booze-soaked lives, it was now. Forcing the waitress to break the law wasn't that big a deal. But, but . . . fuck it. When in Rome—I mean, Mörön . . . I sighed. Tama nodded sorrowfully.

'Two . . . Mongol teas, please,' I said. 'Extra salt.'

The final mörön
www.moron2moron.com/videos/final-moron

It took less than ten minutes for someone to pick us up. A middle-aged man with a white van and a can-do attitude helped us disassemble our bikes and expertly crammed all our gear into the back of his van, which was already full of family-holiday stuff. Batbot's wife and his daughter, a girl of nine or ten with big searching eyes, looked on with expressions somewhere between amusement and annoyance. Batbot made his daughter sit in the front and gestured for us to make ourselves comfortable in the back. As far as I could tell, the family lived in Ulaanbaatar and had been visiting relatives in the east.

'What do you think of Mongolia?' the mother asked. It was a good question. I hadn't seen much of Mongolia, but I'd seen more than enough of my Mörön fantasy.

'Ah, Mongolia is . . . *mash sain?*' I replied.

'*Mash sain?* You speak Mongolian! *Manai kheliig surakhiig oroldoj baigaa gadaagiin xuntei taarsan n yamar sain khereg ve? Toomsorgui bayan juulchid enuugeer zunduu. . .*'

After 'Sorry, no we don't', '*Nyet Russki*' and a few more minutes of increasingly futile pleasantries, the van was quiet.

Tama fell asleep. I lost myself in the view of the flat brown land we'd just flogged ourselves across. It was incredible how fast the scenery moved when you weren't pedalling. After just half an hour of effortless driving we whizzed past the morning's campsite; it looked like an uninviting pile of rocks. It took Batbot and his van fifteen minutes to conquer yesterday's awful two-hour pass. An hour later we passed the picked-over remains of a sheep carcass, next to the ridge where we'd slept two nights ago, where I'd vomited and got pissed on by a mighty black stallion under a curdled moon.

Or had I? I slumped back in the seat and closed my eyes. I felt like our whole journey was going into rewind, or worse—it was being erased . . .

Tama punched me in the ribs until I woke up.

'Doiggus Khaan, check it out!'

'Seen it,' I mumbled, pulling my hat down over my face.

'Bro, I *guarantee* you haven't seen this. It's—us.'

I opened my eyes reluctantly. Tama was waving a scrap of paper at me; I couldn't focus on it. Someone was giggling.

'She drew this weird picture of us.'
'Who?'
'The girl, you moron.'
This is the drawing.
I'm pretty sure I'm the one on the right.

ACKNOWLEDGEMENTS

First and foremost, thanks and bayish lar to Tama Pugsley, for making this whole Mörön thing happen and bringing me along for the ride. And as for him being so ridiculously good-natured about me writing an entire book about him, what can I say, except—*Mash sain!* Zang super zang!

Thanks to everyone at Allen & Unwin for taking a punt on an unpublished munter. To Elise Jones, my surrogate agent and number-one advocate: my first-born son is all yours, whether you want little Batbot or not! A huge thanks to Foong Ling Kong, publisher extraordinaire, for whipping this manuscript into shape and reminding me to keep it simple, even when I couldn't. Thanks to Ann Lennox, Simone Ford and Jo Lyons for editorial wizardry and for asking the right questions. Also thanks to Zaya Khanchiimaa for her excellent translations to and from Mongolian.

Particular and ardent thanks to Laura Jean McKay, for everything that happened after Mörön, and plenty that happened before, writing-wise and otherwise. Laura: you are so great. Thanks to Luke Meinzen, for his integrity, generosity and candour—and for sharing his Mongolian expertise. Double thanks to Nicolas Low for his invaluable feedback, and for going the extra kilometre on the manuscript—twice. Mega thanks to Henry Feltham, for his tenacity and psychopathic attention to detail, not to mention his disturbingly consistent support. Thanks on toast to Puck Murphy for all his video zang, his mad post-production skills and his unceasing commitment to Keeping It Mong. Bukku and Conrad Wedde for the inspired, moronic tunes. Pearly Jacob for additional filming and Benj 'Mongolian Bling' Binks for the Mongoliphilia.

To Benjamin Law, for seeing the book before I did. To Jack Doig, David Woods, Erin Kelly, Russell McGilton, Paulina Olszanka, Liam Pieper, Chris Flynn, Kelly Chandler, Esther Anatolitis and Kelly-Lee Hickey, for reading early drafts and making them better. To Ami Mitchell for the MORON T-shirts and for broad-spectrum awesomeness. To Stuart Mackay, Helen at Seven Summits, Emlyn Hughes, Heaven and Rhino, Freeload, Alice Doig, Sam and Sophie. To Lonely Planet—can't live with it, can complain about it.

Thanks to all who supported early manifestations of Mörön. To Tabatha Fulker and ACF Habitat magazine, Lisa Dempster and the Emerging Writers' Festival, Nillumbik Shire Council and the Laughing Waters residency, and Bhakti Puvanenthiran and the National Young Writers' Festival. To Jenny Gill, Harry Doig, Mary Slater and Andrew Watson, for the glorious productiveness of Hahei. To Jenny and Harry more generally, for being astonishingly great and ever-encouraging parents, even when some might argue the last thing I need is more encouragement.

Finally and most importantly, a heartfelt and badly pronounced bayarllaa! to all the people we met in Mongolia who helped us on our shonky journey. Your hospitality, generosity and good humour are an inspiration. Again, bayarllaa.

Tom Doig has been published in *The Big Issue*, *The Lifted Brow* and *Voiceworks* magazine. His plays include *Survival of the Prettiest*, *Hitlerhoff* and *Selling Ice to the Remains of the Eskimos*. Tom is currently a PhD candidate at Monash University, researching the lived experience of climate change in Australia. *Mörön to Mörön* is his first book.

tomdoig.com